Quality Instruction

Building and Evaluating Computer-Delivered Courseware

Robert T. Hays, Ph.D.

Universal Publishers
Boca Raton, Florida

Quality Instruction:
Building and Evaluating Computer-Delivered Courseware

Universal Publishers
Boca Raton, Florida ● USA
2008

ISBN-10: 1-59942-998-5
ISBN-13: 978-1-59942-998-4

www.universal-publishers.com

Table of Contents

List of Tables

List of Figures

Preface

High quality instruction is essential to ensure people learn the knowledge and skills that will enable them to succeed at their jobs. Computer-delivered instruction (including instruction on the Internet) has the potential to provide much of this needed instruction. Although the military and industry are purchasing large numbers of computer-delivered courses, there a lack of methods, supported by empirical and theoretical literature, to determine if this courseware is of good quality. This is true for all types of instruction. However, it is especially critical for computer-delivered courseware because these often do not include an instructor to make adjustments to the instructional content "on the fly."

The objective of this book is to provide an instructional quality evaluation method (subsequently referred to as the Method) to help instructional developers and instructional program managers determine the quality of their instructional products, both during development and at project completion. The Method also supports the comparison of courseware from different developers or courseware that uses different combinations of instructional media. The Method can be used during all phases of instructional development (i.e., it supports both formative and summative evaluations). Furthermore, it is designed so that an evaluator has the choice of how "deeply" to evaluate, depending on his or her time and other resources.

The Method is based on the results of two earlier efforts. Hays, Ryan-Jones, & Stout (2003) conducted an in-depth review of the literature on learning and instructional evaluation and developed an initial set of evaluation criteria. Hays, Ryan-Jones, & Stout (2005) reviewed additional literature on learning and instructional theories and used these to enhance the initial evaluation criteria and to develop supporting discussions for each criterion. In addition, Likert scaling techniques were used to develop 5-point, anchored rating scales for each evaluation criterion.

The rating scales were designed to "stand alone" if this is the level of evaluation chosen. However, the detailed discussions allow evaluators to obtain additional information on the criteria. The discussions include information on the importance of the evaluation criteria, the empirical support for the criteria, and suggestions for optimizing the instructional quality based on the criteria.

The Importance of Evaluations

Evaluations of instructional programs or products are essential in order to determine if they meet their intended goals. When conducting an instructional quality evaluation, one compares the courseware against one or more standards that have been identified as important contributors to instructional quality. This book presents a set of empirically- and theoretically-based criteria that serve as the standards that enable individuals to evaluate instructional quality.

Two Types of Evaluations

When judging instructional programs and products, there are two main types of evaluations: formative and summative. Formative evaluations are conducted during the developmental stages of program or product development. Formative evaluations are used to identify and correct problems before the instruction is delivered to learners. Summative evaluations are used to assess program or product impacts and outcomes. Summative evaluations are typically conducted after the courseware has been implemented. The results of summative evaluations are used to determine how well the courseware has achieved its intended goals. A saying attributed to Robert Stakes summarizes the distinction between formative and summative evaluations: "When the cook tastes the soup, that's formative; when the guests taste the soup, that's summative." The evaluation Method presented in this book supports both formative and summative evaluations.

The Method

The Method consists of a series of instructional quality criteria that are assigned ratings using anchored Likert scales. It also includes directions for using the scales and detailed discussions about how each of the criteria supports quality instruction. The scales are divided into two main sections: 1) instructional features evaluation criteria, which include four evaluation areas, and 2) user-interface design evaluation criteria, which include three evaluation areas. Each evaluation area includes several evaluation criteria. The scales can be used as a "stand alone" evaluation. They allow an evaluator to use the anchor statements and instructions to conduct a meaningful evaluation of instructional programs or products without any additional information. However, if an evaluator has the necessary time and other resources to conduct a more in-depth evaluation, or if he or she wishes additional information on a criterion, he or she may consult the discussion sections. The detailed discussions of each evaluation criterion include definitions of important terms and summaries of the literature that supports the criterion. The discussions also provide suggested techniques to improve courseware by optimizing the instruction from the perspective of each criterion.

Instructional developers and instructional program managers can use the Method during all phases of instructional product development. They can also use it at the level of detail that their time and resources permit. During program or product development, the method can be used to help ensure that no important facet of quality is overlooked. At program or product implementation, the method can help to determine if the instructional courseware is of the highest quality to meet the instructional needs of the learners.

Organization of the Book

Section I includes two chapters. The first chapter discusses the need for instructional quality and the purpose of the Method. Chapter 2 presents a series of 5-point evaluation scales—one for each evaluation criterion listed in Table 1. All the scales include verbal anchors and some include simple examples. The scales are designed to "stand alone." Using *only* these scales, evaluators with limited time or resources can still conduct a meaningful evaluation. For more in-depth evaluations, the evaluators can consult the discussions in Sections II and III.

Section II includes five chapters, which provide detailed discussions of the instructional features evaluation criteria. If evaluators are able to devote the time and effort, they can "drill down" into deeper levels of information on one or more of the criteria by reading the discussions in this Section. This is strongly recommended for instructional developers. These discussions provide suggestions on "how to" maximize the score on each criterion. They also include summaries of the literature that supports the criterion.

Chapter 3 is entirely devoted to discussions of the first and most important evaluation criterion (the content is presented in a logical manner). This criterion is influenced by all of the other criteria to some extent. It is recommended that evaluators wait to assign a score on this criterion until all of the other scores have been assigned. Chapter 4 continues the discussion of instructional content by presenting details about the other criteria that influence the quality of content presentation. Chapter 5 examines the criteria used to evaluate the instructional activities that are included in the courseware. The type of activities and the way learners interact with the courseware are major determinants of its effectiveness. Chapter 6 includes discussions of the criteria that are used to evaluate how effectively learner performance is assessed during and at the end of the course. Chapter 7 finishes this section with discussions of the criteria used to evaluate the quality of the performance feedback provided to the learners about how the performed in the course.

Section III consists of three chapters, which discuss the user interface evaluation criteria. These criteria involve how the learner interacts with the computer that delivers the instructional content. Chapter 8 examines the criteria used to evaluate the navigation and operation parameters of the courseware. Chapter 9 includes discussions of the criteria that examine the presentation of the content in terms of its appearance and other uses of sensory modalities. Chapter 10 completes this section with discussions about how a learner installs and registers for the course.

Section IV, the final section, consists of two chapters that provide additional elaborations on the basic Method. In Chapter 11, several adaptations of the Method are presented to evaluate the quality of instructional games. Chapter 12 provides additional details on how to use the Method for both formative and summative evaluations and closes with some recommendations about how the Method can be improved.

SECTION I:
A Method for Evaluating
Instructional Quality

The theoretically- and empirically-based Method presented in this book is intended: 1) to help instructional developers design and deliver higher quality computer-delivered courseware and 2) to help instructional program managers procure higher quality computer-delivered courseware. This section includes two chapters. Chapter 1 explains why we need higher quality courseware and Chapter 2 presents a series of rating scales that are used to determine the quality of the courseware.

CHAPTER 1:
Why Quality Instruction?

The Need for Instructional Quality

Effective learning and, ultimately, improved job performance are the goals of all instructional systems. In recent years, many organizations, including academia and those in the public and private sectors, have turned to computer-based instruction and distance learning (e.g., internet-delivered) approaches as alternatives to traditional, lecture-based courses. However, the majority of instructors surveyed by the National Education Association (over 50%) believe that their traditional course in the same subject matter does a better job in meeting educational goals than their distance-learning course (National Educational Association, 2000). This book presents a Method to help improve the quality of all forms of computer-delivered instruction (including web-based courseware).

In order to help ensure that all instructional programs or products meet their instructional goals, instructional developers and project managers need to evaluate them during development and at the time of delivery. This Method will help them in these endeavors. The development of the Method leveraged earlier work on guidelines for designing web-based instruction (Hamel, Ryan-Jones, & Hays, 2000) and a set of initial instructional quality evaluation criteria (Hays, Ryan-Jones, & Stout, 2003). Hays, Ryan-Jones, and Stout (2005) revised the initial set of evaluation criteria and developed the anchored rating scales for each criterion. They also presented discussions of each criterion. This book includes the rating scales and expanded discussions of each of the criteria. It also includes some adaptations of the Method to evaluate instructional games.

Education or Training?

A distinction is sometimes made between education and training. *Education* is often regarded as the teaching of general knowledge, while *training* is believed to focus on the teaching of specific, job-relevant skills. This Method does not dwell on this distinction because it is assumed that both education and training require instruction. In discussions of the evaluation criteria, the term

19

instruction is used to refer to both education and training. Instruction is a structured process through which individuals learn new knowledge and skills. Therefore, learning is the product of the instructional process. If we want effective learning, we need to ensure that the process is working as effectively as possible. The Method provides a way to evaluate the quality of both education and training.

What is Quality?

Most people would agree that quality is important in the products we buy, the items we create, and in our "quality of life." However, less agreement is found when we try to define quality. Hays et al. (2003) discussed some of the ways quality has been defined and conclude that quality is found in the interaction of persons with the world and that it is defined by the standards they set. Botha (2000) described six conceptions of quality, as the term is applied to instructional products.

- *Quality as "exceptional."* In this sense, saying an instructional product is of high quality means that it is something special, distinctive, of high class, and surpassing very high standards. It is an example of "excellence."
- *Quality as "perfection."* This conception of quality means that there are minimal defects (absence of defects) in an instructional product, when measured against a set of standards.
- *Quality as "fitness for purpose."* When an instructional product does the job it is designed for (e.g., it meets its instructional objectives), it can be said to be of high quality.
- *Quality as "facilitating changes" in learners.* When a learner takes a course, it is with the intent of learning new knowledge, skills, and abilities (KSAs), which are influenced by the learner's attitudes (affect). The instructional product is intended to transform the learner. If these changes enable the learner to excel in his or her chosen field, the product can be said to be of high quality.
- *Quality as "value for money."* Instructional products must be "purchased." If the organization that procures the product believes they have received good value for their investment, the product can be said to be of high quality. For

instructional products designed for military and industrial instructional users, the most unambiguous method to determine good value is demonstrated improvement in job performance or alternatively, demonstrated equivalent job performance for lower instructional costs.

The Purpose of the Instructional Quality Evaluation Method

Broadbent and Cotter (2003) observed that the word evaluation is derived from the word "value." A quality evaluation seeks to establish the value of the instructional programs or products that are developed and procured. To accomplish this, the instructional programs or products should be evaluated against criteria that address all of the conceptions of quality listed above. The Method provides a set of criteria that meets this objective. These evaluation criteria are shown in Table 1, which also serves as a summary sheet for accumulating evaluation scores. The evaluation criteria are divided into two main sections: instructional features criteria and user interface criteria. Although many of the criteria apply to all forms of instruction, the main focus of the method is the evaluation of computer-delivered courseware that is designed for use without the presence of an instructor.

Formative and Summative Evaluations

The Method supports both formative and summative evaluations. Formative evaluations are conducted during courseware development. They normally focus on the efforts of the development team so modifications and corrections can be made before they negatively impact learning. Summative evaluations are conducted after the courseware has been implemented. They focus on the effectiveness of the instruction and how learners are able to use their new knowledge and skills. The discussion sections for each criterion include recommendations for how to use the Method for both formative and summative evaluations.

Table 1:
Instructional Quality Evaluation Summary Sheet

Instructional Features Evaluation		
Rating Criteria	Score (1-5)*	
1. Instructional Content		
1.a. The presentation of content is logical (note: rate this after the other criteria).		
1.b. The purpose of the course is clearly stated.		
1.c. The instructional objectives are clearly stated.		
1.d. The content supports each and every instructional objective.		
1.e. The content is free of errors.		
1.f. The content is job-relevant.		
1.g. "Authority" for content is clearly stated.		
1.h. There are clear indications of prerequisites.		
1.i. There are clear indications of completed topics.		
1.j. Sources for more information are available.		
Content Subtotal		
2. Instructional Activities		
2.a. Activities are relevant (all support LOs & job requirements).		
2.b. The learner is required to interact with content.		
2.c. Instruction is engaging (attracts and maintains learners' attention).		
2.d. Instructional media directly support learning activities.		
Activities Subtotal		
3. Performance Assessment		
3.a. Assessments are relevant.		
3.b. Assessments are logical.		
3.c. Assessments are varied.		
Assessment Subtotal		
4. Performance Feedback		
4.a. Feedback is timely.		
4.b. Feedback is meaningful (related to objectives).		
4.c. Positive reinforcement is provided for correct responses.		
4.d. Remediation is provided for incorrect responses.		
Feedback Subtotal		
Instructional Features Subtotal (carry to next page)		

*Note: No matter what the overall score, a score of *one (1)* on *any criterion* should be considered a *major problem* and *requires redesign* of the instructional product. A score of *two (2)* on any criterion should be considered a problem and *may require redesign.*

Table 1:

(Continued)

User Interface Evaluation		
Evaluation Criteria	Score (1-5)*	
5. Navigation and Operation		
5.a. User Interface makes course structure explicit		
5.b. Tutorial is available to explain navigation and operation features.		
5.c. Help function is available to explain navigation & operation features.		
5.d. Includes all necessary navigation and operation controls.		
5.e. Navigation & operation controls are clearly and consistently labeled.		
5.f. Navigation & operation controls are located in consistent place.		
5.g. Navigation & operation controls function consistently.		
5.h. Course show's learner's location.		
5.i. Course show's how learner arrived at location.		
5.j. Course show's estimated time required for each module.		
Navigation & Operation Subtotal		
6. Content Presentation		
6.a. There are no sensory conflicts.		
6.b. All media are clear and sharp.		
6.c. Screens are aesthetically pleasing.		
6.d. Multi-modal presentation of content is used.		
6.e. Multi-media presentation of content is used.		
6.f. Media are easy to use.		
6.g. External hyperlinks are kept to a minimum.		
Presentation Subtotal		
7. Installation and Registration		
7.a. Course does not require installation or learners can install the course without assistance.		
7.b. Minimal "plug-ins" are required.		
7.c. "Optimization" test is available.		
7.d. Technical support is available.		
7.e. Registration is simple & straightforward (or not required).		
Installation and Registration Subtotal		
User Interface Subtotal (from this page)		
Instructional Features Subtotal (from previous page)		
Total Quality Score (sum of subtotals)		

*Note: No matter what the overall score, a score of *one (1)* on *any criterion* should be considered a *major problem* and *requires redesign* of the instructional product. A score of *two (2)* on any criterion should be considered a problem and *may require redesign.*

Description of the Method

The instructional quality evaluation method (the Method) uses anchored rating scales so evaluators can assign a score on each evaluation criterion. The anchor statements below the scales help to standardize the evaluations make the scales easier for the user. The scales are the essence of the method. They are designed to support an evaluation without the need to consult additional information. If an evaluator has limited time or other resources, the scales contain all of the necessary information to conduct a meaningful evaluation. However, if the evaluator has enough resources, he or she may conduct an "in-depth" evaluation. The discussions can also be used to obtain additional information on the importance of a criterion and help the evaluator understand the empirical and theoretical research that supports it. These discussions include definitions of terms and recommendations for designing instructional programs or products. The discussions also include suggestions for locating resources that provide additional details.

The detailed discussions (Sections II and III) are necessary because evaluation of instructional programs or products is not an easy task. The more an evaluator understands the importance of each criterion, the better he or she will be able to assign a score. Evaluation usually requires the evaluator to invest time and attention for a detailed review of the courseware. In essence, the evaluator may have to "take the course," sometimes multiple times from different perspectives (e.g., a novice learner, an experienced learner, an instructor, etc.). An example of the recommended steps to follow in evaluating courseware is shown in Table 2 (Coursestar, 2003). This is a good beginning. However, the Method presented in this book is much more elaborate and quantitative. It allows individuals to evaluate courseware on a comprehensive set of empirically- and theoretically-based criteria that support learning.

Beyond "buzz words". Many existing evaluation approaches recommend criteria, such as "the content has educational value," "presentation of content is clear and logical," "graphics are appropriate," "package is motivational," or "feedback is effectively applied." However, these criteria are seldom explained, nor are they accompanied by some form or "anchored" evaluation scale. Also, the terms used in these criteria are usually left to the user to define. Without specific, standard definitions of terms and explanations of the context where each term is applied, evaluators could actually be evaluating different concepts. Therefore, this Method includes "anchored" evaluation scales and the discussions includes definitions and explanations of all terms and how the terms are used in the context of the evaluation criteria.

A Systems Approach. An *instructional system* (or training system) is the planned interaction of people, materials, and techniques, which has the goal of improved performance as measured by established criteria from the job (Hays, 1992; 2006). The *people* in an instructional system include, but are not limited to: the learner, the instructor, the course developer(s), effectiveness evaluators, administrators, logistics managers, subject matter experts, instructional media designers and implementers, and sometimes on-the-job supervisors. Some of the *materials* in an instructional system are: instructional content, instructional media, devices, documents, job-specific equipment, and evaluation instruments (such as the evaluation scales presented in this book). Some of the *techniques* employed in instructional systems include: needs analysis, instructional design approaches, instructional aids design methods, instructional effectiveness evaluation methods, logistics analysis, and cost-benefit analysis (often called return on investment analysis). Finally, some of the *interactions*, which take place in instructional systems, include those during development and evaluation. They also include instructor-learner interactions, learner-content interactions, and learner-learner interactions that take place during instruction.

Table 2:
Recommended Steps to Evaluate Courseware

Step 1. Run the program briefly to become familiar with its operation and features.
Step 2. Execute the program as a conscientious learner, avoiding intentional or careless errors. Extend the program when possible by interacting as a creative learner would.
Step 3. Execute the program as a careless learner would. Respond incorrectly to test how the program handles learner errors. Repeat the same response and also try giving different incorrect responses. Make other kinds of errors such as typing mistakes, incorrect form of input, content errors, and errors in following directions.
Step 4. Choose a checklist for the evaluation of software adapting it as necessary to fit your own needs. Key factors to consider:

Directions	The directions should be complete, readable, under the user's control, and they should include appropriate examples.
Input	A program should ensure that a user knows when and in what form input is needed. Usually, minimal typing should be required.
Screen formatting	Are the screens easy to understand-not distracting or cluttered?
Documentation	Includes instructional objectives, suggested activities, instruction for teacher modification, and other needed information?

Step 5. Record your evaluation in the appropriate form.

Hays discussed a variety of system concepts that affect the quality of instructional systems (1992; 2006) and web-based instructional products (2001). Foremost among these system concepts is that *any instructional product is part of a larger instructional system.* As a system, a change in any part of the instructional program or product can affect the system as a whole. It is assumed that lack of attention to quality on any criterion can reduce the overall quality of the courseware. This is because a violation of any criterion could affect the instructional quality as measured by other criteria. It is therefore important to *use every criterion* when determining overall quality. Furthermore, a score of *one (1) on any criterion* should be considered to be a *serious problem* and will probably require some level of *redesign* of the courseware. Further explanations are provided in the section on interpretation of scores.

Evaluating instructional programs or products is a difficult and complex task that may require the evaluator to delve into a course with almost as much attention as a learner. For developers, evaluation of their instructional products should be an ongoing process during and after development. Resource constraints (e.g., time, money) can limit the amount of effort a developer devotes to certain elements of a course. Even so, it cannot be emphasized too strongly that each and every one of the criteria in the Method should be evaluated at some level. In addition, if the evaluator finds any major type of distraction that is not addressed in this Method, he or she should consider revising the course.

CHAPTER 2:
THE EVALUATION SCALES

The following scales allow an evaluator to rate computer-delivered instructional programs or products on criteria that are important to the quality of instruction. All of the scales are scored on a 5-point scale ranging from one (1) to five (5). The scales include descriptive anchors to help the evaluator assign a score. Some of the scales also include examples or important things to look for when conducting the evaluation.

To assist the evaluator, the anchor statements use terms like "almost none," "few," "some," "most," and "almost all." A few of the scales contain anchor statements that combine certain features (e.g., few of "this" and some of "that"). It should be noted that the anchor statements are illustrative and should only be used as a guide when scoring. Most of the scales ask the rater to indicate how much, how often, or how extensively a given feature appears in the courseware. To assist in choosing a rating, it may be helpful to think in terms of percentages. Thus, a rating of one (1) is roughly 0-10%, a two (2) is roughly 25%, a three (3) is roughly 50%, a four (4) is roughly 75%, and a five (5) is roughly 90-100%. Use these percentages as a guide in addition to the anchor statements and examples.

An individual evaluator can assign scores on the scales or the scales can be used in a group evaluation. In the second case, the ratings on each criterion could be an average of all the ratings in the group. Reiser and Kegelmann (1994) suggest that instructional products should be evaluated by up to three raters. They further suggest that these individuals can work either independently or together when conducting their evaluations. Group ratings can be consensus scores, assigned after group discussions. This is the recommended approach.

Using the Criteria and Scales During Different Instructional Development Phases. The scales and anchor statements are presented in a form that supports summative evaluations (after implementation). However, the criteria (and scales) can also be used during each of the stages of instructional systems development (ISD). In early ISD stages, the criteria support formative evaluations, without the need to "formally" assign scores on the scales. For example, during the requirements analysis phase, the criteria can be used to help focus the analysis to identify the critical content information, presentation alternatives, and implementation issues. An important part of this analysis is to determine the prerequisites and purpose of the course. This, in turn, will help determine how to structure items of content so they are mutually supportive.

The criteria can also be applied formatively during the development phase to help the instructional developers focus on important design principles and how to include these in the courseware. This can enable the developers to recognize and correct problems before they are "cast in stone." At this stage, the anchor statements for the scales can help the developers evaluate their ongoing efforts.

During the implementation phase, the scales can be iteratively used to help ensure that implementation issues do not conflict with or override important instructional requirements. For example, courseware that requires "plug-ins" (extra software programs) that are not allowed on the learner's computer because of organizational policy would need to be redesigned. Finally, during the evaluation phase, the scales provide the capability to conduct summative evaluations to determine both the strengths of the courseware and also any weaknesses that may be corrected in later iterations. Chapter 12 includes detailed discussions of how to use the Method at each stage of ISD.

The Roles of Different Types of Evaluators. The definition of an instructional system presented in Chapter 1 referred to a variety of people who interact to develop and implement an instructional system. The Method and the discussions that support it focus on three main types of people: program managers, instructional developers, and instructors. Program managers usually control the budget and are ultimately responsible for delivering an effective instructional product. They normally do not develop the courseware, but must make decisions on who to hire to conduct the development and whether they have successfully accomplished their task. The Method can help these managers select the appropriate development team based on how well they address the criteria in their project proposals. During development (e.g., storyboard reviews, interface design meetings, small group tryouts) the program managers can use the criteria to evaluate the progress of the development team. At project completion, the program managers can use the Method to determine if the courseware has met its goals (e.g., is it worth the investment?).

Instructional developers can use the Method to focus the efforts of the development team. Too often resources are devoted to the development of new types of technologies that may not add to the instructional value of the program or product. By using the criteria to focus their efforts, the instructional developers can be confident that they are directing their time and energy toward issues that have been shown to positively affect the effectiveness of instructional programs and products.

Instructors are the persons who must ultimately deliver the instruction. In some cases, they are also involved on program development teams. Instructors can use the criteria to help them develop their lesson plans and to help them determine how to insert the computer-delivered instruction into their larger instructional programs.

In recent times, computer-delivered courseware has been designed to be delivered to learners without instructor assistance. In these cases, it is extremely important that program managers and instructional developers ensure that all of the functions that are normally conducted by the instructor are included in the courseware (e.g., assessment of learner performance, delivery of performance feedback, and remediation of poor performance). The Method can be used to ensure that these instructor functions are designed into the courseware.

The people discussed above have different levels of involvement depending on which stage of ISD they are engaged. Chapter 12 includes a discussion on how program managers, instructional developers, and instructors can use the Method at each ISD stage.

Instructional Features Evaluation Criteria

The criteria in this section are used to evaluate the manner in which the instructional content is designed and organized for presentation to the learner. They do not address the "appearance" and presentation of the content. The criteria that evaluate these issues are found in the "User Interface" section. Additional information on instructional features criteria is provided in the discussion chapters in Section III.

1. Instructional Content

The first evaluation areas consists of instructional features evaluation criteria that deal with how the content is organized so that the learner receives the highest quality instruction from the course. The content should be organized and presented to maximize the probability that learners will learn the knowledge and skills that are needed from the course. This involves motivating learners, gaining and maintaining their attention, and helping them to transfer the learned knowledge and skills to their jobs. The instruction should be designed to include all of the necessary events for effective instruction (e.g., Gagné and Briggs, 1979). It should also help learners develop confidence that they are obtaining the instruction that will support their specific learning needs.

There are a variety of labels for the organizational sections of a course. For example, one method is to label the sections as follows: Course, Module, Lesson, Topic, and Subtopic. In this example, each section following "course" is a smaller, subset of the section preceding it. For the purposes of this Method, no distinction is made between these terms because there is so much variation in how they are used in the instructional development community. In most discussions the terms "topic" will be used.

1.a. The Presentation of Content is Logical

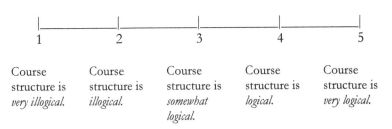

1	2	3	4	5
Course structure is *very illogical.*	Course structure is *illogical.*	Course structure is *somewhat logical.*	Course structure is *logical.*	Course structure is *very logical.*

Instructions: Using the anchor statements above and the list of things to look for below, circle the number that best describes how logically the course content is presented. It is *highly recommended* that evaluators wait to assign a score on this criterion until they have assigned scores on the other criteria.

Note: The logic of content presentation includes both "syntactical logic" (following the rules of language and the logical connection of ideas) and "instructional logic" (following an accepted instructional model of combination of instructional models). Additional information on these two components of logic is presented in Chapter 3.

Things to look for to determine the instructional logic of the content presentation:

- Content structure is clearly visible (e.g., table of contents, course outline; see also Criterion 5.a, Chapter 8 for additional details on how the user interface can make the course structure explicit)
- Instructional content is organized to support learning objectives (see Criterion 1.c, Chapter 4)
- Learning objectives support each other (also see Table 6, Chapter 3)
- No learning objectives conflict (also see Table 6, Chapter 3)
- Content is logically consistent (e.g., is free from internal conflicts)
- Instructional content builds on prior learning
- Content builds in complexity
- Content uses advance organizers and summaries
- Content appropriately emphasizes or highlights important information (e.g., uses cues and signals)

1.b. The Purpose of the Course is Clearly Stated

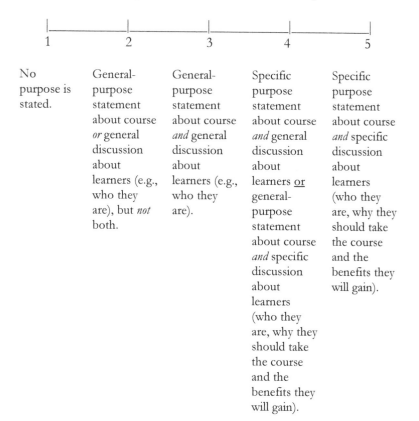

1	2	3	4	5
No purpose is stated.	General-purpose statement about course *or* general discussion about learners (e.g., who they are), but *not* both.	General-purpose statement about course *and* general discussion about learners (e.g., who they are).	Specific purpose statement about course *and* general discussion about learners *or* general-purpose statement about course *and* specific discussion about learners (who they are, why they should take the course and the benefits they will gain).	Specific purpose statement about course *and* specific discussion about learners (who they are, why they should take the course and the benefits they will gain).

Instructions: Using the examples below and anchor statements above, circle the number that best characterizes how the purpose of the course is communicated to the learner.

Examples of Increasing Specificity, Relevance, and Clarity of Purpose Statements:

- (1) N/A
- (2)"The purpose of this course is to teach you to be a better leader." Or "This course is for beginning supervisors."
- (3) "The purpose of this course is to teach beginning supervisors how to be better leaders."

34

- (4) "The purpose of this course is to teach beginning supervisors how to conduct a performance appraisal with their subordinates." Or "The purpose of this course is to teach beginning supervisors to be better leaders so they can better manage their subordinates."

- (5) "Effective performance appraisals are important because they help employees know how they are doing on their jobs, what they need to do to improve their performance, and motivate them to achieve. The purpose of this course is to train beginning supervisors in program management to conduct more effective performance appraisals with their subordinates. After completing this course you, a beginning supervisor in program management, will be better able to conduct performance appraisals with your subordinates that will be meaningful and will help them do a better job."

1.c. The Instructional Objectives Are Clearly Stated

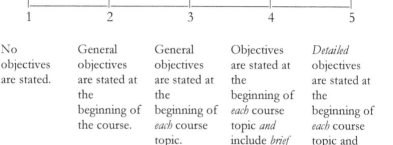

1	2	3	4	5
No objectives are stated.	General objectives are stated at the beginning of the course.	General objectives are stated at the beginning of *each* course topic.	Objectives are stated at the beginning of *each* course topic *and* include *brief* statements describing actions, standards, & conditions.	*Detailed* objectives are stated at the beginning of *each* course topic and include *detailed* statements describing *all* actions, standards, & conditions.

Instructions: Using the anchor statements above, circle the number that indicates how clearly the instructional objectives of the course are communicated to the learner.

Note: If you give a rating of one (1) on this criterion, you must also rate the next criterion (1.d.) as one (1).

1.d. The Content Supports Each and Every Instructional Objective

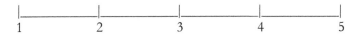

1	2	3	4	5
No instructional objectives are supported.	*Few* instructional objectives are supported.	*Some* instructional objectives are supported.	*Most* instructional objectives are supported.	*All* instructional objectives are supported.

Instructions: Using the anchor statements above, circle the number that indicates how well the course content supports each and every instructional objective.

Note: If the score on 1.c is one (1) you must also give this criterion a score of one (1).

1.e. The Content is Free of Errors

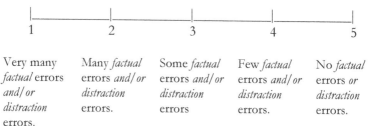

1	2	3	4	5
Very many *factual* errors *and/or* *distraction* errors.	Many *factual* errors *and/or* *distraction* errors.	Some *factual* errors *and/or* *distraction* errors	Few *factual* errors *and/or* *distraction* errors.	No *factual* errors *or* *distraction* errors.

Instructions: Using the anchor descriptions above and the list of types of errors below, circle the number that best indicates how much the course is free of errors.

Types of Errors and Examples:

Factual Errors
- Incorrect definitions
- Incorrect formulas
- Math errors
- Logical errors in examples or presentations
- Other obvious factual errors

Distraction Errors
- Typos
- Mislabeled graphics
- Grammatical errors
- Shifts in tense
- Shifts in voice (e.g., human to computer-generated or changes in accent)
- Unexpected addition of sounds or narration
- Shifts in sound level
- Unexpected changes in control location (see section 5.f.)
- Malfunctions in interface controls (see section 5.g.)
- Activities that do not perform correctly (e.g., drag and drop answers that bounce back even when correct)
- Other obvious distractions

1.f. The Content is Job-Relevant

1	2	3	4	5
None of the content is job-relevant	*Little* of the content is job relevant.	*Some* of the content is job relevant.	*Most* of the content is job relevant.	*All* of the content is job relevant.

Instructions: Using the statements above and the list of techniques below, circle the number, which best indicates the job-relevance of the course.

Ways Content Can Be Made Job-Relevant:

- Includes clear statements linking information to job tasks
- Examples are from the job context
- Exercises are from the job
- Scenarios, vignettes are from the job
- Includes simulations of job processes and equipment
- Shows how interconnections among items support job tasks
- Includes testimonials and stories from experts at the job
- Provides resources for future job support

1.g. "Authority" for the Content is Clearly Stated

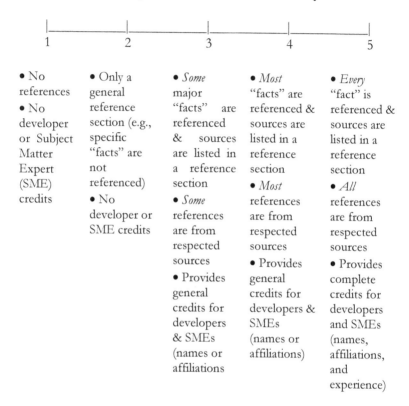

1	2	3	4	5
• No references • No developer or Subject Matter Expert (SME) credits	• Only a general reference section (e.g., specific "facts" are not referenced) • No developer or SME credits	• *Some* major "facts" are referenced & sources are listed in a reference section • *Some* references are from respected sources • Provides general credits for developers & SMEs (names or affiliations	• *Most* "facts" are referenced & sources are listed in a reference section • *Most* references are from respected sources • Provides general credits for developers & SMEs (names or affiliations)	• *Every* "fact" is referenced & sources are listed in a reference section • *All* references are from respected sources • Provides complete credits for developers and SMEs (names, affiliations, and experience)

Instructions: Using the anchor statements above, circle the number, which best characterizes the level of "authority" of the course content.

1.h. There are Clear Indications of Prerequisites

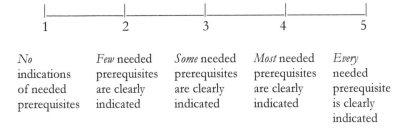

1	2	3	4	5
No indications of needed prerequisites	*Few* needed prerequisites are clearly indicated	*Some* needed prerequisites are clearly indicated	*Most* needed prerequisites are clearly indicated	*Every* needed prerequisite is clearly indicated

Instructions: Using the anchor statements above and the list of ways to indicate prerequisites, circle the number that indicates how well the course indicates needed prerequisites for the learner.

Ways to Indicate Prerequisites:

• Includes statements of any required prerequisite course(s) in the introduction

• Content is sequenced from simple to complex, from basic to detailed, etc.

• Does not allow learner to move to new topic until previous topic has been completed and the learner has been evaluated

1.i. There Are Clear Indications of Completed Topics

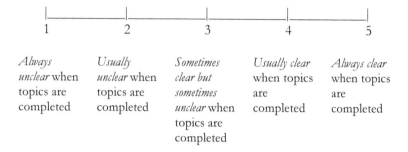

1	2	3	4	5
Always unclear when topics are completed	*Usually unclear* when topics are completed	*Sometimes clear but sometimes unclear* when topics are completed	*Usually clear* when topics are completed	*Always clear* when topics are completed

Instructions: Using the statements above and the examples below for guidance, circle the number that indicates how clearly the course indicates completion of topics.

Indications that a Topic Has Been Completed:

- Unambiguous statements that topic has been completed
- Includes summaries at the end of each topic
- Includes assessments at the end of each topic
- Includes remediation if learner has not mastered each topic
- Completed topic changes color in the table of contents

1.j. Sources for More Information are Available

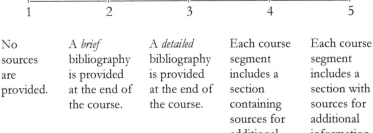

1	2	3	4	5
No sources are provided.	A *brief* bibliography is provided at the end of the course.	A *detailed* bibliography is provided at the end of the course.	Each course segment includes a section containing sources for additional information *and* a detailed bibliography is provided at the end of the course.	Each course segment includes a section with sources for additional information *and* detailed instructions for locating and using the sources for additional information *and* a detailed bibliography is provided at the end of the course.

Instructions: Using the statements above, circle the number that indicates how well the course provides additional information.

(Please go to the next page for Evaluation Area 2, Instructional Activities)

2. Instructional Activities

The second evaluation area includes criteria that deal with the instructional activities that help the learner interact with the content. These activities are essential to help the learner process the knowledge and skills at a deeper level and increase the probability that he or she will be able to perform effectively at some later time (e.g., on the job).

2.a. Activities Are Relevant
(All Support Learning Objectives and Job Requirements)

1	2	3	4	5
No activities or *none* of the activities are relevant	*Few* of the activities are relevant.	*Some* of the activities are relevant.	*Most* of the activities are relevant	*All* of the activities are relevant.

Instructions: Using the anchor statements above and the examples below, indicate how well the course provides relevant activities.
Note: If you rated this criterion as one (1), *do not continue* ratings. This course needs major rework.

Examples of Relevant Activities:
- Role playing in a case study based on real-world issues
- Solving realistic (real-world) problems
- Interacting with realistic simulations
- Identifying the similarities and differences among real-world examples
- Using analogies

44

2.b. The Learner is Required to Interact with Content

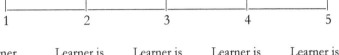

1	2	3	4	5
Learner does not interact with content or only interacts with the interface (e.g., to navigate)	Learner is only required to answer simple factual questions before moving to a new section.	Learner is required to answer simple factual questions and engage in simple activities like "drag and drop" before moving to a new section.	Learner is required to answer factual questions and engage in a variety of activities ranging from simple to complex before moving to a new section.	Learner is required to answer factual questions and engage in a wide variety of activities ranging from simple to complex before moving to a new section.

Instructions: Using the statements above, circle the number that indicates the degree that the learner is "required" to interact with the content of the course.

2.c. Instruction is Engaging
(Attracts & Maintains Learners' Attention)

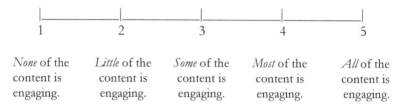

1	2	3	4	5
None of the content is engaging.	*Little* of the content is engaging.	*Some* of the content is engaging.	*Most* of the content is engaging.	*All* of the content is engaging.

Instructions: Based upon *your* experience with the course and the examples below, circle the number that indicates whether you agree or disagree that the instruction is engaging.

Examples:

- Session length is not too long
- Gains and maintains learner attention through appearance of content
- Content is challenging (e.g., builds from simple to complex; uses competition)
- Shows learner that he or she is attaining course objectives
- Uses expert testimonials and real-world examples to make instruction more relevant.
- Engages learner's curiosity and fantasy
- Uses variety in media and instructional methods

2.d. Instructional Media Directly Support Learning Activities

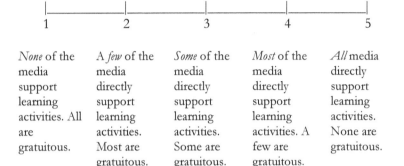

|_____|_____|_____|_____|
1   2   3   4   5

None of the media support learning activities. All are gratuitous.

A *few* of the media directly support learning activities. Most are gratuitous.

Some of the media directly support learning activities. Some are gratuitous.

Most of the media directly support learning activities. A few are gratuitous.

All media directly support learning activities. None are gratuitous.

Instructions: Using the anchor statements above, circle the number that indicates how much the instructional media support the learning activities in the course.

Note: The term *gratuitous* refers to the use of media that are included only because they add glamour or "flash" to the course, but do not add to the instructional value of the course (e.g., they do not explain, elaborate, or clarify).

(Please go to the next page for Evaluation Area 3, Performance Assessment)

3. Performance Assessment

The third evaluation area includes criteria that are used to determine how well the instructional product assesses whether the learners are learning the material.

3.a. Assessments Are Relevant

1	2	3	4	5
None of the assessments are relevant.	*Few* of the assessments are relevant.	*Some* of the assessments are relevant.	*Most* of the assessments are relevant.	*All* of the assessments are relevant.

Instructions: Below is a list of some characteristics of relevant assessments. Read the list and, using the anchor statements above, circle the number that indicates how many of the assessments are relevant.

Note: If you assign a score of one (1) on this criterion, you *must* also assign a score of one (1) to the next two criteria (3.b. & 3.c.).

Characteristics of Relevant Assessments:
- Related to the instructional objectives of the course
- Related to topics and issues that the learner cares about (e.g., will help on job)
- Learner must demonstrate knowledge or skill ("do" versus "know")
- Assessment activities taken from or apply to job requirements

3.b. Assessments Are Logical

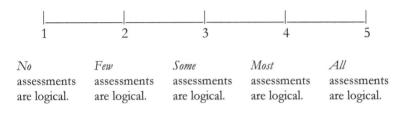

|_____|_____|_____|_____|_____|
1   2   3   4   5

| *No* assessments are logical. | *Few* assessments are logical. | *Some* assessments are logical. | *Most* assessments are logical. | *All* assessments are logical. |

Instructions: Using the list of features of logical assessments and the anchor statements above, circle the number that indicates how many of the assessments are logical. In general, an assessment that has more of the features would indicate a more logical assessment.

Note: If you assigned a score of one (1) to Criterion 3.a., you must also assign a score of one (1) to this criterion.

Features of Logical Assessments:

- Cogently and explicitly support instructional objectives
- Are iterative (assess progress from less to more complex information or tasks)
- Learner expectations are managed by clearly linking assessments to purpose and objectives of course

3.c. Assessments Are Varied

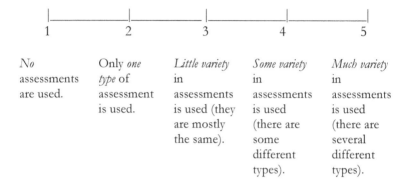

1	2	3	4	5

| *No* assessments are used. | Only *one* *type* of assessment is used. | *Little variety* in assessments is used (they are mostly the same). | *Some variety* in assessments is used (there are some different types). | *Much variety* in assessments is used (there are several different types). |

Instructions: Using the anchor statements above and the examples below, circle the number that best describes how much variety is used in assessment methods.

Note: If you assigned a score of one (1) to Criterion 3.a., you <u>must</u> also assign a score of one (1) to this criterion.

Example Assessments:

- Multiple choice questions on factual information
- Fill in the blank statements of factual information
- True/false statements of factual information
- Completing puzzles based on correct answers

- Drag and drop to match questions and answers
- Role playing of real-world situations
- Simulations of real-world problems
- Assessment games (must include measures of performance)

(Please go to the next page for Evaluation Area 4, Performance Feedback)

4. Performance Feedback

Feedback is an essential component of high quality instruction. If well designed, feedback serves as another instructional opportunity. The fourth evaluation area includes criteria that address how the instructional product provides feedback to learners about how well they are learning the material.

4.a. Feedback is Timely

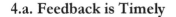

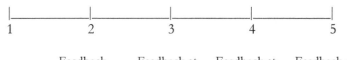

1	2	3	4	5
No feedback is provided	Feedback only at the end of the course.	Feedback at end of each major segment.	Feedback at end every segment.	Feedback at end of each *activity* within a segment.

Instructions: Using the anchor statements above, circle the number, which indicates the timeliness of the feedback, provided in the course.

Note: If you give a one (1) rating on this criterion, you *must* also rate the next three criteria (4.b., 4.c., & 4.d.) as one (1).

4.b. Feedback is Meaningful

1	2	3	4	5
No feedback is provided	*Little* of the feedback is meaningful.	*Some* of the feedback is meaningful.	*Most* of the feedback is meaningful.	*All* of the feedback is meaningful.

Instructions: Using the statements above and the examples below circle the number that indicates how much meaningful feedback is provided to the learner.

Note: If you rated the previous criterion (4.a) as one (1), you must also rate this criterion as one (1).

Examples of meaningful feedback:

- Is based on concrete learning goals (instructional objectives) that are clearly presented to the learners
- Describes the gap between the learner's learning goal and the learner's current performance and suggests how to close the gap
- Focuses the learner's attention on the learning goal and not on failure to achieve the goal
- Is appropriate for the ability level of the learner (e.g., not too complex for novices; detailed enough for experts)
- Provides additional information
- Corrects learner errors
- Asks for clarification
- Debates issues and explains disagreements
- Ties concepts to one another
- Offers insight based on expert experience

4.c. Positive Reinforcement is Provided for Correct Responses

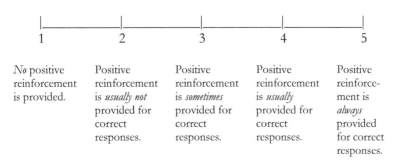

1	2	3	4	5
No positive reinforcement is provided.	Positive reinforcement is *usually not* provided for correct responses.	Positive reinforcement is *sometimes* provided for correct responses.	Positive reinforcement is *usually* provided for correct responses.	Positive reinforcement is *always* provided for correct responses.

Instructions: Using the anchor statements above and the definition of positive reinforcement below, circle the number that indicates how often positive reinforcement is provided for incorrect responses.

Note: If you rated Criterion 4.a as one (1), you *must* also rate this criterion as one (1). Also note, in an instructional context, reinforcement should be more than simply indicating that the answer is "correct."

Definition of Positive Reinforcement

Positive reinforcement is a stimulus (e.g., praise, food, or money) provided after someone emits a behavior that increases the probability that the behavior will occur again. Positive reinforcement can be given in many ways and under many different schedules (e.g., after every behavior [continuous reinforcement], after some number of behaviors [fixed-ratio schedule], after a set time period [fixed-interval schedule]). Specific types of reinforcement and reinforcement schedules must be determined in the context of the course. Ideally, reinforcement should be another instructional experience.

4.d. Remediation is Provided for Incorrect Responses

1	2	3	4	5
No remediation is provided.	Remediation is provided for *few* incorrect responses.	Remediation is provided for *some* incorrect responses.	Remediation is provided for *most* incorrect responses.	Remediation is provided for *all* incorrect responses.

Instructions: Using the examples below and the anchor statements above, circle the number that indicates how often remediation is provided for incorrect responses.

Note: If you rated Criterion 4.a as one (1), you must also rate this criterion as one (1).

Examples of Remediation:
- Explains why the response was incorrect
- Provided in a non-threatening, encouraging manner
- Provides the correct answer or demonstrates correct skill performance
- Encourages the learner to obtain more instruction on correct behavior
- Leads the learner to remedial instruction
- Also see Criterion 4.b.

(Please go to the next page for User Interface Evaluation Criteria [Evaluation Areas 5-7])

User Interface Evaluation Criteria

The User Interface criteria deal with how the instructional content is presented to the learner, how the learner moves through the content, and how he or she controls instructional activities (e.g., playing a video). In general, the user interface should be designed to make things easier for the learner (it should be "learner-centric"). Additional information on these criteria is provided in the discussion chapters in Section III.

(Please go to the next page to begin Evaluation Area 5, Navigation and Operation)

5. Navigation and Operation

This evaluation area includes criteria about how the learner is shown the course structure and provided the means to move about the course and operate the controls for course activities.

5.a. User Interface Makes Course Structure Explicit

1	2	3	4	5
No course structure is shown on user interface.	*Basic* course structure is shown on the user interface (e.g., course outline), *but* does help the learner understand how course segments fit together and support one another.	*Basic* course structure is shown on the user interface (e.g., course outline). Summaries or other methods are used to help the learner understand *only* how the major course segments fit together and support one another.	*Detailed* course outline (expandable as needed) is shown on the interface. Summaries or other methods are used to help the learner understand how *all* course segments fit together and support one another.	*Detailed* course outline (expandable as needed) is shown on the interface. Summaries or other methods are used to help the learner understand how *all* course segments fit together and support one another. When instructionally useful, the GUI allows learner to easily move to different segments of the course.

Instructions: Using the anchor statements above and the examples below circle the number that best describes the user interface of the course.

Example ways to make the course structure explicit:

- Interface includes the course structure as part of its main display and indicates the learner's current location at all times (see also Criterion 5.h).

- Course outline (table of contents) always available and can be expanded to show detailed level

- Course map shows course structure and segments are accessible from course map

- Summaries of course segments are available as "previews."

- Shows history of course segments the learner has completed

- Search function is available to locate information on specific topics

5.b. Tutorial is Available to Explain Navigation & Operation Features

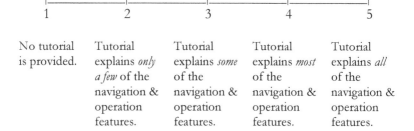

1	2	3	4	5
No tutorial is provided.	Tutorial explains *only a few* of the navigation & operation features.	Tutorial explains *some* of the navigation & operation features.	Tutorial explains *most* of the navigation & operation features.	Tutorial explains *all* of the navigation & operation features.

Instructions: Using the anchor statements above and the examples below circle the number that best describes the tutorial provided with the course.

Ways to design tutorials:

- Walk-through with text and narration
- Animation of moving cursor with text narration
- Animated "guide" (avatar)
- Text and graphics

5.c. Help Function is Available to Explain Navigation & Operation Features

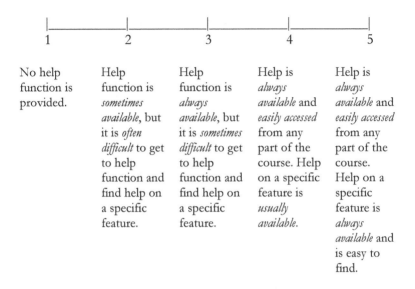

1	2	3	4	5
No help function is provided.	Help function is *sometimes available*, but it is *often difficult* to get to help function and find help on a specific feature.	Help function is *always available*, but it is *sometimes difficult* to get to help function and find help on a specific feature.	Help is *always available* and *easily accessed* from any part of the course. Help on a specific feature is *usually available*.	Help is *always available* and *easily accessed* from any part of the course. Help on a specific feature is *always available* and is easy to find.

Instructions: Using the anchor statements above and the examples below circle the number that best describes the help functions available in the course.

Examples of ways to access help:

- Right-click on a control to access text and narration
- Roll over and pause on control to access text and narration
- Click on help button to ask question or access alphabetical list of instructions or explanations
- Access to specific segments of the tutorial to explain features

5.d. Includes All Necessary Navigation & Operation Controls

1	2	3	4	5
No interaction after course starts. Course leads learner through the material at a predetermined pace.	Includes *few* navigation controls. Little learner control.	Includes *some* navigation controls. Some learner control.	Includes *most* navigation controls. Considerable learner control of media and time on topic.	Includes *all* navigation controls. Learner has complete control of activities and media, time on topic, and movement (except for sequence of instructional segments).

Instructions: Using the anchor statements above and the list of possible navigation and operation controls below, circle the number that indicates if the course includes all navigational controls needed to move through the course and effectively interact with the content (e.g., operate presentation media like video players).

Note: Only consider the navigation and operation controls that are *necessary* in the course (e.g., if no videos are includes then no VCR-type controls are needed and you should not lower the score).

Possible Navigation and Operation Controls:

- Start
- Stop
- Pause
- Resume (may use "start" button)
- Mark place in course (bookmark)
- VCR-type controls for videos (start, stop, pause, rewind, fast forward, etc.)

- Go forward by screen
- Go backward by screen
- Go forward by lesson
- Go backward by lesson
- Return to main menu

- Return to beginning of course
- Print a screen
- Print selected text
- Take notes
- Save a copy of work
- Volume control for audio
- Search function (e.g., keywords)

5.e. Navigation & Operation Controls are Clearly & Consistently Labeled

1	2	3	4	5
None of the navigation & operation controls are clearly and consistently labeled.	*Few* of the navigation & operation controls are clearly and consistently labeled.	*Some* of the navigation & operation controls are clearly and consistently labeled.	*Most* of the navigation & operation controls are clearly and consistently labeled.	*All* of the navigation & operation controls are clearly and consistently labeled.

Instructions: Using the anchor statements above, circle the number that indicates how clearly and consistently the navigation and operation controls are labeled throughout the course. Minimally, your opinion should be based on observing the navigation controls in segments at the beginning, middle, and end of the course and also observing more than one screen within each segment. It is always better to observe more of the course before giving a score.

5f. Navigation & Operation Controls are Located in a Consistent Place

1	2	3	4	5

Almost no controls are located in the same place throughout the course.	*Few* controls are located in the same place through the course.	*Some* controls are located in the same place throughout the course.	*Most* controls are located in the same place throughout the course.	*All* controls are located in the same place throughout the course.

Instructions: Using the anchor statements above circle the number that best indicates how many navigation and operation controls are consistently located. Minimally, your rating should be based on observing the navigation controls in segments at the beginning, middle, and end of the course and also observing more than one screen within each segment. It is always better to observe more of the course before giving a score.

5.g. Navigation & Operation Controls Operate Consistently

1	2	3	4	5

| *None* of the controls operate consistently. | *Few* of the controls operate consistently. | *Some* of the controls operate consistently. | *Most* of the controls operate consistently. | *All* of the controls operate consistently. |

Instructions: Using the anchor statements above, circle the number that best characterizes how consistently the navigation and operation controls operate throughout the course. Minimally, your opinion should be based on using the navigation and operation controls in segments at the beginning, middle, and end of the course and also trying them on more than one screen within each segment. It is always better to try the controls in more of the course before assigning a score.

5.h. Course Show's Learner's Location

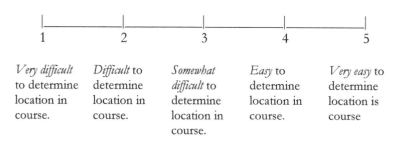

1	2	3	4	5
Very difficult to determine location in course.	*Difficult* to determine location in course.	*Somewhat difficult* to determine location in course.	*Easy* to determine location in course.	*Very easy* to determine location is course

Instructions: Using the anchor statements above and the examples below, circle the number that indicates how easy it is for the learner to know his or her location in the course.

Example Techniques to Help Learner Determine Their Location in the Course:

- Course map (outline) always available with current location highlighted
- Descriptive labels for current topic always available on interface

5.i. Course Show's How Learner Arrived at Location

1	2	3	4	5
Very difficult to determine how one arrived at a location in the course.	*Difficult* to determine how one arrived at a location in the course.	*Somewhat difficult* to determine how one arrived at a location in the course.	*Easy* to determine how one arrived at a location in the course.	*Very easy* to determine how one arrived at a location in the course.

Instructions: Using the anchor statements above and the examples below, circle the number that indicates how easy it is for the learner to know how he or she arrived at a location in the course.

Example Techniques to Help Learner Determine How They Arrived at a Course Location:

- Course map showing "trail" learner has taken through course
- Highlighted "completed" topics on course outline
- Prerequisites must be completed before course "allows" learner to begin a segment

5.j. Course Show's Estimated Time Required for Each Module

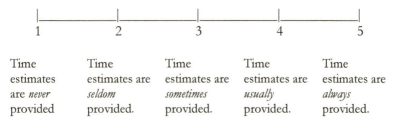

1	2	3	4	5
Time estimates are *never* provided	Time estimates are *seldom* provided.	Time estimates are *sometimes* provided.	Time estimates are *usually* provided.	Time estimates are *always* provided.

Instructions: Using the anchor statements above and the examples below, circle the number that indicates how often the course provides estimated time to complete segments or activities. It is suggested that at least three segments (topics or subtopics) be reviewed to make this determination (more is always better).

Example Techniques:

- Simple statement (e.g., "this module should take about 10 minutes")
- Numerical display (e.g., completed: 3 minutes of 10 minutes)
- Countdown clock
- Sliding scale

6. Content Presentation

The sixth evaluation area includes criteria that deal with how the content is presented. This primarily refers to the appearance or multimedia presentation (combinations of text, graphics, videos, narration, etc.) of the content.

6.a. There Are No Sensory Conflicts

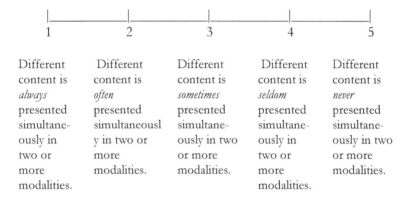

1	2	3	4	5
Different content is *always* presented simultaneously in two or more modalities.	Different content is *often* presented simultaneously in two or more modalities.	Different content is *sometimes* presented simultaneously in two or more modalities.	Different content is *seldom* presented simultaneously in two or more modalities.	Different content is *never* presented simultaneously in two or more modalities.

Instructions: Using the anchor statements above and the examples below indicate how often the course contains sensory conflicts.

(Please see examples on the next page.)

Examples of sensory conflicts:

Media Mix	Example
Text and Audio	Text provides different information from that being presented on an audio track at the same time.
Text and Video	Text provides different information from that being presented in a video being played at the same time.
Text and Conflicting text	Similar to the scrolling text used in some TV news broadcasts. Learner can't attend to both sources.
Video and Audio	Audio track is not synchronized with video or is providing different information.
Sidebars	Extra textual information is provided in a box (sidebar), but the learner does not know when to read this extra information or why it is provided.

6.b. All media are Clear and Sharp

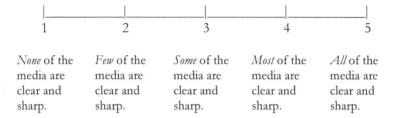

1	2	3	4	5
None of the media are clear and sharp.	*Few* of the media are clear and sharp.	*Some* of the media are clear and sharp.	*Most* of the media are clear and sharp.	*All* of the media are clear and sharp.

Instructions: Using the examples below and the anchor statements above, circle the number that indicates how many of the media in the course are clear and sharp.

Examples of Clear and Sharp Media:

- *Text:* Clear and sharp text is readable for most people without causing eyestrain. The specific font size necessary for readability depends on the medium (e.g., smaller text is easier to read on paper). Larger text is always easier to read.
- *Graphics:* Clear and sharp graphics are large enough that all-important components can be distinguished and any text is readable.
- *Audio:* Clear and sharp audio is loud enough that all words and important sounds (e.g., equipment sounds) can easily be heard and understood.
- *Video:* Clear and sharp video is focused on important components and uses long shots and close-ups to establish the context for those components.

6.c. Screens are Aesthetically Pleasing

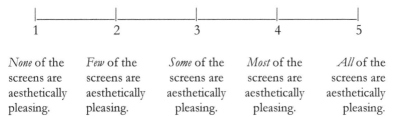

1	2	3	4	5
None of the screens are aesthetically pleasing.	*Few* of the screens are aesthetically pleasing.	*Some* of the screens are aesthetically pleasing.	*Most* of the screens are aesthetically pleasing.	*All* of the screens are aesthetically pleasing.

Instructions: Using the examples below and *your* experience of the course, circle the number that indicates how many of the screens are aesthetically pleasing.

Examples: All aesthetic experience is personal. However, artists use certain principles that result in positive aesthetic experiences for most people. Some of these principles are:

- simplicity
- balance or symmetry
- logical groupings of items by proximity and/or similarity
- colors do not clash
- colors are used to convey important information
- white space is used to separate different ideas and highlight important information

6.d. Multi-modal Presentation of Content is Used

1	2	3	4	5
Only *one* presentation mode is used or multiple presentation modes are randomly used with *no instructional* <u>purpose</u>.	Multiple presentation modes are *seldom* used to reinforce and clarify instructional information.	Multiple presentation modes are *sometimes* used to reinforce and clarify instructional information.	Multiple presentation modes are *often* used to reinforce and clarify instructional information.	Multiple presentation modes are *always* used to reinforce and clarify instructional information.

Instructions: Using the anchor statements above and the examples below, circle the number that indicates how often multi-modal presentation is used in the course.

Note: If you give a one (1) rating on this criterion, you *must* also rate the next criterion (6.e) as a one (1).

Examples of multi-modal presentation:

- An animation is used to clarify a textual description of the movement of oil in an engine
- A video shows the correct placement of text equipment on an electrical panel
- Important points in an audio presentation are emphasized with bulleted text

6.e. Multi-media Presentation of Content is Used

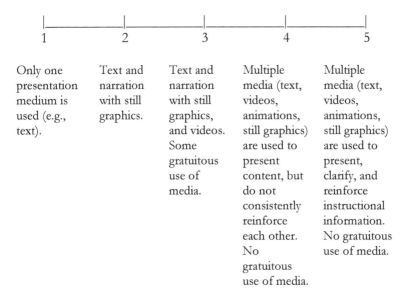

1	2	3	4	5
Only one presentation medium is used (e.g., text).	Text and narration with still graphics.	Text and narration with still graphics, and videos. Some gratuitous use of media.	Multiple media (text, videos, animations, still graphics) are used to present content, but do not consistently reinforce each other. No gratuitous use of media.	Multiple media (text, videos, animations, still graphics) are used to present, clarify, and reinforce instructional information. No gratuitous use of media.

Instructions: Using the statements above and the examples below circle the number that indicates how multiple media are used to present course content. The term *"gratuitous"* means the inclusion of media for no instructional purpose, but only to add "glitz" to the course.

Note: If you rated Criterion 6.d as a one (1), you *must* also rate this criterion as a one (1).

Examples of Instructional Media:
- Classroom lecture (or talking head)
- Video tele-training lecture
- Audio lecture
- Video lecture
- Text instruction
- Animations
- Instructional Games
- Job Performance Aid (JPA)

73

6.f. Media Are Easy to Use

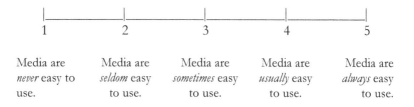

1	2	3	4	5
Media are *never* easy to use.	Media are *seldom* easy to use.	Media are *sometimes* easy to use.	Media are *usually* easy to use.	Media are *always* easy to use.

Instructions: Using the examples below, circle the number that indicates how many of the media are easy to use.

Examples of Easy-to-use Media:
- Standard browser buttons
- Single-click functions
- Familiar VCR-type video controls
- Slide control for audio volume

6.g. External Hyperlinks are Kept to a Minimum

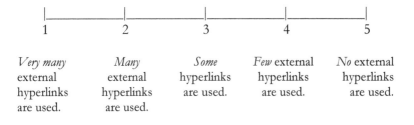

1	2	3	4	5
Very many external hyperlinks are used.	*Many* external hyperlinks are used.	*Some* hyperlinks are used.	*Few* external hyperlinks are used.	*No* external hyperlinks are used.

Instructions: Using the statements above, circle the number that indicates how many external hyperlinks are used in the course. External hyperlinks take the learner to an external site that is not a part of the course itself. The content of the external site cannot be controlled or the site may no longer exist at the time the learner takes the course. These are distinguished from internal hyperlinks that allow the learner to move within the course and are not addressed in this criterion.

(Please go to the next page for Evaluation Area 7, Installation and Registration)

7. Installation and Registration

The seventh evaluation area includes criteria that deal with how the learner installs the course to run on his or her computer.

7.a. Course Does Not Require Installation or Learners Can Install the Course Without Assistance

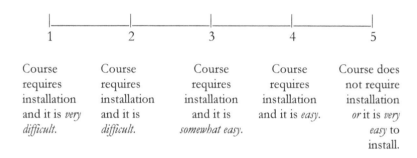

1	2	3	4	5
Course requires installation and it is *very difficult.*	Course requires installation and it is *difficult.*	Course requires installation and it is *somewhat easy.*	Course requires installation and it is *easy.*	Course does not require installation *or* it is *very easy* to install.

Instructions: Using the statements above as a guide, circle the number that indicates how difficult it is to install the course.

7.b. Minimal "Plug-ins" Are Required

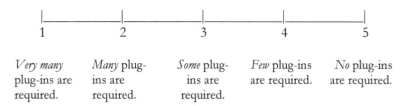

1	2	3	4	5

| *Very many* plug-ins are required. | *Many* plug-ins are required. | *Some* plug-ins are required. | *Few* plug-ins are required. | *No* plug-ins are required. |

Instructions: Using the statements above as a guide, circle the number that indicates how many plug-ins are required to run the course.

Definition of "plug-ins": A plug-in is a program needed to run a portion of a course. For example, a video program may be needed to play the videos in a course. Sometimes plug-ins may be automatically downloaded from the internet.

7.c. "Optimization" Test is Available

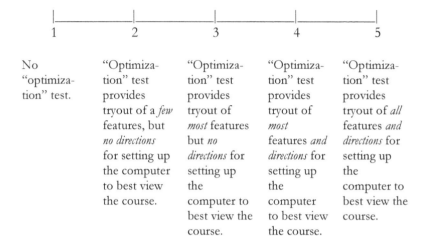

1	2	3	4	5
No "optimization" test.	"Optimization" test provides tryout of a *few* features, but *no directions* for setting up the computer to best view the course.	"Optimization" test provides tryout of *most* features but *no directions* for setting up the computer to best view the course.	"Optimization" test provides tryout of *most* features *and directions* for setting up the computer to best view the course.	"Optimization" test provides tryout of *all* features *and directions* for setting up the computer to best view the course.

Instructions: Using the anchor statements above, circle the number that indicates the quality of the optimization test.

Definition of an "Optimization" Test:

An "optimization" test is a software-based routine that helps the learner try out all of the features of the course to ensure that his or her computer is set up to support the optimal presentation of all media used in the course.

7.d. Technical Support is Available

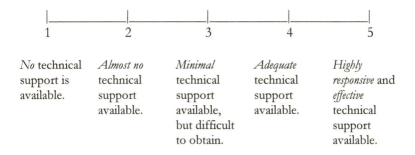

1	2	3	4	5
No technical support is available.	*Almost no* technical support available.	*Minimal* technical support available, but difficult to obtain.	*Adequate* technical support available.	*Highly responsive* and *effective* technical support available.

Instructions: Using the anchor statements above and the characteristics listed below, circle the number that indicates the quality of technical support provided with the course.

Characteristics of Effective Technical Support:
- Easy to obtain
- Responsive to needs
- Available any time

7.e. Registration is Simple and Straightforward
(Or Not Required)

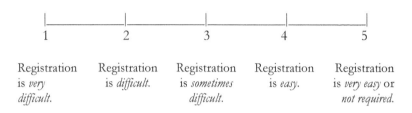

1	2	3	4	5
Registration is *very* difficult.	Registration is *difficult*.	Registration is *sometimes* difficult.	Registration is *easy*.	Registration is *very easy* or *not required*.

Instructions: Using the statements above, circle the number that indicates how easy it is to register for the course.

Note: If registration is *not* required, assign a score of five (5) this criterion.

INTERPRETATION OF SCORES

Once the evaluator has assigned a score on of the criteria, he or she should transfer the scores to the summary sheets (Table 1) and add them to generate an overall score for the instructional product. Table 3 shows ranges of scores and a suggested scheme for the interpretation of the scores. There are 43 evaluation criteria. The highest possible score: 215.

Table 3:
Evaluation Scores and Interpretations

Range of Scores	Interpretation
172 – 215	Extremely well designed instructional product. Scored well on all criteria.
151 – 171	Has potential. Scored well on most criteria, but still has some "loose ends" that could be improved.
129 – 150	Has some strengths, but large deficits. Should focus on improving weaknesses.
108 128	Not enough effort invested in instructional design. Confusing and could lead to frustration. Should go back to the "drawing board."
43 – 107	Inadequate. Little or no consideration of instructional design. Not suitable for most learners.

*Note: No matter what the overall evaluation score, a score of *one (1)* on *any criterion* should be considered a *major problem* that will *require redesign* of the instructional product. A score of *two (2)* on any criterion should be considered a *problem* and *may require redesign*.

Interpretation of Scores for Each Evaluation Area

Looking at the subtotal scores for various evaluation areas can help diagnose specific problems in the course. Table 4 provides guidance for interpretation of subtotal scores. If a problem is found in an evaluation area, the ratings for one or more specific criteria can provide more detailed diagnosis.

Table 4:
Interpretation of Subtotal Scores for Evaluation Areas

Evaluation Areas	Interpretation of Subtotal Scores
Instructional Features	105 is the highest possible subtotal score for all instructional features criteria. A subtotal score below 63 is a problem.
Instructional Content (Evaluation Area 1)	50 is the highest possible subtotal for instructional content criteria. A subtotal score below 30 is a problem.
Instructional Activities (Evaluation Area 2)	20 is the highest possible subtotal score for instructional activities criteria. A subtotal score below 12 is a problem.
Performance Assessment (Evaluation Area 3)	15 is the highest possible subtotal score for performance assessment criteria. A subtotal score below 9 is a problem.
Performance Feedback (Evaluation Area 4)	20 is the highest possible subtotal score for performance feedback criteria. A subtotal score below 12 is a problem.

Table 4:
(Continued)

Evaluation Areas	Interpretation of Subtotal Scores
User Interface	110 is the highest possible subtotal score for all user interface criteria. A subtotal score below 66 is a problem. (See note under Area 7, below)
Navigation and Operation (Evaluation Area 5)	50 is the highest possible subtotal score for navigation criteria. A subtotal score below 30 is a problem.
Presentation (Evaluation Area 6)	35 is the highest possible subtotal score for presentation criteria. A subtotal score below 21 is a problem.
Installation & Registration (Evaluation Area 7)	25 is the highest possible subtotal score for installation and registration criteria. A subtotal score below 15 is a problem.

Presentation of Results

There are a variety of techniques that can be used to present the results of the instructional quality evaluation. The level of detail will depend on the audience. For example, program managers will probably need a summary of the overall effectiveness of the courseware (e.g., do learners perform better after taking the course). They might also need a general summary of problems as involved with either instructional or user interface features. Summary scores can help the program manager allocate resources to address the overall weaknesses of the courseware. On the other hand, instructional developers will need a much more detailed diagnostic report so they can correct specific deficiencies in the courseware.

Verbal or written reports can convey the evaluation results. However, written reports are often difficult to interpret, especially for detailed diagnosis of problems. In most cases, written reports are easier to understand if they are supplemented with some form of visual representation of the scores. Graphical presentation of the evaluation scores can be tailored to the level of detail needed by the audience. The following figures show a suggested graphical presentation of some hypothetical evaluation scores. Figure 1 is a bar chart that shows a sample overall summary of an evaluation. On the left side of Figure 1 the courseware is shown to have received a score of 145 (see above the bar). Table 3 explains that this score indicates that the courseware has some strengths, but also has large deficits. The shading of the bar gives the viewer a quick indication that there may be a problem with the courseware.

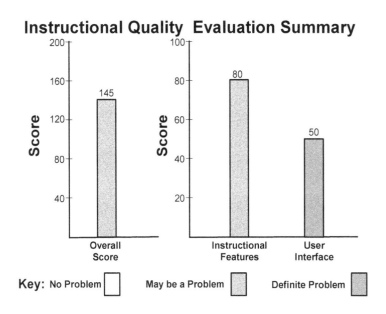

Figure 1:
Sample Overall Summary

More detail is provided on the right side of Figure 1. The two bars show the summary scores for the instructional features and user interface criteria. The instructional features score is 80, which indicates (as shown by the shading of the bar) that there may be a problem with the instructional features of the courseware. However, the shading of the bar showing the user interface score (50) indicates that there is a definite problem with the user interface. Thus, in this example, the overall score for the courseware has probably been lowered by problems with the user interface. This summary indicates that resources for courseware improvement should probably be directed toward improving the user interface.

Additional diagnostic details can be obtained by examining the summary scores for each evaluation area under instructional features and user interface features. Figure 2 shows a hypothetical diagnostic summary. The left side of Figure 2 shows the scores for the four instructional features evaluation areas and the right side shows the summary scores for the three user interface evaluation areas. In this hypothetical diagnostic summary, the score obtained for Evaluation Area 1(instructional content) is 40. This may be a problem as indicated by the shading of the bar. The second Evaluation Area (instructional activities) has a definite problem, as shown by the shading of the bar and the score of 11. The third bar (Evaluation Area 3, performance assessment) shows that there may be a problem. The fourth bar indicates that there is no problem with Evaluation Area 4 (performance feedback). Thus, in this diagnostic sample, the most resources should be devoted to correcting problems with the instructional activities provided in the courseware. If additional resources are available, they should be used to correct problems with the instructional content and performance assessment.

The right side of Figure 2 shows summaries of the three evaluation areas under user interface. These summaries indicate that resources should be directed to correcting problems with the presentation of the content (Evaluation Area 6). This means that

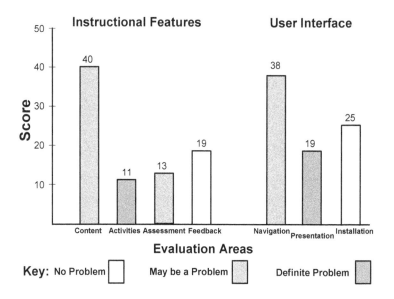

Figure 2:
Sample Diagnostic Summary

the appearance of the courseware (e.g., the combinations of text, graphics, videos, narration, etc.) needs to be improved. No corrections are needed for the installation and registration of the courseware, but some attention should be directed toward improving the navigation and operation of the courseware.

An even more detailed diagnostic report can be obtained by examining the scores on each individual criterion. Figure 3 shows a hypothetical detailed diagnostic summary that shows the scores on each of the criteria in Evaluation Area 1 (Instructional Content). Figure 3 shows that the main problems with the courseware are indicated by the scores on Criterion 1.b (the purpose of the course is clearly stated), Criterion 1.f (the content is job relevant), and Criterion 1.h (there are clear indications of prerequisites). These areas require corrective actions. Once these problems are corrected, additional resources could be directed to other issues that may be problems.

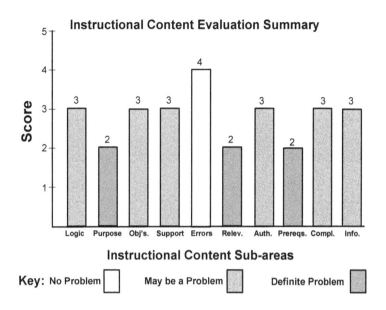

Figure 3:
Sample Detailed Diagnostic Summary

SECTION II:
DETAILED DISCUSSIONS OF
INSTRUCTIONAL FEATURES
EVALUATION CRITERIA

The following discussions provide information to help the evaluator understand and more confidently assign ratings to each of the instructional features evaluation criteria. The chapters in this section present discussions for the instructional features evaluation areas (e.g., Area 1: Instructional Content; Area 2: Instructional Activities; etc.). The discussions begin with directions for using the scales. This is followed by definitions of terms and discussions of concepts and techniques to maximize the quality of instructional products as measured by each criterion. The discussions also provide summaries of some of the literature that supports each criterion.

Learner-Centric Evaluations. In conducting the evaluation, the evaluator should try to think in terms of how the learner will perceive the instructional product. Thus the evaluation should be "learner-centric." For example, if the evaluator is trying to determine if the purpose of the course is clearly stated (criteria 1.b.), he or she should ask whether the learner can understand the purpose of the course. Although it is vitally important for the developer to understand the purpose of the course, this understanding is moot if it is not communicated to the learner.

The Distinction Between Information, Instruction, and Learning. It is often assumed that any source of information (e.g., a web site or a news report) is also instruction. This is because many do not understand the distinction between information, instruction, and learning. Hays (2006) identified the confusion among these terms as one of the major myths in the education arena. Winner (as cited in Iseke-Barnes, 1996, pp. 16-18) maintained that only when information is interpreted and related through critical thought and understanding does it become knowledge (for the purposes of this discussion, knowledge also includes skills and abilities). Instruction is the structured process that helps a learner make this transformation from information to knowledge. Furthermore, it is only when an individual is able to change his or her performance based on the new knowledge that we infer that learning has occurred.

People can learn from information, but it is uncontrolled and unstructured learning that may produce unpredictable results. The instructional process, must, as a minimum, include four elements. First, it must be designed to support specific instructional objectives, which are usually determined by job requirements or the requirements to advance to a higher grade or level of responsibility. Second, instruction must include the opportunity for the learner to interact with the instructional content in a meaningful way. Third, the learner's performance must be assessed to determine if he or she has learned what was intended. Fourth, the results of the assessment must be provided to the learner to either reinforce correct behavior or to provide remediation for incorrect behavior. Merrill (1997) presented a similar description of instruction as consisting of knowledge structure, presentation, exploration, practice, and learner guidance. The instructional process is should also be designed to target learner's attitudes (affect). The learner must be motivated to attend to instructional information so he or she will engage with the information and expend the energy necessary to learn.

The criteria presented in Section I and discussed in this and the following sections to help us determine if the instruction is well designed and implemented. Higher scores on the criteria can give us confidence that the computer-delivered courseware will enable individuals to learn what is required.

This section includes 5 chapters that focus on the criteria used to evaluate the instructional features of the courseware. Chapter 3 and 4 are discussions of the first and most important evaluation area— the manner in which instructional content is designed and organized for presentation to the learner. Chapter 5 discusses the second evaluation area—the instructional activities included in the courseware. Chapter 6 targets the third evaluation area— performance assessment. Performance feedback (the third evaluation area) is discussed in Chapter 7. The "appearance" of the content is discussed in the "User Interface Evaluation" chapters in Section III.

The instructional features criteria discussed below apply to all instructional theories or approaches. However, specific tasks may lend themselves to a specific instructional approach or combinations of approaches (e.g., "behavioral," "cognitive," "constructivist," etc.).

CHAPTER 3:
Instructional Content (Part 1)

This is the first of two chapters that discuss the criteria used to evaluate how well the content is designed and organized for presentation to the learner. This first criterion (the content is presented in a logical manner) is probably the most important of all the instructional evaluation criteria because it is affected by many of the factors that are addressed in the several criteria. Because of its importance, this entire chapter is dedicated to this first evaluation criterion.

1.a. The Presentation of Content is Logical

This criterion is used to evaluate the *structure* of the content and how it is designed to facilitate understanding of the material to be learned. Hays (2006) discussed instruction as a specific type of communication. The purpose of instruction is to transmit information on new knowledge and skills to the learner. Figure 4 is a simple diagram illustrating this process. The figure shows how instruction is a combination of content and the transmission of the content. The instructional content (the information that needs to be learned) is transformed into structured information using one or more instructional approaches (e.g., see the 9 events of instruction presented later in this chapter). This content is then transmitted to the learner using instructional techniques or media. In traditional classroom instruction, the instructor usually creates the instructional structure. In computer-delivered instruction there is often no instructor present, so it is even more vital that this instructional structure be provided in the content. If the content is illogically structured, learners are less likely to form the enduring associations among separate items of information that will help them remember and use what they have learned. Even worse, they may form incorrect associations or patterns among items of information that could lead to poor performance.

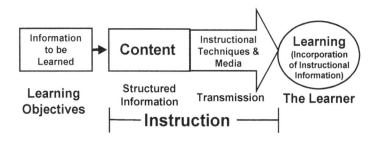

Figure 4:
The Communication of Instructional Content

Using the Scale

As mentioned in the previous chapter, the evaluation criteria and scales should be used differently depending on whether the evaluation is formative or summative. In this context, the following statements apply not only to this scale—they apply to all of the scales. Although the anchor statements for each scale are primarily designed for summative evaluations, the issues that are targeted by each criterion should also be used to focus formative evaluations. During the earliest ISD stages, formative evaluations are less specific and the criteria should be used as guides. At later ISD stages, the formative evaluations become more specific. Finally, after the courseware has been implemented, the scales are used to support detailed summative evaluations. Chapter 12 includes detailed discussions of how different individuals can use the Method during each stage of ISD.

This scale (1.a) rates the course in terms of how logically the instructional information is presented and how the individual pieces of information are related to one another. Evaluators should use the anchor statements and the "things to look for to determine logical presentation" to assign a score on this criterion. It is highly recommended that evaluators wait to assign a score on this criterion until most of all of the other criteria have been assigned a score. This is because many of the other evaluation criteria (e.g., Criterion 1.d: the content supports each and every instructional objective) contribute to the logical structure of the content. Additional information to help raters understand the terms and concepts involved in this criterion and the supporting literature for this criterion is provided in the following sections.

Terms, Concepts, Techniques, and Supporting Literature

This criterion evaluates the logical structure of the course content. It focuses on whether instructional topics are presented in a logical sequence that helps the learner understand how individual topics should fit together to support improved performance. Researchers have studied how individuals form mental patterns (models) of information items. This research has shown that people search for consistency in the information they encounter in all areas of their lives. According to Johnson-Laird, Legrenzi, and Girotto (2004), "Individuals evaluate the consistency of a set of propositions by searching for a model of a possibility in which they are all true. If they find such a model, they evaluate the propositions as consistent; otherwise, they evaluate the propositions as inconsistent" (p. 42). This is also true for information that learners encounter in instructional situations.

A problem arises when an individual is not able to construct a model that provides consistency among pieces of information. Because they strive for such consistency, they may "succumb to illusions of consistency and of inconsistency" (Johnson-Laird, et al., 2004, p. 44). The result of improperly formed models of instructional information is likely to be poorer performance. Thus, the purpose of high quality instructional content should be to guide the learner to form models, patterns, and associations of information that will be more easily retrieved and used when needed. Course content should be designed to follow a logical structure that supports student learning. According to Merrill, "associative memory is composed of a hierarchical network structure" (1983, p. 302). Any information to be learned can be designed so that its structure supports the development of associative memory. Rosch (1978) stated that information can be organized into "basic" concepts and then into more specific (subordinate) or more general (super-ordinate) categories. Associative memory can be aided if the information is clearly structured to support the interrelationships among these levels of specificity.

Two Types of Logic Necessary in Instructional Content

The logical presentation of content can be thought of in two ways: syntactical logic and instructional logic. Syntactical logic refers to whether the content is designed to follow the rules for the correct use of language and the way words and ideas are connected to one another. This type of logic is important in any type of communication not just instruction. For example, a novel will not be appreciated if the reader is unable to connect events into a logical story. Likewise, a technical publication must also present information logically so the reader can understand how specific items of technical information interconnect.

Instructional logic builds on semantic logic to present information in a manner that helps someone learn. Syntactical logic is a necessary part of instructional logic, but it is not sufficient. Instructional logic requires both syntactical logic and specific instructional methods and media that support specific instructional objectives. Guidance on syntactical logic can be found in a wide variety of writing guides (e.g., Hairston & Ruszkiewicz, 1996; American Psychological Association, 2001) and is taught in creative writing courses. Evaluators should consult these sources if they have questions about the syntactical logic of the content. The following sections provide introductions to some of the most influential theories and approaches for designing instructionally logical content.

Gagné's Theory of Instruction

Robert M. Gagné (1973; 1985) and his colleagues (e.g., Gagné & Briggs, 1979) developed a theory of instruction based on the idea that what we know about learning could be systematically related to the design of instruction. Gagné and Rohwer (1969) summarized a large body of research that supported their theory of instruction up to that time. More recent research has continued to support the components of Gagné's theory (e.g., Mayer, 2002; Clark, R. C., 2003).

Components of Gagné's Theory. Driscoll (2002) summarized Gagné's theory of instruction as comprised of three components:
1. The types of capabilities humans can learn (categories of learning outcomes);
2. The internal and external conditions associated with the acquisition of each category of learning outcome; and
3. Nine events of instruction that facilitate a specific cognitive process during learning.

The *categories of learning outcomes* include the following:
1. *Verbal information* or knowing "that" or "what."
2. *Intellectual skills*, which are necessary to apply knowledge.
3. *Cognitive strategies* that help the learner employ effective ways of thinking and learning.
4. *Attitudes*, which are feelings and beliefs that govern one's choices of personal action.
5. *Motor skills* that require executing precise, smooth, and accurately timed movements.

Gagné assumed that each learning outcome requires different *conditions for learning* (e.g., types of instruction). For example, riding a bike (a motor skill) requires different conditions (e.g., practice) than learning the names of presidents (verbal information) or learning to solve math problems (intellectual skill). Many have advocated the completion of a detailed task analysis, to determine what must be learned, prior to developing instructional programs (e.g., Fleishman, 1972; Mayer, 2004).

The Nine Events of Instruction. Although various instructional event models have been developed, one of the most comprehensive is the *nine instructional event model* developed by Gagné and his associates (e.g., Gagné & Briggs, 1979). Gagné believed that there are nine *events of instruction* that are necessary to facilitate the process of learning in general. Table 5 (adapted from Gagné & Briggs, 1979, p. 166) lists the nine events of instruction and some of the conditions of learning that help design effective instructional communications for specific categories of learning outcomes. The instructional logic of content

Table 5:
Nine Instructional Events and Conditions of Learning

Instructional Event	Capability Type and Implications
1. **Gaining attention**: Present a new problem or situation.	• **For all types of capabilities**: Help the learner selectively attend to the important information and stimuli in the task to be learned. Use "interest devices" or short "teasers" to grab learner's attention (e.g., storytelling, demonstrations, incorrect performance and its consequences, why it is important).
2. **Informing the learner of the objective**: Allow the learner to organize their thoughts around what they are about to see, hear, and/or do.	• **Intellectual skill**: Provide a description and example of the performance to be expected. • **Cognitive strategy**: Clarify the general nature of the solution expected. • **Information:** Indicate the kind of verbal question to be answered. • **Attitude**: Provide example of the kind of action choice aimed for. • **Motor skill:** Provide a demonstration of the performance to be expected.

Table 5:
(Continued)

Instructional Event	Capability Type and Implications
3. Stimulating recall of prerequisites: Allow the learner to build on previous knowledge or skills.	• **Intellectual skill**: Stimulate recall of subordinate concepts and rules. • **Cognitive strategy**: Stimulate recall of task strategies and associated intellectual skills. • **Information**: Stimulate recall of context of organized information. • **Attitude**: Stimulate recall of relevant information, skills, and human model identification. • **Motor skill**: Stimulate recall of executive sub-routine and part-skills.
4. Presenting the stimulus material: Chunk the information to avoid memory overload. Structure material following instructional strategies (e.g., Merrill (1997; see Instructional Strategies Section).	• **Intellectual skill**: Present examples of concept or rule. • **Cognitive strategy**: Present novel problems. • **Information**: Present information in propositional form. • **Attitude**: Present human model demonstrating choice of personal action. • **Motor skill**: Provide external stimuli for performance, including tools or implements.
5. Providing learning guidance: Provide instructions on how to learn.	• **Intellectual skill**: Provide verbal cues to proper combining sequence. • **Cognitive strategy**: Provide prompts and hints to novel solution. • **Information**: Provide verbal links to a larger meaningful context. • **Attitude**: Provide for observation of model's choice of action, and of reinforcement received by the model. • **Motor skill**: Provide practice with feedback of performance achievement.

Table 5:
(Continued)

Instructional Event	Capability Type and Implications
6. **Eliciting the performance**: Provide opportunity to practice.	• **Intellectual skill**: Ask learner to apply rule or concept to new examples. • **Cognitive strategy**: Ask for problem solution. • **Information:** Ask for information in paraphrase, or in learner's own words. • **Attitude**: Ask learner to indicate choices of action in real or simulated situations. • **Motor skill:** Ask for execution of the performance.
7. **Providing feedback**: Analyze the learner's behavior and provide them with specific feedback on degree of correctness, reinforcement for correct responses, or remediation for incorrect responses.	• **Intellectual skill**: Confirm correctness of rule or concept application. • **Cognitive strategy**: Confirm originality of problem solution. • **Information:** Confirm correctness of statement of information. • **Attitude**: Provide direct or vicarious reinforcement of action choice. • **Motor skill:** Provide feedback on degree of accuracy and timing of performance.
8. **Assessing performance**: Test to determine if the lesson has been learned.	• **Intellectual skill**: Learner demonstrates application of concept or rule. • **Cognitive strategy**: Learner originates a novel solution. • **Information:** Learner restates information in paraphrased form. • **Attitude**: Learner makes desired choice of personal action in real or simulated situation. • **Motor skill:** Learner executes performance of total skill.

Table 5:
(Continued)

Instructional Event	Capability Type and Implications
9. **Enhancing retention and transfer:** Help the learner use what has been learned (e.g., additional practice, similar problem situations, reviews).	• **Intellectual skill:** Provide spaced reviews including a variety of examples. • **Cognitive strategy:** Provide occasions for a variety of novel problem solutions. • **Information:** Provide verbal links to additional complexes of information. • **Attitude:** Provide additional varied situations for selected choice of action. • **Motor skill:** Learner continues skill practice.

should include all of the necessary events of instruction. Although differing in specifics, most instructional models address some of Gagné's nine events of instruction. For example, Reigeluth and Stein (1983) focused on how to structure the sequence and presentation of the ideas in instructional content, while Keller (1983) focused on how to motivate the learner. Gagné's model provides a comprehensive overview of the entire instructional process and can be made more specific by applying one or more of these other models. As a minimum, the content should be designed to include all nine of the instructional events combined with the appropriate instructional strategies.

Instructional Strategies

Merrill (1997) described instructional strategies as consisting of five parts. He stated that:

> A complete instructional strategy consists of **knowledge structure** consistent with, and appropriate for, the knowledge and skill being taught, a **presentation** consistent with, and appropriate for the kind of knowledge or skill being taught, an opportunity for **exploration** of the ideas

being taught, **practice** with feedback consistent with, and appropriate for, the knowledge or skill being taught, and **learner guidance** consistent with, and appropriate for, the knowledge and skill being taught (Merrill, 1997, online version, p. 2, author's emphasis).

Merrill (1997, online version) described some basic instructional strategies:

- **Information-About Strategy**: "describes features, cautions, and context for some set of entities, activities, or processes" (p. 2). This strategy is contrasted with and used to supplement other kinds of strategies.

- **Parts of ... Strategy**: enables the learner "to identify the name and location (with regard to some whole) of a given part of a device or system" (p. 3).

- **Concept or Kinds of ... Strategy**: enables the learner "to identify unencountered examples of objects, devices, procedures, actions, or symbols as belonging to a particular class" (p. 3).

- **Procedure Strategy**: enables a learner to perform a "series of actions which lead to some desired consequence" (p. 4).

- **Process, Principle or How does ... work Strategy**: helps the learner to predict the consequence of an event given a set of conditions or, given a consequence, to be able to identify the conditions which lead to the consequence.

Teaching Specific Types of Content

Compatible with the general framework of the nine instructional events (Gagné, & Briggs, 1979) and Merrill's (1997) instructional strategies, specific approaches have been recommended to teach different types of content. Summaries of these approaches are provided below. The instructional logic of content should be evaluated based on how well the content follows these recommendations.

Teaching Concepts. Merrill and Tennyson (1977) provided a five-step prescription for teaching concepts. Before beginning, one must first understand what is involved in concept learning. A concept is "a set of specific objects, symbols, or events which are grouped together on the basis of shared characteristics and which can be referenced by a particular name or symbol" (Merrill & Tennyson, 1977, p. 12). One can know that a student has learned a concept when he or she can correctly classify (identify the class membership) of a specific symbol, object, or event. To successfully classify a concept, the student must engage in two psychological processes: generalization and discrimination. "Generalization occurs when a learner exhibits a particular response in one stimulus situation which he/she acquired in a similar stimulus situation. Discrimination occurs when a learner exhibits a particular response in one stimulus situation but a different response in a similar stimulus situation" (Merrill & Tennyson, 1977, p. 13). These should not be confused with association and rule-using behaviors. "Association behavior occurs when a student is asked to associate two specific symbols, objects, or events by being able to name one when shown the other. Rule using behavior occurs when a student is asked to combine objects, symbols, or events from two or more classes by means of some operation to form an object, symbol, or event in a resulting concept class" (p. 13).

According to Merrill and Tennyson (1977), teaching concepts should follow these steps (consult the original for details):

1. *Decide if a Concept Lesson is Needed.* Ask the following questions:
   - Does the material involve new terms? If the answer is yes, a concept lesson is needed for each new term or related set of new terms. Does the material require the student to define new words? If the answer is yes, a concept lesson is needed for each important new word or related set of words.
   - Does the content involve rule using? If yes, a concept lesson is needed for each component concept in the rule.
   - Does the content involve a series of steps or events? If yes, examine each step or event as a potential concept and prepare a concept lesson for those steps or events, which are concepts.
   - Does the material require identification of parts? If yes, decide which parts should be taught as concepts and prepare a concept lessons for those.

2. *Define the Concept.* Follow these steps to define the concept:

- Identify the concept name (a word or symbol which is used to refer to the class as a whole or to examples of the class).
- List critical and variable attributes of the concept. A critical attribute is a characteristic necessary for determining class membership of a given instance. A variable attribute is a characteristic shared by some, but not all, members of the class.
- Write a concise definition of the concept (a statement identifying each of the critical attributes and how they are combined). Definitions can specify conjunctive, disjunctive, relational, or combination relationships between attributes.

3. *Collect an Instance Pool of Divergent Examples Each Matched to a Non-example.* Follow these steps:

- Decide on the form of concept representation (examples) to be used. Indicate the variety needed and eliminate any forms, which do not present the critical attributes.
- The instance pool should be as diverse as possible.
- Each example should be matched to a non-example.

4. *Estimate the Difficulty for Each Instance.* Some symbols, objects, or events in a concept class will be more difficult to classify than others. Instance difficulty can be estimated by determining the probability of a given instance being classified correctly by a sample of students who have been given only a definition.

- Present the instances with their definitions to a portion of the target population.
- Record the number of correct and incorrect responses for each instance and determine the percentage of the sample that identified each instance correctly.
- Construct a frequency distribution of the examples that will show the range of difficulty of the instances.

5. *Prepare a Diagnostic Classification Test.* "A classification test is an instrument which enables the instructor to make valid and reliable inferences about the student's ability to classify newly encountered instances of the concept(s)" (Merrill & Tennyson, 1977, p. 79). Classification behavior is best measured by presenting students with new examples and non-examples of

the concept class and having them identify which are members and which are nonmembers.

6. *Prepare Attribute Isolation.* Use an attention-focusing device (e.g., color, drawings, special symbols, simplified illustrations, etc.) to direct the student's attention to the critical attributes of a specific example; to potentially confusing variable attributes in examples and non-examples; and to the absence of the critical attributes in a specific non-example. Caution: don't use attention-focusing devices merely to emphasize. Be sure to emphasize critical attributes rather than variable attributes.

7. *Prepare an Instructional Strategy.* "An instructional strategy is a specified sequence of presentation forms" (Merrill & Tennyson, 1977, p. 111). Ensure that the instructional strategy includes all five of the components described above: knowledge structure, presentation, exploration, practice, and learner guidance (Merrill, 1997).

Howard (2000) suggested that the more that students practice classifying varied and novel examples, the higher the probability that they will be able to classify new examples in a variety of contexts.

Teaching Causal Principles. According to Merrill (1983), the effective instruction of a cause-and-effect principle follows these steps:

1. Provide a statement of the cause(s) and the resulting effect(s).
2. Next, provide an example (a prototype or worked example of an application of the causal principle in a work setting).
3. Follow this with activities that allow the student to work with the causal principle. These activities should start with simple examples and move to more complex examples. The student should first be asked to describe and label each phase of the cause-and-effect chain in the correct order. Then, when given one phase, he or she should be asked to predict the next phase or the previous phase.
4. Finally, the student should be asked to use the principle to solve increasingly difficult or novel problems.

Teaching Process Knowledge. Merrill (2000) defined process knowledge as "knowledge about how something works. It answers the question, 'What happens?'" (p. 12). For process knowledge, the content should provide a clear narrative description of the process

103

integrated with a visual model of the sequence of events that characterize the process. It should then describe each stage of the process, including the key events that occur at each stage to produce a change that leads to the next stage.

Teaching Procedural ("How To") Knowledge. Procedural knowledge may include a combination of the other knowledge types. Instruction should provide clear step-by-step descriptions of all actions and decisions required to achieve the end goal. It should also include models or demonstrations of the procedure and/or worked examples that provide knowledge of the concepts, processes, and principles involved in the procedure. The student should be given the opportunity to practice the procedure on a variety of problems and in settings that are similar to the work environment where the procedure will be used.

Sequencing the Ideas in Content

The Elaboration Theory of Instruction. Reigeluth and his colleagues developed methods to sequence related ideas in an instructional presentation. Their *Elaboration Theory of Instruction* (Reigeluth & Stein, 1983) builds on the work of Gagné (1968), Ausubel (1968), Bruner (1960), Norman (1973), and many others. It prescribes a simple-to-complex sequence intended to help the learner understand the importance of the different ideas presented, their context, and relationships between them. This approach helps the learner make the instruction meaningful and therefore easier to learn, retain, and remember.

The central concept of Elaboration Theory is the elaboration sequence, "in which: (1) the general ideas *epitomize* rather than summarize the ideas that follow; and (2) the epitomizing is done on the basis of a *single type of content* (Reigeluth & Stein, 1983, p. 343, authors' emphasis). Epitomizing is not a preview or summary. Rather, it presents a few fundamental and representative ideas, examples, and practice opportunities that "convey the essence of the entire content" (p. 343). Reigeluth and Stein (1983) provided examples of epitomes for conceptual, theoretical, and procedural content. The reader should consult the original for details and guidance on the application of Elaboration Theory.

Motivational Aspects of Content

The ARCS Model of Instruction. Keller (1983, 1987) developed a motivational model of instruction. It is based upon earlier work, such as field theory (Lewin, 1935), social-learning theory (Rotter, 1972), and expectancy-value theory (see Steers & Porter [1975] for a review). The model focuses on how to gain and maintain the attention of the learner throughout the instructional process. Keller's model is labeled the ARCS model referring to the four basic categories of motivational conditions:

- **Attention** (originally labeled *interest*) "refers to whether the learner's curiosity is aroused, and whether this arousal is sustained over time" (Keller, 1983, p. 395). The model refers to different types of arousal and recommends various techniques to increase each type. *Perceptual arousal* can be increased by using novel, surprising, incongruous and uncertain events. *Inquiry arousal* can be increased by stimulating information seeking behavior by posing questions or problems or having the learner generate questions or problems to solve. Interest can be maintained by varying the elements of instruction (e.g., switch between information presentation and learner activities that allow them to interact with the content).

- **Relevance** "refers to the learner's perception of personal need satisfaction in relation to the instruction, or whether a highly desired goal is perceived to be related to the instructional activity" (p. 395). Relevance can be increased by providing the learner with concrete examples, with which the learner is familiar (e.g., related to their previous experiences and values). Relevance can also be increased by presenting goal oriented statements and objectives and by explaining the utility of the instruction for the learner's present and future uses.

- **Confidence** (originally labeled *expectancy*) "refers to the perceived likelihood of success, and the extent to which success is under learner control" (p. 395). Confidence can be increased by designing instruction to enable the learner to succeed. The instruction should be challenging, but not overwhelming. Learners should see that their expended efforts directly influence the consequences by receiving relevant and meaningful feedback about their efforts. Positive learner expectations can be increased by helping them estimate the probability of success by presenting performance requirements and evaluation criteria.

• **Satisfaction** "refers to the combination of extrinsic rewards and intrinsic motivation, and whether these are compatible with the learner's anticipations. Satisfaction can be increased by providing learners with opportunities to use their newly acquired knowledge or skills in a real or simulated setting. Then, providing feedback with either reinforcements to sustain the desired behavior or remediation to correct undesired behavior. At all times, learners should perceive that the outcomes of their efforts are consistent with their expectations.

Keller (1987) further subdivided each of the ARCS categories into subcategories and provided suggestions for motivational strategies under each subcategory. A summary of these suggestions is shown in Table 6. Although these motivational strategies are focused on classroom instruction, they can be modified for computer-based instructional delivery. For example, in computer-delivered instruction the content should supplement these strategies with all of the functions of a live instructor (e.g., providing helpful feedback).

Applying the ARCS Model During Stages of Instructional Development. Keller (1987) recommended that the ARCS model be applied at each stage of instructional development. He offered the following suggested activities during each of the following four stages:

- Define:
  - Classify the motivational problem(s) to be solved
  - Conduct an audience analysis to identify motivational gaps
  - Prepare motivational objectives that identify the behavior, conditions, and criteria that apply

Table 6:
Motivational Strategies According to the ARCS Model

Strategy Type	Strategies
Attention Strategies	**A1: Incongruity, Conflict** A1.1 Introduce a fact that seems to contradict the learner's past experience. A1.2 Present an example that does not seem to exemplify a given concept. A1.3 Introduce two equally plausible facts or principles, only one of which can be true. A1.4 Play devil's advocate.
	A2: Concreteness A2.1 Show visual representations of any important object or set of ideas or relationships. A2.2 Give examples of every instructionally important concept or principle. A2.3 Use content-related anecdotes, case studies, biographies, etc.

Table 6:
(Continued)

Strategy Type	Strategies
Attention Strategies (Continued)	**A3: Variability** A3.1 In stand up delivery, vary the tone of your voice, and use body movement, pauses, and props. A3.2 Vary the format of instruction (information presentation, practice, testing, etc.) according to the attention span of the audience. A3.3 Vary the medium of instruction (platform delivery, film, video, print, etc.). A3.4 Break up print materials by use of white space, visuals, tables, different typefaces, etc. A3.5 Change the style of presentation (humorous-serious, fast-slow, loud-soft, active-passive, etc.). A3.6 Shift between student-instructor interaction and student-student interaction.
	A4: Humor A4.1 Where appropriate, use plays on words during redundant information presentation. A4.2 Use humorous introductions. A4.3 Use humorous analogies to explain and summarize.

Table 6:
(Continued)

Strategy Type	Strategies
Attention Strategies (Continued)	**A5: Inquiry** A5.1 Use creativity techniques to have learners create unusual analogies and associations to the content. A5.2 Build in problem solving activities at regular intervals. A5.3 Give learners the opportunity to select topics, projects and assignments that appeal to their curiosity and need to explore.
	A6: Participation A6.1 Use games, role-plays, or simulations that require learner participation.
Relevance Strategies	**R1: Experience** R1.1 State explicitly how the instruction builds on the learner's existing skills. R1.2 Use analogies familiar to the learner from past experience. R1.3 Find out what the learners' interests are and relate them to the instruction.
	R2: Present Worth R2.1 State explicitly the present intrinsic value of learning the content, as distinct from its value as a link to future goals.

Table 6:
(Continued)

Strategy Type	Strategies
Relevance Strategies (Continued)	**R3: Future usefulness** 　　R3.1 State explicitly how the instruction relates to future activities of the learner. 　　R3.2 Ask learners to relate the instruction to their own future goals (future wheel).
	R4: Need Matching 　　R4.1 To enhance achievement striving behavior, provide opportunities to achieve standards of excellence under conditions of moderate risk. 　　R4.2 To make instruction responsive to the power motive, provide opportunities for responsibility, authority, and interpersonal interaction. 　　R4.3 To satisfy the need for affiliation, establish trust and provide opportunities for no-risk, cooperative interaction.
	R5: Modeling 　　R5.1 Bring in alumni of the course as enthusiastic guest lecturers. 　　R5.2 In a self-paced course, use those who finish first as deputy tutors. 　　R5.3 Model enthusiasm for the subject taught.

Table 6:
(Continued)

Strategy Type	Strategies
Relevance Strategies (Continued)	**R6: Choice** R6.1 Provide meaningful alternative methods for accomplishing a goal. R6.2 Provide personal choices for organizing one's work.
Confidence Strategies	**C1: Learning Requirements** C1.1 Incorporate clearly stated, appealing learning goals into instructional materials. C1.2 Provide self-evaluation tools, which are based on, clearly stated goals. C1.3 Explain the criteria for evaluation of performance.
	C2: Difficulty C2.1 Organize materials on an increasing level of difficulty; that is, structure the learning material to provide a "conquerable" challenge.
	C3: Expectations C3.1 Include statements about the likelihood of success with given amounts of effort and ability. C3.2 Teach students how to develop a plan of work that will result in goal accomplishment. C3.3 Help students set realistic goals.

Table 6:
(Continued)

Strategy Type	Strategies

Confidence Strategies (Continued)	**C4: Attributions**
	    C4.1 Attribute student success to effort rather than luck or ease of task when appropriate (i.e., when you know it's true!).
	    C4.2 Encourage student efforts to verbalize appropriate attributes for both successes and failures

	C5: Self-Confidence
	    C5.1 Allow students opportunity to become increasingly independent in learning and practicing a skill.
	    C5.2 Have students learn new skills under low risk conditions, but practice performance of well-learned tasks under realistic conditions.
	    C5.3 Help students understand that the pursuit of excellence does not mean that anything short of perfection is failure; learn to feel good about genuine accomplishment

Table 6:
(Continued)

Strategy Type	Strategies
Satisfaction Strategies	**S1: Natural Consequences** S1.1 Allow a student to use a newly acquired skill in a realistic setting as soon as possible. S1.2 Verbally reinforce a student's intrinsic pride in accomplishing a difficult task. S1.3 Allow a student who masters a task to help others who have not yet done so. **S2: Unexpected Rewards** S2.1 Reward intrinsically interesting task performance with unexpected, non-contingent rewards. S2.2 Reward boring tasks with extrinsic, anticipated rewards. **S3: Positive Outcomes** S3.1 Give verbal praise for successful progress or accomplishment. S3.2 Give personal attention to students. S3.3 Provide informative, helpful feedback when it is immediately useful. S3.4 Provide motivating feedback (praise) immediately following task performance.

Table 6:
(Continued)

Strategy Type	Strategies
Satisfaction Strategies (Continued)	**S4: Negative Influences** S4.1 Avoid the use of threats as a means of obtaining task performance. S4.2 Avoid surveillance (as opposed to positive attention). S4.3 Avoid external performance evaluations whenever it is possible to help the student evaluate his or her own work.
	S5: Scheduling S5.1 Provide frequent reinforcements when a student is learning a new task. S5.2 Provide intermittent reinforcement as a student becomes more competent at a task. S5.3 Vary the schedule of reinforcements in terms of both interval and quantity.

- Design:
  - Generate a list of potential motivational strategies for each of the motivational objectives
  - Review the list of potential strategies and select the ones to be used. The strategies should follow five guidelines: (1) they should not take up too much instructional time, (2) they should not detract from the instructional objectives, (3) they should fall within the time and money constraints of the development and implementation aspects of the

instruction, (4) they should be acceptable to the audience, and (5) they should be compatible with the delivery system (including the instructor's personal style and preferences).

- Develop:
  - o Prepare any special materials that are required
  - o Integrate the materials with the instruction
- Evaluate:
  - o Conduct development try-out (formative evaluations)
  - o Assess the motivational outcomes (as well as learning outcomes). Judge motivational outcomes using direct measures (e.g., persistence, intensity of effort, emotion, and attitude).

Recent research has tested the effects of designing computer-assisted instruction (CAI) based on the principles of the ARCS model (Song & Keller, 2001). Three types of CAI were designed and presented to different groups of learners. Motivationally minimized CAI contained the minimal number of motivational strategies. Motivationally saturated CAI included a large number of motivational strategies, which were presented to all learners, regardless of their motivational needs. Motivationally adaptive CAI provided motivational strategies targeted to the immediate needs of each learner. In this condition, motivated learners were not presented with motivational strategies that might distract them. The learners' levels of motivation and attention were continuously assessed during instruction. Results showed that the motivationally adaptive CAI was more effective than either of the other approaches.

Guidance on the Structure of Content

The purpose of instruction is to provide new knowledge to the learner. This knowledge must be structured in a manner that can be used at a later time. Citing several researchers, Glaser and Bassok (1989) stated that "the way knowledge is structured influences its accessibility, and knowledge representation determines understanding and influences problem solving (p. 633). Thus, the way the learner structures his or her knowledge is affected by the structure of the instructional content. The information in the instructional content should be presented in a consistent style in terms of writing (e.g., voice, grammar, and notations), use of instructional media, and appearance (see the User Interface Section). In addition, there are several design techniques that can improve the structure of instructional content.

Boettcher (2003) defined *structure* as "something arranged in a definite pattern of organization" (p.1). She maintains that well structured content supports the building of foundations for complex knowledge, helping the learner to integrate isolated facts into more complex, organized knowledge. This is an important point that is sometimes lost in the rush to include all content. It should be organized to allow the learner to gradually progress from the basic foundations of information to the organization of more and more complex material (e.g., as recommended in Elaboration Theory).

Merrill (1983) stated that "associative memory is composed of a hierarchical network structure" (p. 302). Any basic concept that is learned may be related to other concepts that are either more specific (subordinate) or more general (super-ordinate). Associative memory uses the relationships among these categories to both store and retrieve information. For example, the basic concept "carrot" is a subordinate concept of the category "vegetables" and a super-ordinate concept of the category "baby carrots." Learning to distinguish between and use the relationships among these categories helps in both learning and memory.

Nitsch (1977) provided support for the idea that learning is facilitated by structuring instruction to use the hierarchical nature of memory. Like Bransford and his colleagues (1986; 1989), she maintained that the initial instruction on a topic should be structured so that learners can establish a firm contextual basis for understanding the new concept (see Criterion 1.f). Nitsch (1977) found that providing concrete examples in additional to definitions "can have a positive influence upon subjects' subsequent ability to use their knowledge of the concepts" (p. 15). She refers to this as the "contextualization" of knowledge. She also found that providing a variety of examples in different contextual domains "resulted in a much more flexible ability to use the conceptual information" (p 37). This contextual variety made initial learning more difficult but facilitated the learners' ability to "decontextualize" the knowledge so they could apply it in new situations and different contexts. Thus, content should be structured to help the learner create the conceptual hierarchy that will assist in retrieving and using learned concepts.

Structural Areas of Content. Boettcher (2003) discussed four structural areas of content and observed that there are nuances of interaction between all four.

1. The first structural area involves presentation of "content for which an organization is clearly visible and in which concepts are presented clearly and precisely" (p.1).
2. The presentation should be semantically well structured to support instruction (e.g., simple concepts are fully explained and then used as building blocks to explain more complex concepts).
3. The content should be structured to support learner needs (e.g., presented at the reading level of the audience).
4. Finally, it should be technologically well structured (e.g., technology is not used gratuitously, but only to support content).

Below are brief descriptions of some techniques that can be used to structure content to help learners learn more effectively.

Advance Organizers. One of the techniques that help learners easily see the organization of the content is to use advance organizers. *Advance organizers* are "subsuming concepts" (Ausubel, 1960, p. 267) that help learners mobilize most relevant aspects of the instructional information to create the cognitive structures that facilitate learning and memory. They are "concepts introduced before material is covered which are on a more general or abstract level than the material which is to be covered" (Chesebro & McCroskey, 1998, p. 449). Ausubel (1960, pp. 269-271) demonstrated that advance organizers, such as background information that is more concrete than the abstract information that may follow it, improved learners' memory.

Advance organizers provide a conceptual structure or framework to aid the encoding of information and also to help the learner activate prior knowledge and relate it to the new information. They are especially useful in helping the learner make distinctions and comparisons between similar concepts.

Ausubel (1968) identified two types of advance organizers:

1. *Expository Organizers*: Are used with unfamiliar material to set the stage for learning new concepts. For example, when teaching the American Revolution, introduce stages common to all revolutions as a framework for the new information.
2. *Comparative Organizers*: Are used to aid the integration of new ideas by comparing and contrasting them with similar concepts that have already been learned. For example, atomic structure can be taught by discussing the similarities and differences between electrons circling a nucleus and moons orbiting around a planet.

Ausubel and Youssef (1963) compared the effects of comparative organizers using two groups of learners. They gave one group a comparative organizer (a brief textual comparison of the relationships between Christianity and Buddhism) prior to assigning both groups a long reading assignment on Buddhism. Later, the group that received the comparative organizer recalled more of the text.

Use of Signals and Cues. "A signal is any technique used to make some elements of a text or document more salient than other elements" (Clark, R. C., 2003, p. 74). Signals can include topic headings, typographical cues like italics or color, overviews, outlines, highlighting, and pointer phrases such as *results in...*, *therefore...*, or *because of....* Lorch and Lorch (1996) compared the learning effects of signaled and unsignaled text. They found that the use of signals helped learners recall more from complex text, but not from simple text. This finding has also been extended to the use of signals in narration (Mautone & Mayer, 2001).

Use of Summaries. Another technique is to use summaries at the end of each section of material and reviews throughout the course. These help the learner to perceive the patterns among different pieces of information presented in the course.

Activating Existing Knowledge. It is widely accepted that learning requires that new knowledge be presented in a way that activates and builds on existing knowledge (Bower, Clark, Lesgold, and Winzenz, 1969; Halpern and Hakel, 2003). This is true for both the knowledge that a learner brings to the course and also for the new knowledge that is gained during the course. It can be assumed that learners taking an introductory course will know very little about the subject matter. However, they still may bring misconceptions about topics in the course and these misconceptions may have to be corrected prior to presenting new information. Learners taking a refresher course will know much more about the subject matter, but may need to reorganize that knowledge for new purposes or update it based upon new insights about the topics. In either case, the information presented in the course should be structured to help the learner expand existing information structures and build new ones.

Helping the learner build on existing knowledge can help to avoid the distractions of interesting, but non-relevant instructional information. Garner, Gillingham, and White (1989) tested the effect of "seductive details" (interesting by non-relevant information) on the ability of adults and seventh graders to remember important details from a paragraph of text. They found that the seductive details reduced the performance of both groups. However the adults were still able to remember some important details. These researchers assumed that the difference between adults and children is because the adults had more extensive domain knowledge. This previous domain knowledge enabled them to more readily classify the new information as important or simply interesting. Instructional materials should be designed to minimize "seductive details" while providing a logical structure that relates the new material to the learners' existing knowledge.

An instructional technique that has been shown to help activate a learner's existing knowledge base is the use of *analogies* (Stepich & Newby, 1988). This technique is discussed in the context of instructional activities (Chapter 5).

Levels of Content Structure. Similar to Rosch's (1978) categorization approach, Boettcher (2003) believed that job-relevant knowledge and skills may require one of three different levels of content structure (also see Chapter 4, Criterion 1.f).

- The first level presents core concepts and principles.
- The second level includes content with well-structured problems with known solutions.
- The third level consists of content with less-structured, complex problems without known solutions.

Ideally, as learners advance from novice to expert, they will proceed through these three levels, gradually building their understanding by

119

engaging in learning activities at each level. Table 7 lists some of the structural characteristics and requirements at each level of content (Boettcher, 2003).

Table 7:
Structural Characteristics of Three Levels of Content

Content Level	Structural Characteristics
Level one: **Core concepts and principles**	• Provides descriptions of core concepts (may use various media dynamically) • Provides means for learners to rehearse and interact with processes • Helps learner cluster and chunk information • Clearly shows relationships and patterns among core concepts • Reveals differentiations and distinctions among concepts • Links core concepts with current issues in job area
Level two: **Well-structured problems with known solutions**	• Presents consistent elements of the problem sets • Reveals patterns inherent in the problems • Reveals sources and types of knowledge that contribute to problem solutions • Chunks and clusters the elements of the solutions • Gradually increases the complexity of the applied rules and principles • Engages the learner in the solutions (perhaps through the use of simulations or other interactive activities)
Level three: **Less-structured, complex problems without known solutions**	• Provides complex, real-world scenarios and case studies • Engages the learners in solving complex problems where neither the elements or solutions are known (e.g., through use of simulations nor other activities that involve complex interactions among problem elements or interrelated problems) • Provides explanations of real-life problems from experts, including testimonials on their "solutions"

Scaffolding. A teaching strategy that addresses how to help learners build on prior knowledge and internalize new information is called scaffolding. It is based on Lev Vygotsky's sociocultural theory (Van Der Stuyf, 2002). Vygotsky advocated that learners be supported at their current level of competence while encountering new information. These temporary supports or scaffolds are withdrawn as the learner's abilities increase until he or she is able to complete the task or master the concepts independently.

McKenzie (1999) described eight characteristics of scaffolding. Scaffolding:

1. Provides clear directions to reduce learners' confusion about what they must do to meet the expectations of the learning activity.
2. Clarifies purpose by helping learners understand why the problem, issue or decision is important and why they should care about it.
3. Keeps learners on task by providing a pathway through the progression of activities.
4. Clarifies expectations by providing examples of quality work, rubrics, and standards that define quality work.
5. Directs learners to worthy sources so they can avoid confusing, weak, and unreliable information.
6. Reduces uncertainty, surprise, and disappointment by testing lessons to eliminate distractions and frustrations to the extent possible.
7. Provides efficiency by helping focus the learner on the work effort.
8. Creates momentum by concentrating and directing the learner's energy toward accumulating insight and understanding.

Metaphors. Remelhart and Norman (1981) maintained that analogical reasoning is the most common way that people apply knowledge learned in one domain to another domain (e.g., one task to another). One technique that can assist the learner apply such analogical reasoning is to use an intuitive *metaphor* for the learner to interact with the content (Reeves, 1994 as summarized in Botha, 2004). These metaphors might be books, bookshelves, space exploration, buildings with different rooms, college campuses, or many others. Jones and Okey (1995) recommended that the metaphor should reflect the nature of the content. For example, a student learning auto repair could access various lessons by clicking on a portion of an automobile (e.g., the fuel system, the transmission, the brakes). Henke (2001) recommended that the metaphor be designed to be obvious to the learner. He also recommends that the course should use navigation styles that are consistent with the metaphor. Chapter 8 (Evaluation Area 5: Navigation & Operation) provides discussions of the scales that evaluate the design of the user interface to better support learning.

Learner Control. The ability for learners to control the presentation of content is often described as one of the potential advantages of computer-based and web-delivered instruction (e.g., Hannafin and Sullivan, 1995). However, some evidence (e.g., Niemiec, Sikorski, and Walberg, 1996) indicates that "as the extent of learner control over various aspects of instruction increases, learning may decrease" (Clark, R., 2003, p. 14). Some studies do show that there are benefits of some limited forms of learner control, such as control over the pacing of a multimedia presentation (Doherty, 1998; Mayer & Chandler, 2001; additional information is provided in the discussion on the use of multimedia in Chapter 9). Course designers need to provide learner control of pacing and other types of "surface" control, but retain the control of the order of instructional topics and instructional activities.

Size of Instructional Segments. Many recommend that the instructional content should be organized and presented in small, manageable steps (Norman, 1976; Dick and Carrey, 1996; Texas Education Agency, 2003; Trollinger, 2003). Jones and Okey (1995) explained that instructional segments should be small so the learner is not overwhelmed by too much information. The learners need to be able to gradually integrate the new information into their existing knowledge and build new knowledge structures. Jones (1989) referred to the presentation of content in small segments as "progressive disclosure." Therefore, only the material that is relevant to the specific objective of the segment should be presented at any one time. The learner should know when a segment has been chosen and when it has been completed (Criterion 1.i). Furthermore, it should be readily apparent to learners if they have completed all of the prerequisite topics prior to beginning a new segment of instruction (see Criterion 1.h). This approach reduces the perceived complexity of the content and allows the learner to reflect on its meaning.

Sequencing Learning Objectives. Mayer, Mathias and Wetzell (2002) demonstrated the value of teaching related concepts prior to the task or process that is the focus of the lesson. They preceded a multimedia lesson on the mechanical processes of how brakes work with pre-lessons on each individual component in the braking system. No matter what medium was used (e.g., text or multimedia), learning was better with the pre-lesson than when all of the information was presented at once.

The handbook on Instructional Systems Development (Department of Defense, 2001) provides guidance on how to structure a course in terms of the sequence and hierarchy of learning objectives (LOs). The following discussion is a very brief summary of portions of this guidance. Relationships among LOs can also be used to logically sequence a course. "The four most important relationships in sequencing are 1) dependent, 2) supportive, 3) independent, and 4) conflicting" (Department of Defense, 2001,p. 86). Table 8 provides a summary of these relationships.

When evaluating a completed course or plans for course development (e.g., storyboards), the evaluator should consider the following issues (additional details can be found in the handbook). Since most tasks are made up of subtasks, it is important that learners learn the subtasks in the proper sequence. A learning hierarchy is a "map that depicts the relationship of various LOs and their sequence" (Department of Defense, 2001, p. 83). This hierarchy specifies the most effective and efficient learning sequence.

Early in content development, each learning object (for all tasks and subtasks) needs to be classified as either a Terminal Learning Objective (TLO; what the learner will accomplish when successfully completing the instruction for a task) or an Enabling Learning Objective (ELO; what the learner must attain in order to accomplish a terminal objective).

The next step is to cluster or group the ELOs and TLOs into "logical and meaningful portions of training such as units, lessons, or segments" (Department of Defense, 2001, p. 85). Clustering of LOs can be based upon those requiring common prerequisites, those with relationships to the same system or type of action; those requiring common knowledge or skills; or those requiring the same learning approach (e.g., taught by demonstration).

Table 8:
Possible Relationships Among Learning Objectives

Type of Relationship	Description of Relationship
Dependent	• Knowledge and skills in one LO are prerequisite to those in the other LO. • To master one of the LOs, it is first necessary to master the other. • LOs must be arranged in the sequence indicated by the knowledge and skills hierarchy
Conflicting	• Knowledge and skills in one LO conflict in some respect with those in another LO. • Mastering one LO may cause difficulty in mastering the other LO. • LOs must be taught closely together, directly addressing the conflicting elements between the two LOs.
Supportive	• Knowledge and skills learned in one LO makes learning easier in the other LO. • Mastering one LO transfers to other, making learning of the other easier. • LOs should be placed close together in the sequence to permit optimum transfer of learning from one LO to the other.
Independent	• Knowledge and skills in one LO are unrelated to those in the other LO. • Mastering one LO does not simplify mastering the other. • In general, the LOs can be arranged in any sequence without loss of learning efficiency.

Then, the LOs are sequenced within the course using some combination of the following techniques: job performance order, chronological order, cause and effect order; critical order, simple-to-complex order, complex-to-simple order, or known-to-unknown order.

For dependent LOs, it is important that the content be structured to present the material in the appropriate sequence (see Criterion 1.h). On the other hand, supportive LOs should be integrated with each other in instructional events or activities. As Malcolm (2000) observed, instructional events are often "not integrated with each other even when they support the same performance need" (p. 3). He offers an example of instruction for customer service representatives. These courses often teach telephone skills and application system skills separately, even though the real job requires them to be performed simultaneously. This is, as he paraphrases Gloria Gery, "like giving people the threads of learning and expecting them to knit together competent on-the-job performance" (p.3). Content should be designed to do this weaving for learners so they can experience learning while doing the interwoven tasks that are more representative of the real work they will have to do.

Relationships Among Models of Instruction and Evaluation Criteria

Educational researchers have proposed various models of how to organize instructional sequences. As discussed above, different models focus on different aspects of the instructional process. Regardless of the model they choose, most instructional developers agree that *teaching different types of knowledge and skills requires different conditions for learning* (Gagné, 1985). "If an instructional experience or environment does not include the instructional strategies required for the acquisition of the desired knowledge or skill, the effective, efficient, and appealing learning of the desired outcome will not occur" (Merrill, 2000, p. 1).

Table 9 shows how the instructional models discussed above relate to the nine events of instruction and to some of the instructional evaluation criteria. Although the nine events appear to indicate a sequential approach to instruction, in fact, instruction is much more of an iterative process. For example, gaining attention is

Table 9:
Instructional Models and Evaluation Criteria

9 Events of Instruction (Gagné & Briggs, 1979)	Evaluation Criteria	ARCS Model (Keller, 1983, 1987)	Component Response Theory (Merrill, 1983)	Elabora-tion Theory (Reigeluth & Stein, 1983)
1. Gaining Attention	1.b. The purpose of the course is clearly stated	Attention (Interest)		
2. Informing learner of objective	1.c. The instructional objectives are clearly stated	Relevance		
3. Stimulating recall of prerequisites	1.h. There are clear indications of prerequisites			
4. Presenting the stimulus material	1.a. The content is presented in a logical manner		4 types of content (facts, concepts, procedures, & principles)	Epitomizing (layers of instruction)
5. Providing learning guidance	2.a. Activities are relevant 2.c. Instruction is engaging		Four presentation forms (general expository, general inquisitory, instance expository, & instance inquisitory)	

Table 9:
(Continued)

9 Events of Instruction (Gagné & Briggs, 1979)	Evaluation Criteria	ARCS Model (Keller, 1983, 1987)	Component Response Theory (Merrill, 1983)	Elaboration Theory (Reigeluth & Stein, 1983)
6. Eliciting the performance	2.a. Activities are relevant 2.b. Learner is required to interact with content	Confidence (Expectancy)	Three types of performance (find, use, & remember)	
7. Providing feedback	Performance feedback (all criteria in section 4)			
8. Assessing performance	Performance assessment (all criteria in section 3)			
9. Enhancing retention and transfer	2.a. Activities are relevant 4.b. Feedback is meaningful	Satiofaction		

necessary at the beginning of instruction, but this attention must be maintained throughout the entire instructional process. Likewise, feedback should not be presented solely at the end of the instruction, but rather as an ongoing process throughout. The four types of content in Merrill's Component Response Theory (Merrill & Tennyson, 1977) were summarized above. The reader should also consult Merrill (1983) for additional discussions and updates of his types of content, presentation forms, and types of performance. Elaboration Theory and the ARCS Model were also summarized above.

For the development of instructional products, it is also important that logical decisions be made about other instructional issues. For example, specific instructional activities or instructional media should be chosen logically. These issues are discussed in the context of other evaluation criteria (e.g., Instructional activities in Chapter 5 and content presentation in Chapter 9).

CHAPTER 4:
Instructional Content (Part 2)

The last chapter discussed the importance of presenting content in a logical manner. Several additional criteria affect the logical presentation of content. These criteria are discussed in this chapter.

1.b. The Purpose of the Course is Clearly Stated

The purpose of a course sets the stage for both learners and developers. A learner should not have to guess why he or she is taking a course or how the course will support his or her job performance.

Using the Scale

This scale rates the course in terms of how specifically the purpose of the course is communicated to the learner. Evaluators should use the anchor statements and example purpose statements to help assign a rating on this criterion.

In early formative evaluations, the criterion and anchor statements should be used as guides and the evaluator should place less emphasis on assigning a score. However, they should sensitize the developer to the importance of purpose statements and help them make the statements specific, relevant, and clear. In later formative evaluations, the evaluator should take more care in assigning scores so they can be used to diagnose and correct problems. Finally, in summative evaluations, the anchor statements should be strictly followed to assign scores. Additional information to help the evaluator understand this criterion is provided in the discussion below.

Terms, Concepts, Techniques, and Supporting Literature

Understanding the purpose or a course enables learners to establish the relevance and appropriateness of the course (Bostock, 2004, citing Tweddle, Avis and Waller, 1998). This information should be presented at the beginning of the course as a general, "high level" declaration of who should take the course (e.g., novices, journeymen, or experts; persons from a particular job series; persons wishing to change jobs), what is to be accomplished in the course (e.g., what general topics will be covered), why they should take the course (e.g., how it will improve their job performance), and the benefits they will gain from the course (e.g., help advance their career or help them obtain certification). The "high-level" messages in the purpose statement should be used to guide the development of more specific learning objectives (see 1.c).

The purpose of a course also has implications for how content is designed and presented. For example, if the purpose is to provide initial instruction, the learner will need the content to be presented in a very structured manner that ensures that each new piece of information is integrated with previous information and mental structures. On the other hand, refresher instruction, where the learner only needs a specific piece of information to accomplish a specific task or has forgotten something needed on his or her job, might be designed to allow a learner to browse to find that information.

There is a considerable amount of empirical data that indicate the importance of a clearly stated purpose for the course. For example, the first major step in learning is the forming of meaningful associations among pieces of information (Miller, J. G., 1978). The context in which information is presented has a major effect on how these associations are formed (Miller, G. A., Heise, & Lichten, 1951; Klatsky, 1975). These associations must be deeply processed (encoded into long-term memory; LTM), which is believed to consist of a network of associations (Brown & McNeill, 1966; Craik & Lockhart, 1972; Anderson & Bower; 1972; 1973; 1974). Furthermore, it is widely recognized that humans can only attend to a limited amount of information at any one time (Broadbent, 1963; Klatsky, 1975). Therefore, humans must select the information on which they focus their attention (Norman, 1976). It is therefore critical that, during the instructional process, the learner's attention is directed toward the critical information that must be learned. A clearly stated purpose for the course is the first step in this direction of attention. It is so important that Gagné and Briggs (1979) identify it as one of their 9 events of instruction.

A clearly stated purpose can serve as an "advance organizer" (Ausubel, 1960; Mautone & Mayer, 2001). It prepares the learner to attend to the important details that will follow. A clearly stated purpose statement can also help learners filter out "seductive details" that can interfere with the learner's attention to important instructional information (Garner, et al., 1989; Harp & Mayer, 1998). The effects of "seductive details" were also discussed in Chapter 1 under Criterion 1.a and will also be discussed in Chapter 9 (Criterion 6.e) on the use of multimedia. The discussion under Criterion 6.e highlights the need to avoid irrelevant, extraneous words, pictures, and sounds. It is easier to identify such irrelevant information if the purpose of the course is clearly stated.

A clearly stated purpose is especially important for adult learners. Some educators believe that adults are better able to engage in self-directed learning than younger learners (e.g., Knowles, 1989; Hiemstra & Sisco, 1990; Brookfield, 1995). One of the assumptions behind this belief is that adult learners are "problem-centered and interested in immediate application of knowledge" (Merriam, 2001, p. 5). Thus, a clearly stated purpose will help the adult learner focus and maintain his or her interest and attention on the course.

Another area, which supports the need for a clearly stated purpose, is research on motivation. Learners must be motivated to learn and one of the strongest motivators is an objective and obtainable goal (Locke & Bryan, 1966; Magill, 1980). The relevance of the material is also a factor in motivation (Ausubel, 1968). Thus, a well stated purpose for the course helps the learner begin the process of setting goals and establishing the relevance of the material to be learned.

1.c. The Instructional Objectives are Clearly Stated

An instructional objective (often called a learning objective or LO) is "a statement of what the learner will do after the lesson or module to demonstrate that they [*sic*] have understood the content or acquired the skills included in the lesson" (Clark, R. C., 2003, pp. 73-74). Another definition of an LO focuses on the performance requirement after the learner has completed the objective, "A LO is a precise statement of the capability... a student is expected to demonstrate the condition under which the KSA is to be exhibited, and the standard of acceptable performance" (Department of Defense, 2001, p. 78).

Using the Scale

This scale is used to determine how well the instructional objectives are clearly stated. As with all the criteria and scales, evaluators should use them as guides during formative evaluations. During later formative evaluations and summative evaluations the evaluator should be more careful when assigning scores because they can be used diagnostically. The anchor statements below the scale should be used to help determine the score to assign on this criterion. Additional guidance is provided in the discussion below. Remember, if you assign a rating of one (1) on this criterion, you *must* also assign a rating of one (1) on Criterion 1.d (the content supports each and every instructional objective).

Terms, Concepts, Techniques, and Supporting Literature

The instructional objectives should follow from and support the "high-level" purpose of the course (see Criterion 1.b.). They should provide more specificity in terms of how the learner will benefit from each course module, unit, lesson, or topic. Nash (2003) adds another requirement: that they describe how the learner will achieve the objective. Finally, the objectives should also help learners relate different course topics to one another, so they understand how their progression through the course helps them build and expand on their knowledge and skills.

Gagné and Briggs (1979) argue that a clearly stated instructional objective is an important step in gaining and maintaining the learner's attention. It is so important that they call it out as the second of their nine events of instruction (see Table 3).

As discussed above (Criterion 1.b.), adult learners are especially interested in the objectives of a course or a course segment. These objectives can be made more relevant if they indicate how they will benefit the adult learners in their jobs or careers. As such, they can also serve as "advance organizers" (Ausubel, 1960) to help learners structure the information for better encoding and retrieval.

Much of the research supporting the need for clearly stated instructional objectives is the same as those studies that supported the need for a clearly stated purpose for the course (1.b). This research includes the need for information to be relevant (Ausubel, 1968), motivating (Locke & Bryan, 1966; Magill, 1980), and capable of holding the learner's attention (Norman, 1976). Additional empirical support comes from data on the formation of associations (Miller, J. G., 1978) and the context in which information is presented (Miller, G. A., Heise, & Lichten, 1951; Klatsky, 1975). A clearly stated instructional objective can aid the learner to deeply process the associations and encode them into long-term memory (LTM). As several studies have shown (Brown & McNeill, 1966; Craik & Lockhart, 1972; Anderson & Bower; 1972; 1973; 1974) more deeply processed information is more readily remembered. In addition, clearly stated instructional objectives also aid learners to attend to the most important information that must be learned (see Broadbent, 1963; Klatsky, 1975; Norman, 1976 on selective attention).

Goal-setting theory (Locke, 2000) maintains that "specific difficult goals lead to better performance than 'do your best' or easy goals and that goal effects are moderated by feedback and goal commitment" (p. 415). Locke and Bryan (1966) found support for this theory. They found that the performance and intensity of effort was higher for those given specific goals when compared to those told to "do your best." Thus, a clearly stated instructional objective should help to motivate the learner by making the learning goals more specific.

Rothkopf and Billington (1979) compared the reading times and eye movements in two groups of readers. One group was given goals prior to reading and the other group was not given goals. They found that readers who were given goals spent less overall time reading, but more time on the goal-relevant information. They also showed better recall of the goal-specific information than background information. Similar results were reported in a comparison of learning from computer lessons that either included or excluded learning objectives (Cavalier & Klein, 1998).

Catrambone (1998) conducted four experiments that demonstrated improved problem-solving performance when subjects were given labels for groups of steps that formed subgoals. Such subgoals are similar to separate instructional objectives that support the overall purpose of the course. When learners are shown the relevance of the instructional objectives, they should learn better.

Clearly stated instructional objectives also help the instructional developers. Merrill (1983) recommends that objective statements should include "a classification of the type of learning involved;

affective, psychomotor, intellectual skills, verbal information, or cognitive strategies" (p. 290). The purpose of this classification is to help instructional developers determine the necessary conditions for learning.

A complete instructional objective should meet the following requirements (Trollinger, 2003, citing Dick and Carey, 1996; Clark, D., 1995b; Nash, 2001; and Department of Defense, 2001):

- A statement identifying the learners
- A statement of what the learners will be able to do (their capabilities)
- A description of the context (conditions) in which the skills will be applied
- A description of the tools that will be available to the learners
- A statement of how the learner will achieve the objective
- An indication of how the objective relates to other objectives in the course

As can be seen from the above definitions, an instructional objective contains three main parts: 1) a description of an *observable action* in terms of performance or behavior; 2) at least one *measurable criterion* (standard) that states the level of acceptable performance in terms of quantity, quality, time, or other measures; and 3) the actual *condition(s)* under which the task will be observed.

Observable Action. The *action* or behavior states what a learner will do to demonstrate that he or she has learned what is required. It must include an action verb such as "*type* a letter," "*lift* a load," or "*select* a menu option." Each objective should cover only one behavior and should include *only one verb*. If multiple behaviors or complicated behaviors are required, the objective should be broken down into *enabling objectives* that support the main *terminal objective*. Department of Defense (2001, pp. 50-52) provided a job aid for constructing instructional objectives. It includes a set of standardized action verbs to use for different types of learning tasks. This job aid is reproduced as Table 10.

Measurable Criterion (standard). The standard of performance answers questions such as "How many?" "How fast?" or "How well?" A single instructional objective can contain more than one measurable criterion depending on the complexity of the task. However, Don Clark (1995b) cautioned that one should not fall into the trap of using only a time constraint because it is not easy to find

Table 10:
Job Aid for Selecting Action Verbs

KNOWLEDGE	
Verbs	**Learning Level & Definition**
Advise; Answer; Brief; Calculate; Define; Elaborate; Express; Identify; Inform; Instruct; List; Name; Read; Recall; Recommend; Recount; Specify; State; Tell	**Learning Level:** Fact Learning **Definition:** Verbal or symbolic information (e.g., names, formulas, facts, etc.).
Appraise; Compile; Compose; Compute; Encrypt; Estimate; Evaluate; Format; Forward Measure; Outline; Route	**Learning Level:** Rule Learning **Definition:** Using two or more facts in a manner that provides regularity of behavior in an infinite variation of situations.
Check; Condense; Edit; Delete; Implement; Initiate; Pause; Resume; Set up; Start; Stop	**Learning Level:** Procedure Learning **Definition:** Performing step-by-step actions in the proper sequence
Allocate; Arrange; Assign; Categorize; Classify; Collate; Compare; Confirm; Consolidate; Contrast; Correlate; Cross-check; Designate; Differentiate; Discriminate; Distinguish; Distribute; Divide; Eliminate; Extract; Finalize; Group; Label; Level; Match; Organize; Rank; Realign; Redistribute; Reexamine; Reorganize; Restate; Schedule; Select; Separate; Sort; Task; Template; Translate; Tune	**Learning Level:** Discrimination Learning **Definition:** Grouping similar and dissimilar items according to their distinct characteristics.
Analyze; Annotate; Apply; Change; Combine; Conclude; Convert; Create; Criticize; Decide; Defend; Derive; Design; Determine; Diagram; Discover; Draft; Effect; Explain; Extend; Find; Generalize; Generate; Hypothesize; Illustrate; Infer; Investigate; Locate; Manipulate; Modify; Plan; Predict; Produce; Project; Resolve; Revise; Search; Solve; Summarize; Synthesize; Triage; Use; War game	**Learning Level:** Problem Solving **Definition:** Synthesizing lower levels of knowledge for the resolution of problems.

Table 10:
(Continued)

SKILLS	
Verbs	**Learning Level & Definition**
Detect; Feel; Hear; Scan; See; Smell; Taste; Visualize	**Learning Level:** Perception (Encoding) **Definition:** Sensory stimuli that translate into physical performance.
Assault; Carry; Creep; Depart; Fall; Hold; Jump; List; Pull; Run; Stay; Swim; Throw; Turn; Twist; Wear	**Learning Level:** Gross Motor Skills **Definition:** Manual dexterity in the performance of physical skills.
Advance; Control; Follow; Guide; Hover; Land; Maneuver; Regulate; Steer; Take off; Track; Traverse	**Learning Level:** Continuous Movement **Definition:** Tracking or making compensatory movements based on feedback.
Able; Assist; Challenge; Cross; Delay; Guard; Prepare; Prime; Ready; Set; Stand to	**Learning Level:** Readiness **Definition:** Having readiness to take a particular action.

Table 10
(Continued)

SKILLS (Continued)	
Verbs	**Learning Level & Definition**
Access; Activate; Actuate; Adjust; Administer; Align; Archive; Arm; Assemble; Balance; Breach; Calibrate; Camouflage; Center; Charge; Clean; Clear; Close; Collect; Connect; Cover; Debrief; Debug; Decontaminate; Deliver; Dispose; Disseminate; Drive; Egress; Elevate; Emplace; Employ; Engage; Energize; Enter; Establish; Evacuate; Exchange; Fill out; Fire; Fit; Fuel; Ground; Harden; Hoist; Initialize; Input; Insert; Inspect; Install; Integrate; Mount; Move; Navigate; Obtain; Open; Operate; Order; Park; Perform; Place; Plot; Police; Position; Post; Press; Pressurize; Process; Procure; Provide; Publish; Raise; Range; Reach; Receive; Record; Reestablish; Rotate; Save; Secure; Send; Service; Shut down; Sight; Signal; Splint; Squeeze; Stockpile; Store; Stow; Strike; Submit; Supervise; Support; Sweep; Take; Take charge; Tap; Test; Tighten; Trace; Transfer; Transmit	**Learning Level:** Mechanism **Definition:** Performing a complex physical or mental skill.
Destroy; Diagnose; Dig; Disassemble; Disconnect; Disengage; Dismantle; Dispatch; Displace; Display; Intercept; Isolate; Issue; Jack; Launch; Load; Log; Lubricate; Maintain; Manage; Refuel; Release; Relocate; Remove; Repair; Replace; Replenish; Reset; Retrieve; Return; Transport; Treat; Troubleshoot; Type; Unload; Update; Utilize; Write; Zero	**Learning Level:** Mechanism (Continued) **Definition:** Performing a complex physical or mental skill.

Table 10
(Continued)

SKILLS (Continued)	
Verbs	**Learning Level & Definition**
Acclimatize; Accommodate; Adapt; Ambush; Attach; Bypass; Conduct; Deploy; Direct; Draw; Evade; Infiltrate; Lay; Lead; Map; Neutralize; Occupy; Orient; Pack; Patrol; Prevent; Program; Protect; Queue; Reconcile; Recover; Reduce; Relieve; Suppress; Tailor; Temper; Train	**Learning Level:** Adaptation **Definition:** Modifying a complex physical or mental skill to accommodate a new situation.
Cause; Construct; Contrive; Correct; Initiate; Invent; Make; Originate	**Learning Level:** Origination **Definition:** Creating a new complex physical or mental skill to accommodate a new situation.
ATTITUDES	
Attend closely; Listen; Listen attentively; Monitor; Observe; Perceive; Reconnoiter; Recognize; Show awareness; Show sensitivity; Wait	**Learning Level:** Receiving (Perception; Situation Awareness) **Definition:** Demonstrating mental preparedness to perceive the normal, abnormal, and emergency condition cues associated with the performance of an operational procedure.

Table 10
(Continued)

ATTITUDES (Continued)	
Verbs	**Learning Level & Definition**
Accomplish; Achieve; Acknowledge; Announce; Ask; Communicate; Complete; Complete assignment; Comply; Demonstrate; Describe; Encode; Execute; Give; Indicate; Interpret; Notify; Obey rules; React; Report; Request; Respond; Resume; Show	**Learning Level**: Responding (Interpreting) **Definition:** Demonstrating mental preparedness to encode operational cues as indicators of normal, abnormal, and emergency conditions associated with the performance of an operational procedure.
Alert; Appreciate; Approve; Assess; Authenticate; Belief; Cancel; Choose; Judge; Justify; Prioritize; Propose; Quality; Reassess; Review; Share; Study; Validate; Verify	**Learning Level:** Valuing (Judgment) **Definition:** Demonstrating the ability to judge the worth or quality of normal, abnormal, and emergency cues associated with the performance of an operational procedure.

Table 10
(Continued)

ATTITUDES (Continued)	
Verbs	**Learning Level & Definition**
Allow; Alter; Assume; Command; Coordinate; Enforce; Ensure; Influence; Prescribe; Serve	**Learning Level:** Competence (Application of resource management strategies and tactics.) **Definition:** Demonstrating the mental preparedness to make decisions using prioritized strategies and tactics in response to normal, abnormal, and emergency condition cues associated with the performance of operational procedures.
Conceive; Conjecture; Develop; Devise; Formulate; Imagine; Innovate	**Learning Level:** Innovation (Generation of new resource management strategies and tactics) **Definition:** Demonstrating the mental preparedness to make decisions by generating the results expected upon completion of prioritized strategies or tactics in response to normal, abnormal, and emergency cues associated with performance of an operational procedure, and generating prioritized strategies and tactics in response to abnormal or emergency cues.

another measure of performance. A time limit should only be used when it is required under normal working conditions.

Conditions of Performance. In addition to stating the conditions under which the task will occur, this portion of an instructional objective identifies the tools, procedures, materials, aids, or facilities to be used in performing the task. It is often expressed with a prepositional phrase such as "without reference to the manual" or "using a volt-ohm meter."

Example Instructional Objectives. Don Clark (1995b) provided four examples of instructional objectives (p. 5-6 of 22). They are shown in Table 11.

Table 11:
Four Example Instructional Objectives

Example 1: *Write a customer reply letter with no spelling mistakes by using a word processor.*
   • Observable Action: write a customer reply letter
   • Measurable Criteria: with no spelling mistakes
   • Conditions of Performance: using a word processor
Note: If more than one type of word processor or computer is used in the organization, the objective should be more specific (e.g., *Given a personal computer, Word for Windows, and a printer, create a printed customer reply letter with no spelling mistakes.*)
In general, the larger the organization and the more technical the task, the more specific the conditions should be spelled out.

Example 2: *Copy a table from a spreadsheet into a word processor document within 3 minutes without reference to the manual.*
   • Observable Action: copy a table from a spreadsheet into a word processor document
   • Measurable Criteria: within 3 minutes
   • Conditions of Performance: without referencing the manual

Example 3: *Smile at all customers, even when exhausted, unless the customer is irate.*
Note: This example includes a variable.
   • Observable Action: smile
   • Measurable Criteria: at all customers
   • Conditions: even when exhausted
   • Variable: unless the customer is irate

Example 4: *After training, the worker will be able to load a dumptruck within 3 loads with a scooploader, in the hours of darkness, unless the work area is muddy.*
   • Observable Action: load a dumptruck
   • Measurable Criteria: within 3 loads
   • Conditions: with a scooploader in the hours of darkness
   • Variable: unless the work area is muddy

1.d. The Content Supports Each and Every Instructional Objective

Once the learner has been told the instructional objectives of a course segment, the content should provide all the necessary information and instruction to allow the learner to meet each objective (Nash, 2003).

Using the Scale

This scale is used to rate the course in terms of how many instructional objectives are supported by the course content. Like the other scales, it should serve as a guide during early formative evaluations. During later formative evaluations and during summative evaluations, more care should be taken when assigning scores. Evaluators should refer to the anchor statements below the scale to help them assign a score on this criterion. Additional information to help the evaluator assign a score is provided in the discussion below. Remember, if you assigned a score of one (1) on Criterion 1.c, you *must* also assign a score of one (1) on this criterion.

Terms, Concepts, Techniques, and Supporting Literature

Determining if the content supports each instructional objective is easier if the objectives are clearly stated (Criterion 1.c). However, if an objective is stated, but has no supporting content, it cannot be learned. On the other hand, the content should not include gratuitous information that does not support the instructional objectives.

The consequences of not meeting the instructional objectives or purpose of the course are likely a loss of learner motivation and poorer performance on the job. The data on the effects of "seductive details" are relevant here (Garner, et al., 1989; Harp & Mayer, 1998). When information is introduced that is not relevant to the instructional objectives, the learner's attention may be diverted to this irrelevant information and may never be refocused on the instructionally important information.

1.e. The Content is Free of Errors

Learners will have more faith in the quality of the course and probably attend more closely to the instruction if they can see that the content is free of errors. If, on the other hand, they observe many typographical errors, grammatical errors, mathematical errors, contradictory definitions, or errors in the organization of the course (e.g., sections that are numbered incorrectly), they may suspect that the course developers were equally careless in terms of the factual accuracy of the content.

Using the Scale

This scale is used to evaluate the course in terms of how many factual and/or distraction errors are found in the courseware. During early formative evaluations, the scale should serve as a guide to help avoid factual and distraction errors. During later formative evaluations and during summative evaluations, scores on the scale should be used to diagnose errors so they can be corrected. The evaluator should use the anchor statements below the scale to help determine the score to assign on this criterion. A list of types of factual and distraction errors is also included below the scale. Additional guidance to help the evaluator is provided in the discussion below.

Terms, Concepts, Techniques, and Supporting Literature

Factual Errors and Distraction Errors. Content errors can occur in two forms: factual errors and distraction errors. *Factual errors* are those that are commonly called "mistakes." They can include mistakes such as:

- Incorrect definitions
- Incorrect formulas
- Mathematical errors
- Logical errors in examples or presentations
- Incorrect numbering of course segments
- Feedback that identifies an incorrect answer as correct
- Other obvious factual mistakes

Related to factual errors are *distraction errors* that misdirect the attention of the learner from the important instructional information in the content. Factual errors can also be distractions, but may be more difficult to locate than other types of distraction errors. Distraction errors are particularly troublesome because the learner may not be aware that he or she is distracted. However, if learners are thinking about something other than the instructional information, they will probably learn less effectively. Distraction errors can include:

- Typographical errors
- Mislabeled graphics
- Grammatical errors
- Shifts in tense
- Shifts in voice (e.g., human voice changes to computer-generated voice or human voice changes to another accent)
- Unexpected addition of sounds or narration, such as one page of a web-delivered course suddenly having narration when the rest of the pages had no narration (also the reverse)
- Shifts in sound level
- Unexpected changes in control locations (see section 5.f)
- Malfunctions in interface controls (see section 5.g.)
- Other obvious distractions

There are a number of ways that the design of content can increase a learner's faith in its factual accuracy. First, the course should be thoroughly reviewed to minimize or eliminate obvious errors. The textual content should be grammatically correct and free of typographical errors. Mistakes in definitions should be eliminated by closely reviewing sources to ensure they are authoritative (e.g., articles from professional journals or widely used guidebooks or instructions). Numerical calculations should be checked for accuracy and illustrative examples should be thoroughly reviewed by subject matter experts (SMEs) for both factual and logical errors. Care should be taken to ensure the reliability of the content by eliminating internal contradictions like conflicting definitions, confusing examples, or feedback that identifies incorrect answers as correct or correct answers as incorrect. In addition, a glossary containing the definitions of each important term should also be provided and used as the baseline for review of terms throughout the course.

Some of the empirical support for this criterion is found in the literature on selective attention (Broadbent, 1963; Klatsky, 1975; Norman, 1976). Errors in the course can become distracters, leading the learners' attention away from the most important information. This is similar to the effect of "seductive details" (Garner, et al, 1989; Harp & Mayer, 1998). It is especially critical to avoid errors in asynchronous courses, which do not have an instructor to monitor and redirect the learners' attention.

It is also important to minimize errors in introductory courses. Novices are not as familiar with the nuances of a topic as experts (Wickens & Hollands, 2000, p. 255). The novices may become even more distracted because they don't know which errors are important and which are only nuisances.

1.f. The Content is Job-relevant

Using the Scale

This scale is used to evaluate the courseware in terms of the amount of content that is relevant to the learner's job. Like all the other scales, it should be used as a guide during early formative evaluations and as a diagnostic tool during later formative and summative evaluations. Anchor statements and a list of ways to make content job-relevant are found below the scale. The evaluator should use these to help assign a score on this criterion. Additional information to help the evaluator is provided in the discussion below.

Terms, Concepts, Techniques, and Supporting Literature

Often people are "forced" to take instruction that they perceive as a waste of time (e.g., "sensitivity" training, "risk management" training). This may be a reason why transfer of learning to job performance is often disappointing. "Most of the research on employee training clearly shows that although millions of dollars are spent on training in the public sector, there is little empirical evidence linking training to improved job behavior or employee attitudes" (Haskell, 2001, p. 5 cited in Clark, R. C., 2003, p. 136).

Educational researchers have looked at the differences between experts and novices in how they organize important knowledge and skills in a domain. It has been shown that experts have developed a more complex model of a topic area and are able to attend to more subtle features of the topic when solving problems (e.g., Chi, Feltovich, & Glasser, 1981). Bransford and his colleagues (Bransford, Sherwood, Vye, & Rieser, 1986; Bransford, Franks, Vye, & Sherwood, 1989) argue that instruction that focuses only on facts does not guarantee that the learner will be able to use that knowledge in later situations. "Our data suggest that fact-oriented acquisition permits people to remember information when explicitly prompted to do so, but it does not facilitate their ability to use this information spontaneously to solve new problems" (Bransford, et al., 1989, p. 479). They recommend that instruction should provide information in the context of solving relevant problems. Furthermore, they found that problem-oriented activities lead to "greater spontaneous use of the acquired information to aid in problem solving" (p. 477).

The relevance of the instructional material affects the learner's attention (Broadbent, 1963; Klatsky, 1975; Norman, 1976), motivation (Locke & Bryan, 1966; Magill, 1980; Ausubel, 1968), and depth of processing of the content (Brown & McNeill, 1966; Craik & Lockhart, 1972; Anderson & Bower; 1972; 1973; 1974). Therefore, in addition to stating the purpose of the instruction (1.b) and what the learner should be able to do after the instruction (1.c), the learner should be able to relate the content to requirements of his or her job (i.e., it should be job-relevant). This means learners should be able to readily perceive that the content is meaningful in the context of the job and that it supports their job requirements (Dick and Carrey, 1996; Texas Education Agency, 2003; Trollinger, 2003). As discussed under Criterion 1.a, Nitsch (1977) and Bransford and his colleagues (1986, 1989) argued that the instruction on a topic should be structured so that learners can establish a firm contextual basis for understanding the new concept. This contextual basis should include concrete, job-relevant examples.

The content should be free of jargon and only use terms that are defined and job-relevant. Some of the techniques that can make content more job-relevant include: use of real-world examples from the job area, testimonials from experts in the field, or use of realistic scenarios

The Texas Education Agency (2003) recommended that learners be given the ability to "customize" the instruction to meet their specific needs. However, Jones and Okey (1995) citing Jones (1989) caution that "browsing" through a course should not be indiscriminate or uncontrolled. Rather, they recommend that content be designed and organized so that all learners are given instruction on "required" topics (e.g., those that everyone in an occupational field must master). Then additional, related, detailed content could be presented in a manner that allows them to "drill down" into this content through more and more levels of information to the appropriate level of the topics that is most relevant to their needs. This can be done using pop-up menus, buttons, hot text, or other methods.

1.g. The "Authority" for the Content is Clearly Stated

As discussed above (1.e), the learner needs to feel confident that the content is factually accurate. Although it is fairly easy for the learner to determine if the course is free of surface errors, it is more difficult for a learner to judge the factual accuracy of the content. This is especially true if the learner is a novice in the subject area.

Using the Scale

This scale is used to evaluate the quantity and quality of references and credits that are provided to substantiate the "authority" for the content. Formatively, it should serve as a guide to remind developers to include appropriate references and credits. During summative evaluations, the score on this criterion should indicate instances when additional references or credits are needed. The evaluator should use the anchor statements below the scale to help assign a score on this criterion. Additional information to assist the evaluator is provided in the discussion below.

Terms, Concepts, Techniques, and Supporting Literature

The content presented in an instructional product consists of a number of factual assertions or claims. The justification for these assertions relies on their support evidence or the *authority* behind the claims. Zarefsky (2001) discussed several types of evidence that can support factual assertions. One type of justification is social consensus or common knowledge. Secondly, they can be justified by objective data (e.g., examples, statistics, tangible evidence, or historical documents). Finally, the credibility of the information can be judged by the credibility of the source of the information. That is, the competence and trustworthiness of the source.

Social consensus may appear straightforward, with statements like, "Everyone knows such and such" perceived as the only justification necessary. However, one must be aware that common knowledge may not always be correct knowledge. It is always better to supplement social consensus with other justifications. Indeed, Bell (2005) cautioned that statements like "everyone knows such and such" are propaganda techniques. He believes that critical thinkers should not fall into the trap of believing such statements.

In terms of objective data, one must look to the methods used to collect the data and the logic behind their interpretation. In most cases, an evaluator or a learner does not have the expertise to judge whether these methods were correctly employed. Therefore, one must rely on "experts," such as review boards or individuals with experience in the field. In these cases, it is the credibility of the source that is actually being used as justification.

There are several questions that one might ask to reduce doubts about the credibility of an information source. First, one could ask, "Is the person an authority in the field?" This can be supported if the individual has made the factual assertions in respected forums (e.g., scientific journals, books, professional meetings). Second, one could ask, "Does the person have a vested interest?" Eagly, Wood, and Chaiken (1978) found that communicators were judged as being less biased and more persuasive when they made arguments against their own self-interest. If the communicator appears unbiased and unselfish, the message is likely to be perceived to be based on compelling evidence. Credibility can also be judged by asking a third question, "Do other credible sources disagree?" These are the types of questions that should be asked by instructional developers when assembling the content for a course.

Learners do not judge the credibility of a course by asking specific questions like those above. Perceptions of source credibility are easily manipulated. For example, Miller, Moruyama, Beaber, and Valone (1976) found that listeners judged speakers as more credible if they spoke at a rapid rate. This result should not be justification for rapid narrations. Rather, the findings emphasize the importance of considering the listener's perception when evaluating "authority."

Learner confidence in the authority of content can be expected to increase if the origin of the content is made apparent as well as the qualifications of the individuals who provided the content (the subject matter experts) and created the instruction (the instructional developers). This is even true for the reviewers of the course (e.g., "an instructional quality review was conducted by..."). This information should be made available to the learners in a bibliography and collection of resumes and summary statements that are easily accessed from the course. Furthermore, any disclaimers or cautions about the content (e.g., disagreements among experts, theories versus facts, etc.) should be provided to the learners (Bostock, 2004).

Another way to increase learner confidence is to ensure that the content is current (e.g., includes dates for all references and the version of the course). The latest references, as well as "classic" references should be included and updated periodically. Periodic reviews of examples, simulations, and testimonials should also be conducted to ensure that they are providing the most up-to-date information on the topic.

1.h. There are Clear Indications of Prerequisites

As discussed in Chapter 3 (Criterion 1.a), the structure of instructional information can positively or negatively affect the learning experience. Gagné (1968; 1985) strongly argued that instruction should be built as a hierarchy of information. This also is the basis for the Elaboration Theory of Instruction (Reigeluth & Stein, 1983). This hierarchy should be readily apparent to the learner. One way to help ensure that the learner is attending to the appropriate level of this informational hierarchy is to clearly indicate the prerequisites for any course or course segment. The indications of prerequisites serve as guideposts for the learner and help to ensure that he or she is taking the appropriate segment of instruction.

Using the Scale

This scale is used to evaluate the course in terms of how many of the needed prerequisites are clearly indicated. Evaluators should use the anchor statements below the scale and the list of ways to indicate prerequisites to help them assign a score on this criterion. Additional information on this criterion is provided in the discussion below.

Like all of the scales, this one should be used as a guide during early ISD stages and as a diagnostic tool during later ISD stages.

Terms, Concepts, Techniques, and Supporting Literature

As previously discussed (1.a), learners should proceed through a course in small meaningful steps (Gagné, 1968). Before beginning each step, the learner should have completed all required prerequisite topics. Catrambone (1998) demonstrated that labeling groups of steps in examples helped learners understand these meaningful steps or subgoals. Royer (1979) reviewed several theories of transfer and concluded that "relevant previous learning can facilitate the acquisition of current instruction" (p. 53). Prerequisites provide the essential information that is required by the learner to organize and structure new instructional information.

In an introductory course, the learners should not have to worry about prerequisites because the course should be designed to guide them through the content in the appropriate sequence. However, learners could overlook important prerequisites in a more advanced course. This could lead to confusion and frustration when they have not learned this prerequisite knowledge or mastered these necessary skills. In all cases, the introduction or course overview should provide clear statements about requirements for prerequisite courses. Within a course, each topic should include an introductory discussion about prerequisite topics.

1.i. There are Clear Indications of Completed Topics

Learners should always know when they have completed a topic. They should not have to wonder whether new information is part of the current topic or the beginning of a new topic. A clear indication of topic completion enables the learner to cognitively pause and consolidate the information presented.

Using the Scale

This scale is used to rate the course on how clearly the completion of topics are indicated in the courseware. Evaluators should use the anchor statements below the scale and the list of indications of completed topics to help them assign a score on this criterion. Additional information on this criterion is provided in the discussion below. During formative evaluations, the scale and anchor statements should serve as guides to remind developers to include indications when learners complete each topic. During later formative evaluations and during summative evaluations the scores should be used to identify topics that do not have clear indications when they are completed. These indications should then be added to the courseware.

Terms, Concepts, Techniques, and Supporting Literature

A learner should not have to wonder if he or she has completed a topic. The structure of the course should provide the cues that the learner completed a topic. Some of these structural cues include summaries of the important information, interactive activities (Chapter 5, Criterion 2.a), or some form of assessment (Chapter 5, Evaluation Area 3) to determine if the learner has learned the material and is ready to move forward. Performance feedback (Chapter 6, Evaluation Area 4) should then be provided to either reinforce correct behaviors or to provide remedial instruction if the learner has not demonstrated that the material has been learned correctly. In all cases, the learner should be provided with an unambiguous message (or multiple messages using various techniques) that the topic has been completed. For example, a topic on the table of contents could change color when it has been successfully completed.

1.j. Sources for More Information are Available

Every learner does not take a course for the same reason. The requirements of a learner's job may lead him or her to desire or need additional information on the topics presented in the course. Sources for this additional information should be made available and instructions provided to access these sources.

Using the Scale

This scale is used to evaluate the course in terms of how well the course provides sources for additional information. At early formative stages, it should be used as a guide to remind developers to include sources for additional information. During later formative evaluations and during summative evaluations, it should be used to identify instances where learners should be directed to additional information. Evaluators should use the anchor statements below the scale to help them assign a score on this criterion. Additional information on this criterion is provided in the discussion below.

Terms, Concepts, Techniques, and Empirical Support

No course can provide all information on any given topic nor is this a goal that should be pursued. The goal of instruction should be to achieve the purposes and instructional objectives of the course. Many learners will wish to learn more about some of the topics in the course. Some of this additional instructional information can be provided as "drill down" options in the course. However, most additional information will be found in other sources. The course should provide easy-to-follow instructions or directions to find this information. Some of the sources might be additional courses, literature, professional organizations, schedules for meetings, etc. In all cases, the developers and maintainers of the course should ensure that the information from the sources is current (e.g., the date the information was last verified), the directions to the sources are correct, and that the sources are still available.

Chapter 5:
Instructional Activities

"Time plus energy equals learning" (Chickering & Gamson, quoted in Graham, Cagiltay, Craner, Byung-Ro, & Duffy, 2000). This short phrase captures one of the most important concepts of instruction. The learner must invest time and energy in order to learn. He or she should not be a passive recipient of instruction. Rather, the instructional product should be designed so the learner is an active participate in the learning process and is encouraged and enabled to think more about the subject or practice the required skills. This chapter provides discussions of the criteria that deal with what the learner does during the course.

2.a. Activities are Relevant (All Support LOs and Job Requirements)

Activities should be designed to support the learning objectives (LOs) of the course. The instructional activities should provide the learners with the necessary skills, knowledge, and experience to meet the goals and objectives of the course and, ultimately, their job.

Using the Scale

This scale is used to rate how many instructional activities included in the course are relevant. During early formative evaluations, the scale and anchor statements should be used as guides. During later formative evaluations and during summative evaluations, the scale and anchor statements should be used to assign a diagnostic score. Use the anchor statements below the scale and the examples of relevant activities to help assign a score on this criterion. Remember, if you assign a rating of one (1) on this criterion *do not continue*. The course needs to be reworked. Additional information to help the evaluator understand the importance of relevant activities is provided in the discussion below.

153

Terms, Concepts, Techniques, and Supporting Literature

According to Rumelhart and Norman (1981, p. 358), analogical reasoning is the most common way that people apply knowledge learned in one domain to another (e.g., from one job task to another or from an instructional situation to a job situation). Instructional activities should be designed to help the learner develop analogical reasoning by exposing the learner to natural, relevant operations and information from the target domain.

The learner should find the instructional activities meaningful. That is, the learner should be able to easily see how the learning objectives are supported by the activities (Perry, 2003). The learner should also easily perceive that the activities are job-relevant (i.e., they have face validity). Some examples of relevant activities include:

- Role playing in a case study based on real-world issues
- Solving realistic (real-world) problems
- Interacting with realistic simulations
- Identifying the similarities and differences among real-world examples
- Using analogies

Information on these activities is provided in the sections below.

Role Playing

Role-playing is a type of activity, which allows the learner to put him or herself into a realistic situation in which he or she may use the information he or she is trying to learn. Taylor, Renshaw, and Jensen (1997) assessed the use of role playing exercises in either a paper-and-pencil or computer-based format for learning information about the probability of a volcano eruption. They also manipulated whether the role-playing scenarios were framed positively (e.g., it is estimated that no eruption will occur) or negatively (e.g., it is estimated that an eruption will occur). Results indicated that computer-based role-playing enhanced learning. Furthermore, in the computer-based condition, there was no effect of the type of framing. These results should be regarded with caution because of differences between the computer-based and paper-and-pencil exercises that could also have affected the results (e.g., novelty, timing of feedback, use of animation, etc.).

Problem Solving

Mayer, Dow, and Mayer (2003) conducted a series of four experiments to examine some of the variables that affect learner performance in a problem-solving task. In all the experiments, the learners were presented with explanations from an agent (Dr. Phyz). In the first experiment, the learners were given explanations on the operation of electric motors by either an on-screen agent or as on-screen text. The group receiving narration performed better than the text group on the problem-solving transfer test.

In experiment 2, the role of interactivity was examined. Learners were presented with explanation of lightning formation and they either were allowed to control the pace of the explanations or were presented with non-interactive messages that were not under their control. The learners in the interactive group generated significantly more answers on the problem-solving test than the non-interactive group. The same procedure was tried again but the transfer test was administered one week after the learning session. In this case, the interactive group also outperformed the non-interactive group.

In their third experiment, half of the learners were given pre-questions to guide their learning of electric motors. This group performed better than the group that did not receive the pre-questions. The researchers assumed that the pre-questions required the learners to more deeply process the information and to think about the information prior to and during the learning session. The results provide support for the self-explanations principle (people learn better when they are prompted to provide explanations during learning).

Finally, in their fourth experiment, they examined the role of the agent's on-screen image. No performance differences were found between the group who learned with an image of the agent present during narration and the group who was only given narration without an image of the agent. The results indicate that the presence of an agent may not always enhance learning and may even be distracting. This is probably affected by the nature of the task and the characteristics of the agent. Indeed, Stout and Sims (2005) argued the presence of agents may be beneficial for instruction on some types of tasks (e.g., the need for learners to be able to react to facial expressions or body movements in specific ways).

Simulations

Instructional simulations are usually created by combining a variety of media attributes (e.g., sound, motion, and text). The term *simulation* should not be confused with *simulator*. A simulator is a type of device, which "(a) attempts to duplicate the essential features of a task situation and (b) provides for direct practice" (Kinkade & Wheaton, 1972, p. 671). A simulation, on the other hand, does not have to be any type of equipment (although it may involve the use of equipment). Morris and Thomas (1976) define a simulation as "the ongoing representation of certain features of a real situation to achieve some specific training objective" (p. 66). They go on to define a simulator as "the media through which a trainee may experience the simulation" (p. 66).

The Department of Defense (1997) identified three types of simulations: live, virtual, and constructive.

- *Live Simulation*s involve real people operating real systems. An example is the Multiple Integrated Laser Engagement Simulation (MILES). This system, a precursor of the laser tag game, uses laser emitters and receivers attached to weapons so troops can practice in realistic conditions.

- *Virtual Simulations* involve real people operating simulated systems. A flight simulator and a driving simulator are examples of virtual simulations.

- *Constructive Simulations* involve simulated people operating simulated systems. Real people make inputs into the simulation and the simulation determines the outcomes of the exercise. Two examples are a computer-controlled war game or a simulation of the activities of a team dealing with an oil spill.

These three types of simulations are not mutually exclusive and are often combined in a given instructional exercise.

The use of simulations has been an effective instructional approach for tasks with strong perceptual-motor components such as flying an airplane (Valverde, 1973; Waag, 1981; Flaxman & Stark, 1987; Hays & Singer, 1989; Hays, Jacobs, Prince & Salas, 1992). Simulations have also been shown to be effective for teaching cognitive concepts like statistics. Lane and Tang (2000) compared the performance of learners given a simulation illustrating the statistical concepts of probability with those given textual explanations. The learners who were given the simulation outperformed the learners trained with a textbook.

Swaak and de Jong (2001) studied the learning effectiveness of simulations for teaching physics principles. They found that the simulations enhanced the learning of the principles. Furthermore, they found that activities (exercises) designed to help the learner structure the simulation as a learning experience contributed most clearly to their effectiveness.

Determining the Characteristics of Simulations. No instructional simulation can capture all of the characteristics of a real situation. If it did, it would be the real situation, not a simulation. Each of the possible characteristics that can be simulated adds to the cost of the simulation and increases its development time. Furthermore, for instructional purposes, it is often desired to omit certain characteristics of the real situation so the instruction can focus on specific tasks. Thus, it is of vital importance to determine which characteristics of the real situation can and should be simulated. A conceptual metaphor that can help simulation designers make these important choices is simulation fidelity.

Simulation fidelity is the degree of similarity between the simulated situation and the operational situation that is simulated. This degree of similarity can be conceptualized under two major dimensions: (1) the physical characteristics of the simulation (e.g., visual, spatial, kinesthetic); and (2) the functional characteristics of the simulation (e.g., the informational (stimulus) and action (response) options provided by the simulation).

Baum, Reidel, Hays, and Mirabella (1982) confirmed the separate and interactive effects of the physical and functional dimensions of fidelity in a perceptual-motor task. They concluded that in fidelity research, it is not sufficient to study general levels of fidelity. Rather, fidelity must be operationalized in terms of at least two dimensions: physical and functional similarity.

Physical fidelity is how the simulation looks; the physical characteristics of the simulation. *Functional fidelity* is how the simulation works or provides the necessary information to support the task. These two fidelity dimensions are related (e.g., if the physical characteristics of the simulation are changed, its functional fidelity will also change). In general, the functional requirements of the simulation should dictate its physical characteristics.

The functional fidelity (the information or stimulus and response options) is how the simulation provides required information and interaction opportunities so the learner can learn the task. Depending upon the task, the information can come through any of the senses. For example, if a learner is learning to fly a plane in a simulated cockpit, and the task is to fly at a specific altitude, then the simulated altimeter must be represented in enough detail that the learner can read the altitude. On the other hand, if the instructional task is only to locate the display next to the altitude indicator, then the simulation does not need to include a functioning altimeter.

In order to respond to the information (act), the user must have the ability to make input to the simulation. For example, if the learner needs to learn how to change altitude, a simulated control device must actually move and this movement must result in a change in the simulated altitude.

The instructional developer and simulation designer must ask questions like:

- "What information does one need to accomplish the task?"
- "How does one obtain this information?"
- "What actions must one take to accomplish the task?"
- "How does one take these actions and what feedback information informs one that the task has been accomplished correctly?"

Answers to these types of questions help determine the functional requirements of the simulation. These functional requirements then drive the decisions about how to design the physical characteristics of the simulation. Additional details on the concept of fidelity may be found in Hays and Singer (1989) and Hays (2006).

Working with Examples

Using examples can be a useful technique when the learning task involves problem solving and the learners are novices. Ruth Clark defined *worked examples* as "a step-by-step demonstration of how to perform a task or solve a problem" (Clark, R. C., 2003, p. 51). Paas (1992) compared the effects of worked examples (practice exercises) on learning geometry problems. One group was given conventional instruction using 12 practice problems. A second group studied worked examples followed by four practice problems. The worked examples group spent less time studying, yet scored higher on a test than did those in the conventional group. The worked examples group also scored higher on different types of problems that required applications of the principles taught. Zhu and Simon (1987) found that worked examples allowed learners to finish a three-year mathematics course in two years.

It should be noted that experienced learners do not appear to benefit from worked examples. Kalyuga, Chandler, Tuovinen, and Sweller (2001) studied trade apprentices learning to write programs for circuits. In the early sessions, the learners benefited from the worked examples. However, in later sessions, solving problems was found to be a more effective approach. They concluded that novices benefit from worked examples, but those with more experience benefit just as well from less structured problem solving strategies (see also Tuovien & Sweller, 1999). Based on their research, Kalyuga et al. (2001) provide the following instructional design recommendation: "A series of worked examples should be presented first. After learners become more familiar with the domain, problem solving (as well as exploratory learning environments) can be used to further enhance and extend acquired skills" (p. 588).

Atkinson (2002) studied the instructional effects of using an animated pedagogical agent to deliver instructional information about worked examples. He found that learners exposed to an animated narrator outperformed those only given textual explanations of the examples. Baylor and Ryu (2003) studied learners' perceptions of pedagogical agent personal characteristics. They found that animated agents were perceived as more "instructor like" and "engaging." However, the learners' perception of agent credibility was found to be the same with either a static or animated agent.

Moreno and Mayer (2004) examined the role of personalized agent messages in a computer-based simulation used to teach college students about the characteristics of plants. They found that the learners who received personalized agent messages performed better than those who received non-personalized messages on both retention and problem-solving transfer tests. This and other research on pedagogical agents has implications for how learners interact with content (see Criterion 2.b) and ways to make the content more enjoyable (see Criterion 2.c).

Using Analogies

"An instructional analogy is an explicit, non-literal comparison between two objects, or sets of objects that describes their structural, functional, and/or causal similarities" (Clark, R. C., 2003, p. 111). Analogies can help the learner understand instructional information by relating the new information to familiar knowledge. For example, Newby, Ertmer, and Stepich (1995) found positive learning benefits from the use of analogies when teaching physiological concepts.

Stepich and Newby (1988) stated that there are four parts that make up an analogy:

1. A *subject*, which is the new information to be learned (e.g., the functions of red blood cells).
2. An *analog*: some existing knowledge that can be compared to the subject (e.g., trucks).
3. A *connector*, which shows the similarity between the subject and the analog (e.g., red blood cells function like trucks...).
4. A *ground*, which describes the similarities and differences between the subject and the analog (e.g., a common function between red blood cells and trucks is they are both transporters of materials; a difference is that blood cells are biological and trucks are mechanical).

Stepich and Newby (1988) provided guidelines for constructing and presenting analogies. When constructing an analogy, they recommended following the memory aid ABCD:

- **A**: Analyze the subject to determine the most important things the learner needs to understand and the characteristics that make the subject unique or novel.

- **B**: Brainstorm potential analogs and list the concrete items that have the same or similar attributes as the subject.

- **C**: Choose an analog. From the list of candidates, eliminate those that are not likely to be effective (e.g., those not familiar to the learners, those difficult to understand, and/or those that do not closely match the relevant attributes of the subject). Choose the analog or analogs from those that remain

- **D**: Describe the connector and ground. Provide a clear and thorough description of the similarities and differences between the subject and analog.

When presenting an analogy, they recommended follow the memory aid ADAPT:

- **A**: Analogize early. Present the analogy during the initial description of the subject.
- **D**: Deliver in combination format. Use combinations of verbal and pictorial formats (or other media combinations).
- **A**: Assimilate elaborations. As you elaborate the subject, assimilate the added information to the analog.
- **P**: Provide practice. Allow the learners to apply the subject information and provide corrective feedback.
- **T**: Test. Provide new situations where the learner can apply the subject information.

2.b. The Learner is Required to Interact with Content

"Requiring" interaction means that the course should be designed so that the learner must engage in some form of activity where he or she uses the content in some meaningful way.

Using the Scale

This scale is used to evaluate the course in terms of how it is designed to promote interaction between the learner and the content. As with all the scales, this one should be used as a guide during early formative evaluations. During later ISD stages greater care should be taken to use the scale to assign diagnostic scores, which can target required improvements in the courseware. Use the anchor statements below the scale to help assign a rating on this criterion. Additional information on this criterion is provided in the discussion below.

Terms, Concepts, Techniques, and Supporting Literature

All of the activities discussed under Criterion 2.a (relevance) are also applicable here. However, in addition to relevance, the activities should be designed to help the learner interact with the material to be learned. Interactive activities help the learner to integrate new information into existing mental structures and/or develop the necessary motor skills required to perform the task. In all cases, the learner should be assessed (formally or informally) on how his or her performance demonstrates that he or she is meeting the instructional objectives (see Evaluation Area 3 in Chapter 5) and should be provided feedback on the quality of his or her performance (see Evaluation Area 4 in Chapter 6).

Najjar (1988) defined interaction as "mutual action among the learner, the learning system, and the learning material" (p. 314). He cites several studies that show a positive effect on learning with computers when learners use an interactive interface. However, this interactive interface is only beneficial if it encourages learners to cognitively process the learning material. In other words the material must be cognitively engaging (see Criterion 2.c).

Types of Interactions. Sims, Dobbs, and Hand (2001) discussed several types of interactivity that encompass both human-computer interactions and human-human interactions. These include interactions between: learner and learner, learner and teacher, teacher and content, teacher and teacher, learner and interface, and learner and content. It is only the last two (learner and interface and learner and content) that are within the scope of this guide since the focus is on the evaluation of asynchronous instruction without the presence of an instructor or other collaborative learners. Learner and interface interactions deal with how the learner navigates through the course and provides various inputs when required. Learner and interface criteria are evaluated in the User Interface section. Learner and content interactions are evaluated under this criterion.

Interaction with Content. One definition of learning is "a relatively permanent change in someone's knowledge based on the person's experience" (Mayer, 2002, p. 3). Once the person has learned the new information, he or she needs to be able to use it to help learn new things or to perform a task. This is usually referred to as transfer of learning. Transfer is facilitated by meaningful instruction and interaction with content (Mayer, 2002). Some types of cognitive interaction with information include thinking about the information, reflecting on its implications, discussing how it relates to other topics in the course, hypothesizing how the new information could improve task performance, comparing one source of information to another, and classifying the information into job-relevant categories. These types of interactions promote active learning, which has been shown to be more effective than passive learning (e.g., Dickinson, 1978). Mayer (2002) discussed numerous instructional methods to help learners interact with content to promote meaningful learning. These include: 1) presentation of concrete examples, 2) methods to make examples more relevant (e.g., case-based learning), 3) guiding cognitive processes, 4) teaching strategies to make learning active, and 5) teaching problem-solving strategies.

Another activity that promotes learning is to have the learners produce information rather than being presented with the information. Called the "generation effect," (Slamecka & Graf, 1978) it "is one of the most robust findings in the experimental psychology literature" (deWinstanley & Bjork, 2002, p. 22). These authors indicated that the generation effect has been shown in a variety of learning areas from mathematics to reading comprehension.

Practice. "One major activity separates the gifted amateur from the professional: practice" (Norman, 1976, p. 199). Many studies have shown the advantages of spreading practice sessions over time (distributed practice) as compared to a single practice session (massed practice). For example, Duncan (1951) allowed one group to practice in one session that was three times as long as the total time another group practiced in distributed sessions. He found that the distributed practice group outperformed the massed practice group.

How does one tell if the learner has practiced enough? Several sources of data indicate that more practice is always better. Experts at difficult tasks (e.g., playing the piano or flying a high-performance jet) continuously practice to refine their skills and keep them current (Schneider, 1985). It has also been shown that the overlearning of a task can result in better retention of skills. Overlearning occurs when learners engage in additional practice after they have learned a task to an established criterion level. The additional practice helps them "automate" the learned skills and helps ensure that they will be able to perform the skill after a prolonged retention interval or under stressful conditions.

Schendel and Hagman (1982) investigated the effects of overlearning on a disassembly-assembly task. They trained three groups of soldiers until they could all perform the task to criterion levels. The control group received no additional instruction. The two experimental groups received 100% overtraining on the task. One of the experimental groups received the overtraining immediately and the other experimental group received the overtraining 4 weeks after initial instruction. Eight weeks after initial instruction all three groups took a retention test. The first trial on the retention test served as the measure of retention. The results showed that both of the overlearning groups outperformed the control group. The

163

performance of two overlearning groups did not differ. The results indicate that overlearning is as effective for improving retention as retraining on the tasks.

Hagman and Rose (1983) reviewed 13 experiments on the retention of learned tasks in the military context. Some of their conclusions from this review are as follows:

- Retention can be improved with repetition (practice) both before and after task proficiency has been achieved. This supports the overlearning principle.
- Retention is better when task repetitions are spaced rather massed during instruction.
- Retention can be improved through the use of instructional methods that are tailored for the specific instructional environment. For example, if instruction is to be conducted in a military field environment, the specific variables that make this environment unique need to be determined and accounted for when designing the instructional approach.

The Institute for Higher Education Policy (IHEP) in their evaluation framework for e-learning maintains that courses should be designed to require learners to engage in analysis, synthesis, and evaluation as part of course requirements (Broadbent and Cotter, 2002). The Texas Education Agency (2003) recommends that instructional interactions should vary according to the desired type of learning outcomes. For example, learners who need to learn about concepts might engage in an activity where they have to identify and categorize the differences and similarities among concepts. Learners required to learn a procedure, might participate in a simulated activity where they have to arrange procedures sequentially or identify a procedural step that is incorrect. Learners learning psychomotor skills might need to interact with a hands-on simulation or an equipment mock-up.

The content should be presented in such a way that it encourages interaction by asking for varied kinds of inputs (Bangert-Drowns and Kozma, 1989). However, there should not be too many inputs required and they should be relevant to the instructional objectives, not "just for the sake of it."

Thibodeau (1997), an instructional developer and designer of interactive courseware for the U. S. Army, provided the following two suggestions for designing content to encourage learner-content interaction.

- Break the content into small units, each followed by an interactive exercise
- The interactions (e.g., questions) should provide an opportunity for the learners to use what they have just learned.

Two techniques that can be used to increase the level of learner-content interaction are to enable learners to annotate text or summarize the information in their own words. Some research indicates that "annotating text while reading improves comprehension" (Dembo and Junge, 2003, p. 58). There is additional research that indicates that learners "who summarize readings comprehend and recall more than those who do not" (Dembo and Junge, 2003, p.56). Course designers could include mechanisms that allow learners to engage in these interactive activities.

Although most research on interaction has been conducted in the context of lecture-based or web-supplemented courses (using the web as an adjunct to the lecture, such as posting the syllabus, answering questions, or conducting discussion groups), it is reasonable to assume that interaction is also an important component of learning in asynchronous courses. Milheim (1995) stated that "the interaction between the computer and the learner may be one of the most important aspects of effective computer-based learning" (p. 163). Zirkin and Sumler (1995) concluded from their review of the research literature that "The weight of evidence...was that increased learner involvement by immediate interaction resulted in increased learning..." (quoted in Roblyer and Ekhaml, 2000, p. 1). This is also true for computer- or web-delivered instruction. However, in the authors' experience, modeling the role of the instructor is one of the most important, yet difficult aspects in designing computer- or web-delivered instruction. Instructional developers need to try and put themselves into the role of the learner—anticipating frequently asked questions and areas of confusion. Content and activities should address these questions and areas because there is no instructor to fill this role. Formative evaluations are a good method to help identify these important issues and questions.

In any case, it is more likely that learners will interact with content if it is presented in an engaging manner. Evaluating how much of the content engages the learner is the topic of the next criterion.

Interactivity Assessment Scales for Instructor-mediated Courses. Roblyer and Ekhaml (2000) and Roblyer and Wiencke (2003) provided a rubric for the design of interactivity for instructor-mediated distance learning courses. If you are evaluating an instructor-mediated, computer-delivered course you may wish to use the following interactivity assessment scales that were adapted from their rubric.

Instructions: Read the statements below each scale and circle the number that best characterized the course on each rating element. Sum the scores to give an overall summary of interactivity (higher scores indicate a better level of interactivity). This summary score may then be used to assign a score or contribute to the assignment of a score on Criterion 2.b. The scores on each separate rating element can be used to diagnose specific interactivity problems.

Element 1. Social/Rapport-Building Designs for Interaction

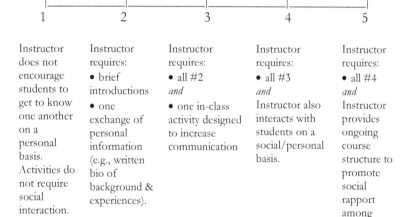

1	2	3	4	5
Instructor does not encourage students to get to know one another on a personal basis. Activities do not require social interaction.	Instructor requires: • brief introductions • one exchange of personal information (e.g., written bio of background & experiences).	Instructor requires: • all #2 *and* • one in-class activity designed to increase communication	Instructor requires: • all #3 *and* Instructor also interacts with students on a social/personal basis.	Instructor requires: • all #4 *and* Instructor provides ongoing course structure to promote social rapport among students and instructor.

Element 2. Instructional Designs for Interaction

1	2	3	4	5
Only one-way delivery of information (e.g., lectures or text delivery) and student products based on information	Instructional activities: • only student-instructor communica-tion (asking/respo nding to questions)	Instructional activities: • #2 *and* • student – student communica-tion (e.g. discussion pairs or small groups)	Instructional activities: • #3 *and* • students develop products cooperatively (e.g., in pairs or small groups).	Instructional activities: • #4 *and* • groups share feedback with other groups

Element 3. Interactivity of Technology Resources

1	2	3	4	5
Fax, Web pages (text and/or graphics).	• E-mail, Listserv, conference/ bulletin board (2-way asynchronous exchange of info.)	Technologies: • all #2 *and* • chat room or other technologies (synchronous exchange of info., primarily written)	Technolo-gies: • all #4 *and* • 1-way visuals (e.g., teleconferenc ing) and 2-way voice .	Technolo-gies: • all #5 *and* • visual technologies that allow 2-way synchronous visual and voice (instructor-student & student-student)

167

Element 4. Evidence of Learner Engagement

1	2	3	4	5
By end of course, most students (50%-75%) are *replying to* messages from instructor but only when required; messages are sometimes unresponsive to topics and tend to be either brief or wordy & rambling.	By end of course, most students (50%-75%) are *replying to* messages from instructor *and* other students, *both* when required *and* on a voluntary basis; replies are usually responsive to topics but are either brief or wordy & rambling.	By end of course, all or nearly all students (90%-100%) are *replying to* messages from instructor *and* other students (*both* required & voluntary); replies are *always responsive* to topics but sometimes are either brief or wordy & rambling.	By end of course, most students (50%-75%) are *both replying to and initiating* messages (*both* required and voluntary); messages are detailed and responsive to topics and usually reflect and effort to communicate well.	By end of course, all or nearly all students (90%-100%) are *both replying to and initiating* messages (*both* required and voluntary); messages are detailed, responsive to topics, and are well-developed communications.

Element 5. Evidence of Instructor Engagement

1	2	3	4	5
Instructor responds only randomly to student queries; responses usually take more than 48 hours; feedback is brief and provides little analysis of student work or suggestions for improvement.	Instructor responds to *most* student queries; responses usually are within 48 hours; feedback sometimes offers some analysis of student work and suggestions for improvement.	Instructor responds to *all* student queries; responses usually are within 48 hours; feedback usually offers some analysis of student work and suggestions for improvement.	Instructor responds to *all* student queries; responses *usually* are prompt (i.e., within 24 hours); feedback *always* offers *detailed analysis* of student work and suggestions for improvement.	Instructor responds to *all* student queries; responses are *always* prompt (i.e., within 24 hours); feedback *always* offers *detailed analysis* of student work and suggestions for improvement along with additional hints and information to supplement learning.

2.c. Instruction is Engaging (Attracts and Maintains Learners' Attention)

In order to learn, learners must attend to the instruction. One of the most important design decisions is how to gain and maintain the learners' attention, or how to "engage" them with the content.

Using the Scale

This scale is used to evaluate the course in terms of how much of the content engages the learner (attracts and maintains attention). The scale should be used as a guide during early formative evaluations. During later formative evaluations and summative evaluations, evaluators should carefully assign a score on this scale. The scores should then be used diagnostically to help direct efforts toward correcting deficiencies and making the courseware more engaging. Use the anchor statements below the scale and the list of examples to help assign a rating on this criterion. Additional information to help understand this criterion can be found in the discussion below.

Terms, Concepts, Techniques, and Supporting Literature

Issues of engagement are closely related to those of motivation (see discussion of ARCS Model under Criterion 1.a, Chapter 3). Richard Clark (2003) stated that course designers can increase and maintain engagement by "helping students connect their personal goals and interests to course goals, ... and by helping students maintain their confidence in achieving the course goals" (p. 20). He also stated that there are three types of motivational goals for instruction: 1) active engagement (motivating the learner to start the learning activity); 2) persistence (motivating the learner to continue to work towards the instructional goal in a focused way, despite distractions); and 3) mental effort. In attempting to help learners invest mental effort, Clark cautions that "instructional strategies and complex screen displays risk overloading working memory and causing 'automated' cognitive defaults where mental effort is both reduced and directed to non-learning goals" (p. 23).

Nash (2003, p. 5) observed that there are always multiple ways to achieve an instructional objective. Even the most interesting and well-designed presentation format can become boring if it is overused. It is more likely that the learners' attention will be maintained if a variety of methods are used for presentations and demonstrations.

Some of these methods include audio and video lectures, audio and video testimonials by experts, animations, videos of real-life examples, or even still graphics combined with text (as well as the methods and activities discussed under Criterion 2.a). Whatever combination of methods is used, developers should ensure that each method is carefully designed to use its strengths and avoid its weaknesses. Several other techniques have been recommended to enhance learner motivation and engagement with instructional content (see Allessi & Trollip, 1991; deWinstanley & Bjork, 2002).

Attention

The content should be designed to gain and maintain attention throughout each lesson. Techniques to provoke attention can be divided into two groups:

- Those that are involved with the appearance of the content (e.g., the use of color, brightness, graphics, and animation). Care should be taken to ensure that the combination of these techniques result in aesthetically pleasing pages (see Chapter 9, Criterion 6.c).
- Those involved with the presentation and organization of the content (e.g., the use of sound, music, humor, novelty, or storytelling).

Gaining Attention. Several methods have been suggested to gain the attention of learners, such as using the novelty and complexity of the stimulus. *Novelty* of a stimulus gains attention because it arouses the curiosity of the learner to direct him or her to the stimulus. Travers suggests three ways to make a situation novel: 1) using a stimulus that has not been presented recently; 2) presenting the stimulus in a new or unfamiliar context or setting; and 3) presenting a stimulus that has never been used before.

Travers (1972) cited research that suggests individuals are more likely to attend visually to an object that is more *complex* than to one which is less complex. For example, babies will fixate on a more complex diagram hanging over their heads than a simple one. People also tend to visually attend more to a person's eyes and mouth rather than any other portions of the face. This may be because there is more information in a smaller space.

Care must be taken when using attention-getting techniques. For example, humor that illustrates a point or helps place it in the context of a real-world situation is useful. Humor that is not used appropriately can actually become a distraction. Thus, it is important to creatively mix the attention-gaining techniques, but only to support well organized content that helps the learner integrate concepts that are built upon one another (see Chapter 3). To accomplish this, the techniques and interactive activities should always be situated in meaningful, job-relevant contexts (see Criterion 1.f).

Maintaining Attention. It is not sufficient to only gain attention, the learner's attention must be directed to the information to be learned and it must be maintained until the information is learned. Patricia deWinstanley and Robert Bjork (2002) pointed out that we have known for decades that "divided attention results in poorer memory than full attention does" (p. 20). They further observed that recent research indicates that divided attention is most detrimental during the encoding of information (Iidaka, Anderson, Kapur, Cabeza, & Craik, 2000; Naveh-Benjamin, Craik, Gravrilescu, & Anderson, 2000).

The term *vigilance* has come to be used as s synonym for maintaining attention. Most vigilance research has followed similar procedures. Subjects are asked to monitor something like a radar screen until a designated signal appears. The subject's task is to report when the signal is noticed. N. H. Mackworth, a British psychologist, conducted one of the earliest vigilance studies during World War II. Mackworth's results demonstrated that during a two-hour period, "the subject's ability to detect a specified signal markedly decreased each half hour" (Magill, 1980, p. 103).

Other vigilance studies have focused on the factors that affect a person's ability to maintain attention. For example, Wilkinson (1963) examined the effects of sleep deprivation on subjects' ability to tap a series of specified points when corresponding lights appeared in a certain order. The results indicated that most errors were committed by subjects who were sleep deprived and who performed the task in a quiet situation. The least errors were committed by subjects with normal sleep who performed in a quiet situation. With sleep-deprived subjects, a noisy environment seemed to help performance, whereas the performance of subjects with normal sleep was hindered by noise.

Broadbent (1958, Chapter 6) reviewed what he termed "theories of vigilance decrement." One theory postulates that people lose attention because the surroundings are monotonous. Another suggests that if a signal is very infrequent, an individual's arousal level will deteriorate during the time of the activity. A third theory suggests that the incoming information is "filtered" in some way so that only part of the information reaches the perceptual system. Each of these theories may contribute to the explanation of vigilance problems.

These theories and vigilance research data suggest several ways instructors and instructional developers can aid the maintenance of attention. First, instruction can sensitize learners to important cues that help the learner prepare to detect a signal. For example, a baseball coach can instruct an outfielder to make each pitch a signal event to begin preparation that directs the player's attention to a hit ball. Words of encouragement or instructions directed toward the learner can also help prevent his or her attention from wandering. Thirdly, Mackworth found that providing immediate knowledge of results after each of the signals to be detected maintained subjects' proficiency for longer periods of time. Finally, the instructional environment should never be permitted to become boring or monotonous. Practice drills should be kept short enough that they remain effective.

Challenge. A learner is more likely to remain engaged with content if it is designed to provide and maintain increasing levels of challenge. Csikszentmihalyi (1990) examined how persons perform optimally in a variety of situations, from sports to academics. He used the term *flow* to describe "the state in which people are so involved in an activity that nothing else seems to matter; the experience itself is so enjoyable that people will do it even at great cost, for the sheer sake of doing it" (p.4). The flow experience occurs when we find the balance between challenge and boredom. As one develops greater knowledge or skills, learning activities must offer more challenge to keep the learner from becoming bored. However, if the learning activity is too challenging, the learner may become anxious and withdraw his or her attention. Thus, facts, concepts, and activities should increase in complexity and difficulty as the learner progresses through the course, but at a reasonable rate. Developers

173

can determine a reasonable rate of increasing challenge by conducting formative evaluations of the content with a small number of learners.

Competition can be used as a technique to help keep the learner engaged as he or she progresses toward greater levels of difficulty. There are at least four types of competition that can be used in an instructional product: competition with other learners, with the computer, with the clock, or with him- or herself. It is important that the learner understands the goals of the competition and that these goals are stated in an unambiguous manner (e.g., the number of questions that must be answered correctly in order to advance to the next level or section).

A difficult task for the evaluators using this method is to determine whether the content "challenges" the learner. How can someone looking at a course determine if it is challenging? There is no definitive answer to this question. However, the evaluator can assume a higher level of challenge if the structure of the course includes some of the following characteristics:

- Learning objectives are based on critical and difficult job tasks (Some evaluators [e.g., program managers] may not have access to this information, but course developers should keep this in mind throughout design and development.)
- Content progresses from easy to difficult information
- Content progresses from simple to complex activities

As mentioned previously, another way to challenge the learner is through activities that encourage him or her to generate information. This activity, sometimes called the *generation effect*, has been shown to be a powerful method of learning (Slamecka & Graf, 1978; deWinstanley & Bjork, 2002).

Confidence. Another technique to help keep the learner engaged is to maintain his or her confidence that he or she is meeting the instructional objectives of the course. That means the objectives must be clearly stated (Criterion 1.b) and the instructional content designed to support them (Criterion 1.c). In addition, the learner should be given opportunities to be successful as he or she engages in learning activities and given encouragement (reinforcement) when performing as expected (Criterion 4.c, Chapter 7). Engagement can be enhanced by using *adjunct reinforcement*, such as following a less engaging activity (e.g., a drill) with an enjoyable activity (e.g., a game).

Stuart, Brown, and Draper (2004) allowed learners to use an electronic voting machine (handset) to answer questions and obtain feedback in class. These researchers hypothesized that the learners would ask more questions and be more open to feedback because the system allowed them to retain their anonymity. They found that the learners liked using the handsets and felt more confident in their learning. The effectiveness of this approach has not yet been compared to traditional classroom lectures or other instructional approaches. However, in computer- and web-delivered courses, without an instructor's presence, the implication is that non-graded assessments where learners can take risks and receive feedback might build their confidence and increase their level of engagement.

Lack of confidence in their ability to interact with the internet has been shown to be associated with opposition to web-based instruction (Thompson & Lynch, 2003). These researchers surveyed 257 college students and found that those with weak Internet self-efficacy beliefs were also inclined to resist web-based instruction ($r = -.29$). The design of the user interface is one way to help the learner develop and maintain self-confidence. Discussions on how to design learner-friendly interfaces are found in the chapters in Section III.

Maintaining satisfaction. If a learner is satisfied that he or she is attaining the objectives of the course, it is more likely that he or she will remain engaged. A learner's satisfaction can be maintained by giving supportive feedback (see Chapter 7) that encourages the learner and keeps the learner informed of how well he or she is progressing through the course. The feedback is likely to be more effective if it shows learners how what they are learning can be useful to them.

Curiosity and fantasy. A learner's inherent curiosity can be used as a method to maintain engagement. Sensory curiosity can be aroused by the use of novel, unexpected sounds and visual stimuli. Cognitive curiosity can be aroused by incorporating elements of surprise or by giving only partial information and then stimulating the learner's desire to know more. Learners' natural tendency to fantasize can also be used to keep them engaged. For example, engagement can be improved by having the learners participate in an imaginary role-playing situation that helps them use the information they are trying to learn.

Curiosity that leads to exploratory behavior is not always beneficial for learning specific tasks. Martens, Gulikers, and Bastianes

(2004) compared learners with high intrinsic motivation to those with lower levels of intrinsic motivation. They found that the highly motivated learners engaged in more explorative study behavior. However, the learning outcomes of these learners were not better than the learners who did not engage in as much explorative study. These results indicate that explorative behaviors need to be directed to ensure that they focus on important instructional information.

Variety. Learners will be less likely to become bored if the content includes a variety of presentation methods (e.g., text, graphics, color, sound, videos, or expert testimonials). Variety can also be introduced by using several different voices (male and female) for narrations. This also makes it easier to update a course because the original narrator does not have to be located to change or add narrations.

A variety of response options (e.g., mouse, keyboard, touch-screens, joysticks, etc.) can also encourage engagement. However, as Bangert-Drowns and Kozma (1989) cautioned, there should not be too many inputs required, nor should required inputs change "just for the sake of it." Furthermore, the learner should always understand which type of input is required.

Session length. Finally, learners should not be expected to concentrate for inordinate periods of time. Lessons and activities should be short enough that they can be completed before learners become bored. Optimal session length will depend on task type and complexity. Formative evaluations can help determine the maximum length of each instructional segment.

2.d. Instructional Media Directly Support Learning Activities

Instructional media can be very attractive and can provide instructional benefits. However, they can also distract from the instruction if they are not used to directly support learning activities.

Using the Scale

This scale is used to evaluate the course in terms of how many instructional media found in the course directly support learning activities. The scale and anchor statements should serve as guides during early formative evaluations. At these ISD stages there is no need to "formally" assign a score. However, during later formative evaluations and summative evaluations, greater care should be taken to assign a score. This score should then be used to identify instances when media do not support learning activities. The non-supportive uses of media should then be eliminated or corrected. Use the anchor statements below the scale to help assign a rating on this criterion. Additional information to help the evaluator understand this criterion is provided in the discussion below.

Terms, Concepts, Techniques, and Supporting Literature

Every effort should be used to maintain the learners' engagement with the instructional content. Media (graphics, videos, animations, etc.) can be powerful tools to engage learners. However, as Ruth Clark, referring to the work of Richard Clark, stated "more than 50 years of research indicate that what causes learning is *not* the technological delivery device but the instructional methods that facilitate human cognitive learning processes" (Clark, R. C., 2001, p.29).

Media should only be used to "facilitate and enhance learning" (Texas Education Agency; 2003, F.1) by directly supporting the content and instructional objectives. Malcolm (2000) maintains that many courses include too much "glitz," which he defines as "gratuitous graphics and audio that do not support learning, much less doing" (p. 2). Media should never be included gratuitously because they can become distractions. When an instructional medium enhances the instruction and engagement it should be used. If it does not add instructional value, it should be omitted. Some of the legitimate uses of media include:

- Simplifying content
- Reinforcing content
- Helping the learner to make connections among pieces of information
- Illustrating learning goals

Although some studies evaluate the effectiveness of whole multimedia applications (e.g., Hansen, Resnick, & Galea, 2003), they seldom systematically evaluate the specific multimedia characteristics that lead to effectiveness. The work of Mayer and his associates is a notable exception (Mayer, 2003; Mayer & Anderson, 1991). A detailed discussion of media principles is provided in Chapter 9 (Criterion 6.e).

Chapter 6:
Performance Assessment

Learners need to interact with instructional content in order to incorporate new information into their existing mental structures (knowledge) and to develop proficiency on the actions that support the tasks being trained (skills). It is essential that learners be assessed to determine if they are learning what is intended and at the required level of proficiency. However, the American Association for Higher Education (AAHE, 2004) warned that assessments must be linked to specific goals (e.g., instructional objectives; see Criteria 1.a and 1.b) or they risk becoming an "exercise in measuring what's easy, rather than a process of improving what we really care about" (p.1). Furthermore, they should not be an end in themselves, but rather a "vehicle for educational improvement" (p. 1). Assessments can be formal (e.g., results of quizzes) or informal (participation in a non-graded activity). The criteria discussed in this chapter concern the design of these assessments. The next chapter provides discussions on the criteria used to evaluate how to provide feedback to the learner on the results of the assessments.

3.a. Assessments are Relevant

It is generally agreed that the performance of learners needs to be assessed regularly during instruction to ensure that they are on track and learning the required material. These assessments are only useful if they meet these goals. Any assessment that does not measure learner performance on knowledge and skills that support the objectives of the course should not be included.

Using the Scale

This scale is used to evaluate how many of the assessments included in the course are relevant to the needs of the learners and the instructional objectives of the course. Like all of the scales, it should be used as a guide during early formative evaluations and as a diagnostic tool during later formative and summative evaluations. Use the anchor statements and list of characteristics of relevant assessments found below the scale to help assign a rating on this criterion. If you assign a rating of one (1) on this criterion, you *must* also assign a rating of one (1) on Criteria 3.b and 3.c. Additional information on this criterion is provided in the discussion below.

Terms, Concepts, Techniques, and Supporting Literature

To be considered relevant, assessments should be connected to issues and questions that the learner really cares about (AAHE, 2004). This means that each and every assessment should, at a minimum, be linked to the instructional objectives of the course and should assess what the objective says it will assess. In addition, adult learners care about being able to do their job more effectively and advancing in their careers. Thus, assessments should measure the skills and knowledge that are required on the learner's job. Furthermore, they should measure not just what the learners know, but what they can do with what they know (AAHE, 2004). This can be accomplished by designing the assessments to measure more than just factual recall. A well-designed assessment will require the learner to show understanding of the material by solving problems, relating pieces of information together, synthesizing common issues or identifying critical differences across different examples, or demonstrating skills and creativity in a realistic simulation. These types of assessments should then be used as the basis for feedback that is also relevant (see Chapter 7, Criterion 4.b).

Assessments not only help determine if the information has been learned. They can also have a beneficial role in the learning process. Carrier and Pashler (1992) conducted four experiments to determine the learning benefits of retrieving an item from memory. They found that learners who attempted to retrieve target items from memory, outperformed learners who merely studied the items. They conclude that these results provide support for the hypothesis "that retrieving an item from memory has beneficial effects for later retention above and beyond the effects due to merely studying the item" (p. 639). Thus, relevant assessments should be considered another learning activity.

Dempster (1996) cited numerous studies that support the general learning benefits of taking tests. He also cites several studies that demonstrate the "test-spacing effect." This "refers to the fact that spaced tests are more effective than massed tests" (p. 323). This effect is probably similar to the distributed-practice effect discussed in Chapter 5 under Criterion 2.b (e.g., Duncan, 1951). The type of assessment can influence learners in terms of how much they study, the study approach they take, and what content they learn. Scouller (1998) found that learners prepare differently for multiple-choice exams and essay assignments. Learners were more likely to perceive multiple-choice exams as assessing factual knowledge and essays as requiring deeper understanding. Thus, they were more likely to use surface learning approaches (recall and reproduction) when preparing for multiple-choice exams. Conversely, they were more likely to use deep learning strategies (development of meaning and understanding) when preparing for essay assignments. These results indicate that multiple-choice assessments may be more useful when attempting to capture the learner's ability to recognize correct material, but essays may be more useful for assessing the learner's deeper level of understanding. This is not to say that a well constructed multiple-choice can never capture a learner's deeper level of understanding. However, these types of multiple-choice questions are very difficult to compose.

3.b. Assessments are Logical

The positive effects of assessments, discussed above, are not likely to be achieved if they are not logically designed. The learner must understand the purpose of the assessments and how they support the instructional purposes of the course or course segment.

Using the Scale

This scale is used to evaluate how many of the assessments used in the course are logical. It should be used as a guide in early ISD stages to help design logical assessments. In later ISD stages, the scores should be assigned and used to diagnose and correct illogical assessments. Use the anchor statements below the scale and the list of features of logical assessments to help assign a rating on this criterion. Remember, if you assigned a score of one (1) on the previous Criterion (3.a.), you must also assign a score of one (1) on this criterion. Additional information on this criterion is provided in the discussion below.

181

Terms, Concepts, Techniques, and Supporting Literature

How do we determine that an assessment is "logical?" This does not refer to the "science" of logic, which deals with the canons and criteria of inference and demonstrations of the principles of reason. In the context of instructional quality, logical refers to "using reason in an orderly cogent fashion" (Webster's, 1977). An assessment is logical if it is cogently designed to support the instructional objectives of a lesson or course. Below are some issues that should be considered to determine if assessments are cogently designed.

Assessments as Process. Assessments should be part of an ongoing process, not "episodic" (AAHE, 2004, p. 1). This means that the assessments should be constructed as a linked series of activities over time that provides a way of monitoring learner progress towards meeting the instructional objectives of the course. Assessments that are designed in this manner provide information that is cumulative and that is focused on the explicitly stated purpose of the lesson and course. This information can be used not only to improve learner performance, but also to improve the assessments themselves.

The authors have met course developers who advocate the use of "discovery assessments." These are "free play" exercises where the learner explores or discovers important information and this "discovery" is the assessment. There is little or no data on the effectiveness of this approach. However, if used, one should be cautious to avoid frustrating the learner with endless loops where he or she must search for the correct response.

Managing Learner Expectations. Learners should be prompted to help them understand what types of responses are expected and what is considered successful performance (e.g., the standards against which their performance will be judged). The prompts should reflect the user's language rather than computer codes or numbers. Responses should require the least amount of typing and should be "forgiving" enough to cope with errors of format, such as capitalization (Reeves, 1994 as summarized in Botha, 2004).

Learner expectations can be managed by helping them set realistic learning goals. Magill (1980) provided several guidelines for setting goals that are relevant to this Method.

1. *Set objective goals.* Goals should be stated in terms of a number or some other objective form rather than "do your best."

2. *Set goals that are meaningful.* The goal should have meaning to the person. For example, asking a learner to hit 6 out of 10 targets is not as meaningful as stating that 6 out of 10 is an above average score.
3. *Set goals that are obtainable.* Challenging, yet obtainable goals tend to increase motivation. However, an unobtainable goal may lead to failure and poorer performance (Nelson, 1978).
4. *Set goals on the basis of past experience.* Learners who have succeeded in the past will usually expect to succeed in the future. Courses should be designed to help learners develop a pattern of success (e.g., move from simple to complex activities).

3.c. Assessments are Varied

Learners can become bored if every assessment is the same throughout the course. To make the course more interesting, relevant, and engaging, a variety of assessment techniques should be used at different places in the course.

Using the Scale

This scale is used to evaluate how many different types of assessments are used in the course. During development, the scale should be used as a guide to remind developers to create a variety of assessments. During later formative evaluations and summative evaluations, scores should be assigned on the scale. These scores should then be used diagnostically to identify redundant assessment types and identify when other types of assessments should be developed. The anchor statements and list of example assessments can help you assign a score. Remember, if you assigned a score of one (1) on Criterion 3.a. (relevance of assessments), you must also assign a score of one (1) on this criterion. Additional information to help understand this criterion is provided below.

183

Terms, Concepts, Techniques, and Supporting Literature

The American Association for Higher Education recommends that assessments be multidimensional (e.g., employ a diverse array of methods). These methods should include measures of knowledge (e.g., quizzes) and also measures of performance (e.g., simulations, role-play) over time to "reveal change, growth, and increasing degrees of integration" (AAHE, 2004, p.1). Variety helps maintain the learner's interest, but more importantly, it provides a number of diverse perspectives on the learner's performance.

Chapter 7:
Performance Feedback

The concept of feedback originated in the branch of engineering known as control theory (Moray, 1981). A special case of feedback (also known as knowledge of results, KOR) has long been recognized as an important aspect of instruction. Performance feedback is the information provided to the learner concerning his or her performance on the assessments (or other interactive activities) in an instructional event (Annett, 1969; Holding, 1965). Performance feedback can be used as a reinforcing stimulus to shape and maintain behavior (Fry, 1963; Skinner, 1968) and to locate and correct errors (Anderson, Kulhavy, and Andre, 1972; Gagné and Briggs, 1979; Bardwell; 1981; Holding, 1987). It has even been shown that the removal of feedback increases a person's annoyance, boredom, and carelessness (Elwell and Grindley, 1938). Based on years of research on the value of KOR for a large variety of cognitive and motor tasks, Magill (1980) stated that it is considered "as the strongest and most important variable involved in learning" (p. 220). Thus, it is important that the learner's performance be assessed throughout the instructional process and that he or she receives feedback on the adequacy of his or her performance. The previous chapter included discussions on criteria to evaluate the design of assessments; this chapter includes discussions on criteria to evaluate the design of performance feedback.

4.a. Feedback is Timely

Using the Scale

This scale is used to evaluate the timeliness of the feedback provided to the learner. The scale should be used as a guide during early formative evaluations and as a more formal diagnostic tool during later ISD stages. Use the anchor statements as a guide to help assign a rating on this criterion. Remember, if you assign a score of one (1) on this criterion, you *must* also assign a score of one (1) on Criteria 4.b, 4.c, and 4.d. Additional information on this criterion is provided in the discussion below.

Terms, Concepts, Techniques, and Supporting Literature

As a general rule, feedback should be provided immediately or soon after an assessment. Learners should be informed, in an unambiguous manner, of the quality of their performance. Then, they should immediately be either reinforced for correct performance or provided remediation for incorrect performance. Learners should not be allowed to proceed to new information that requires understanding of previous information.

In a classic study, Bilodeau, Bilodeau, and Schumsky (1959) demonstrated that learners practicing a motor task without feedback performed poorly. However, the learners who received feedback after each trial improved their performance consistently over twenty trials. When feedback was withdrawn after either two or six trials, the learners' performance deteriorated after that point.

Feedback that is provided too soon may interfere with performance of the task itself. For example, for a simple motor task, Weinberg, Guy, and Tuppler (1964) found that the optimal interval for feedback was 5 seconds. Feedback given 1 second after task completion interfered with task performance. Feedback provided after 10 and 20 seconds did not result in either better or poorer performance, although the authors speculate that with longer intervals, some forgetting may occur. Specific timing decisions for feedback should be based on formative testing to ensure optimal feedback intervals.

One should also be cautious about providing continuous concurrent feedback. Concurrent feedback is "supplementary information presented to the learner during the actual action" (Schmidt & Wulf, 1997, p. 509). Concurrent feedback (or variants) is often used in simulator training (e.g., showing pilots their location with respect to a glide path during landings). Performance problems may occur when the feedback is withdrawn during actual task performance because they can become dependant on the feedback as a performance aid (sometimes called a "crutch" effect). "In other words, continuous concurrent feedback appears to enhance performance during practice when the feedback is operating, but it does not contribute to learning and may even degrade learning, as measured on retention and transfer tests" (Schmidt & Wolf, 1997, p. 510). The authors point out that there are a few exceptions to this generalization. Most notably, very complex tasks may benefit from some form of concurrent feedback. However, for most tasks, it is probably better to provide feedback shortly after task completion or allow additional practice without the feedback before transfer to real-world performance.

4.b. Feedback is Meaningful

Using the Scale

This scale is used to evaluate how much of the feedback in the course is meaningful to the learner. During development, the scale should serve as a guide to remind developers to create meaningful feedback. In later ISD stages, the scores on the scale can be used to diagnose problems with feedback. Once identified, these problems can be corrected so that the courseware provides only meaningful feedback. Use the anchor statements below the scale and the examples of meaningful feedback to help assign a rating on this criterion. Remember, if you assigned a score of one (1) on Criterion 4.a, you *must* also assign a one (1) on this criterion. Additional information to help understand this criterion is provided below.

Terms, Concepts, Techniques, and Supporting Literature

Although feedback is widely regarded as essential to quality instruction, it is not always effective. Kluger and DiNisi (1998) reviewed a large amount of research on feedback conducted in both natural settings and laboratories. They reported that one third of the studies showed that feedback had a negative effect on performance. Another third of the studies showed no effect. "In only one third of the studies did feedback increase performance" (Clark, R., 2003, p. 18). How can this be? Clark believes that "learning problems appear to be caused by feedback that is not focused on clear performance goals and current performance results" (p. 18).

Practice tests can be useful to highlight learning goals and to help the learner focus his or her attention. Sly (1999) found that the use of practice tests improved the performance of learners on a computer-managed learning package. The practice tests may have functioned as formative assessments, providing feedback to help the learners concentrate on the important instructional information.

Although "it is doubtful that any feedback strategy will work equally well for all learners" (Clark, R., 2003, p.19), feedback is more likely to improve learning and performance if it:

- Is based on concrete learning goals (instructional objectives) that are clearly understood by the learners
- Describes the gap between the learner's learning goal and the learner's current performance and suggests how to close the gap
- Focuses the learner's attention on the learning goal and not on failure to achieve the goal

Furthermore, feedback should explain or show how what the learners have learned can be useful to them. This is especially true for adult learners who need to transfer their learned knowledge and skills to the work place (see Criteria 1.f. and 3.a).

Bonk (1999) maintained that meaningful feedback should include a combination of as many of the following as possible. It should:

- provide additional information
- correct errors
- ask for clarification
- debate issues and explain disagreements
- tie concepts to one another
- offer insight based on expert experience

In addition, feedback should be objective; not based on the preferences of a particular instructor or expert.

4.c. Positive Reinforcement is Provided for Correct Responses

Positive reinforcement increases the behaviors that it follows. It also serves other important instructional functions, as discussed below.

Using the Scale

This scale is used to evaluate how often positive reinforcement is provided as part of the feedback for correct responses. Like all of the scales, this one should be used as a guide during early ISD stages and as a diagnostic tool during later stages of ISD. Use the anchor statements and the definition of positive reinforcement to help assign a rating on this criterion. Remember, if you assigned a score of one (1) on Criterion 4.a. (timeliness of feedback), you *must* also assign a score of one (1) on this criterion and the following criterion (4.d.). Additional information on this criterion is provided in the discussion below.

Terms, Concepts, Techniques, and Supporting Literature

When the learner has performed correctly (e.g., provided the correct answer or demonstrated a skill correctly) the feedback should acknowledge and reinforce this correct performance in a positive, encouraging way. There is sometimes confusion about the terms reinforcement, reward, and punishment. Reinforcement always strengthens behaviors. However a reinforcer can be either positive or negative. A *positive reinforcer* is any event (i.e., stimulus) "which serves to strengthen responses preceding its occurrence" (Baron, Byrne, & Kantowitz, 1978, p. 120). Positive reinforcers increase the probability that an individual will respond again in the way he or she responded prior to experiencing the reinforcer. This is what most people think of as a reward.

A *negative reinforcer* is any event "which strengthens responses leading to its termination or removal" (Baron, Byrne, & Kantowitz, 1978, p. 120). In negative reinforcement, the organism strengthens behaviors that allow it to avoid or terminate uncomfortable or annoying stimuli. When a negative reinforcer is removed, the individual is more likely to behave the way he or she did prior to the removal of the aversive stimulus. On the other hand, *punishment* always reduces behaviors. A punisher is some type of unpleasant stimulus that follows a behavior. Its unpleasantness reduces the likelihood that the organism will behave in the same manner.

Figure 5 illustrates the differences between positive reinforcement, negative reinforcement and punishment, as determined through experiments with rats. The top row of the figure illustrates positive reinforcement. When a rat presses the lever, it is presented with food. This increases the rat's tendency to press the lever. On the other hand, the second row of the figure illustrates negative reinforcement. In this case, the rat experiences a shock until it presses the lever. This behavior turns the shock off and results in an increased tendency for the rat to press the lever. Both types of reinforcement increase the tendency to emit a behavior.

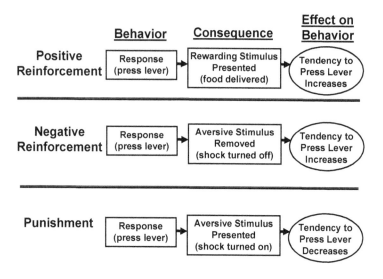

Figure 5:
Positive and Negative Reinforcement and Punishment

Punishment, as illustrated in the bottom row of Figure 5 tends to decrease behavior. In this example, the rat experiences a shock each time it presses the lever. This results in a decrease in the tendency for the rat to press the lever.

Years of research with animals and humans support these general, behavioral principles. In summary, there are two ways to increase the likelihood of a behavior: (1) provide a reward (positive reinforcement) or (2) remove an aversive stimulus (negative reinforcement). In contrast, there are also two ways to decrease the likelihood of a behavior: (1) provide an aversive stimulus (punishment) or (2) take away the rewarding stimulus that follows (is contingent on) a response. The focus on this criterion is on positive reinforcement, geared toward increasing the likelihood of a correct response from the learner. Punishment is never recommended.

Chi, Siler, Jeong, Yamauchi, and Housmann (2001) reviewed several studies on the use of feedback. They concluded that feedback can "guide" learners in the sense of encouraging them to either stay on the same track of reasoning or problem solving (confirmatory

190

feedback) or to change direction or goal (remedial feedback; see 4.d below). It should be noted that positive reinforcement should always be more than just stating that the learner has given a "correct" answer. As discussed under Criterion 4.b, feedback should be meaningful. Reinforcement can be designed to be another learning opportunity by helping the learner to understand the relevance of his or her correct performance and how this performance can be used as the foundation for building associations with new instructional information.

4.d. Remediation is Provided for Incorrect Responses

Learners do not always perform as required by the program of instruction. When performance is incorrect, the course should not just tell them they are "wrong." Rather it should be designed to provide corrective information that will help learners understand their errors and move them back onto the correct learning path.

Using the Scale

This scale is used to evaluate how often remediation is provided to the learner when he or she has given an incorrect response. The scale should be used as a guide during early formative evaluations and as a diagnostic tool during later formative and summative evaluation. Use the anchor statements below the scale and the list of examples of remediation to help you assign a rating on this criterion. Remember, if you assigned a score of one (1) on Criterion 4.a, you *must* also assign a score of one (1) on this criterion. Additional information to help you to understand this criterion is provided in the discussion below.

Terms, Concepts, Techniques, and Supporting Literature

When a learner has not performed as desired (e.g., provided an incorrect answer or did not demonstrate correct skill performance), Bangert-Drowns and Kozma (1989) recommended that the feedback should:

- Provide the correct answer or demonstrate correct skill performance

191

- Explain why the response was incorrect
- Encourage the learner to obtain more instruction on correct behavior
- Lead the learner to this remedial instruction

These characteristics of feedback make it more meaningful to the learner (see Criterion 4.b for an additional discussion on meaningful feedback).

In all cases the feedback should be provided in a non-threatening, encouraging manner. Learners can be demotivated by feedback that is too negative, but their motivation can be increased if the feedback provides the tools to help them succeed and makes them feel confident that they can achieve their goals.

Chi (1996) maintained that corrective feedback is "critical in problem solving in that it effectively reduces searches down the wrong paths of a search space" (p. 535). The course should be designed not only to provide detailed feedback on incorrect responses, but also to either take the learner back through the discussion or to state the instructional information in a different way until the learner has mastered the content. This type of remediation can help learners avoid unproductive "dead ends" and incorrect learning paths.

Section III:
Detailed Discussions of
User Interface Evaluation Criteria

The following discussions provide information to help the evaluator understand and more confidently assign ratings to each of the user interface evaluation criteria. The discussions begin with directions for using the scales. This is followed by definitions of terms and discussions of concepts and techniques to maximize the quality of instructional products as measured by each criterion. The discussions also provide summaries of some of the literature that support each criterion.

Learner-Centric Evaluations. In conducting the evaluation, the evaluator should try to think in terms of how the learner will perceive the instructional product. Thus the evaluation should be "learner-centric." For example, if the evaluator is trying to determine if all necessary navigation and operation controls are included (Chapter 8, Criterion 5.d), he or she should ask whether *the learner* can access and use the controls for all required purposes, *not* whether a computer programmer can use them.

No matter how well instruction is designed, it still must be delivered to learners in some manner. When computers are the chosen delivery method, it is the user interface that shapes the quality of the instructional delivery. Instruction has been delivered using computers for decades. During this time, many insights have been developed about the design of user interfaces. Table 12 summarizes ten interface design heuristics that are believed to enhance the usability of human-computer interfaces (Nielson, 1994). Most of these can be adapted or modified to support computer-delivered instruction. Three other classics in the field are: Nielson (1993), Norman (1988), and Shneiderman (1998). Courseware developers and managers should carefully consult the

Table 12:
Computer Interface Usability Heuristics

Ensures visibility of system status	The software keeps the user informed about what is going on through appropriate and timely feedback (e.g., "clicking" sound to indicate an action has been completed).
Maximizes match between the system and the real world	The software speaks the users' language rather than jargon. Information appears in a natural and logical order.
Maximizes user control and freedom	Users are able to exit locations and undo mistakes. Note: learners should not be able to change the instructional sequence, especially for novice learners. More experienced learners or those taking refresher courses may be allowed more control.
Maximizes consistency and matches standards	Users do not have to wonder whether different words, situations or actions mean the same thing. Common operating system standards are followed.
Prevents errors	The design provides guidance, which reduces the risk of user errors.
Supports recognition rather than recall	Objects, actions and options are visible. The user does not have to rely on memory. Information is visible or easily accessed whenever appropriate.
Supports flexibility and efficiency of use	The software allows experienced users to use shortcuts and adjust settings to suit.
Uses aesthetic and minimalist design	The software provides an appealing overall design and does not display irrelevant or infrequently used information.
Helps users recognize, diagnose and recover from errors	Error messages are expressed in plain language, clearly indicate the problem and recommend a solution.
Provides help and documentation	The software provides appropriate online help and documentation, which is easily accessed and related to the users' needs.

guidance provided these and other experts in the area of human-computer interface design. Molich and Nielsen (1990) and Nielson (1993) recommended some additional usability principles. These principles include:

1. *Simple and natural dialogue.* Dialogues should not contain information that is irrelevant or rarely needed. Every extra unit of information in a dialogue competes with the relevant units of information and diminishes their relative visibility. All information should appear in a natural and logical order.

2. *Speak the users' language.* The dialogue should be expressed clearly in words, phrases, and concepts familiar to the user, rather than in system-oriented terms.

3. *Minimize the users' memory load.* The user should not have to remember information from one part of the dialogue to another. Instructions for use of the system should be visible or easily retrievable whenever appropriate.

4. *Feedback.* The system should always keep users informed about what is going on, through appropriate feedback within reasonable time.

5. *Clearly marked exits.* Users often choose system functions by mistake and will need a clearly marked "emergency exit" to leave the unwanted state without having to go through an extended dialogue.

6. *Shortcuts.* Accelerators—unseen by the novice user—may often speedup the interaction for the expert user such that the system can cater to both inexperienced and experienced users.

This section includes 3 chapters. Chapter 8 is a discussion of the criteria that evaluate the navigation and operation features of the courseware. Chapter 9 provides discussions of the criteria that address the appearance and modes of content presentation. Chapter 10 includes discussions of criteria used to evaluate the installation and registration for the course.

Chapter 8:
Navigation and Operation Criteria

Navigation refers to two aspects of how the learner relates to a course: 1) his or her perceived *ability to move* through the course in an intentional manner, and 2) the learner's *orientation*, or the degree to which the learner knows where he or she is in the course and how to get to another part of it. Navigation should be designed to support the delivery of instruction in the sequence and manner that is consistent with the purposes and instructional objectives of the course. Navigation should never be difficult for or distracting to the learner. Once the learner has reached the desired location, he or she may need to operate the controls necessary to access a content delivery medium (e.g., play a video or start an animation). The operation controls should be easy to use to avoid distracting the learner.

5. a. User Interface Makes Course Structure Explicit

The user interface is the "portal" that lets the learner into the course. Its design can support the instructional objectives of the course by reflecting and supporting the structure of the course.

Using the Scale

This scale is used to evaluate how well the design of the user interface reflects the structure of the course and helps the learner understand that structure. This scale and the other user interface evaluation scales are very important during early ISD stages. The design of the user interface can expend large amounts of resources and once the interface is created, it is very difficult to make major changes. Therefore, it is very important to use this and the other user interface scales as design guides during interface development. During later ISD stages, the scale should be used diagnostically to identify areas where the interface could be improved to make the course structure more explicit. Use the anchor statements below the scale and the list of examples to help assign a rating on this criterion. Be cautious when rating a course that allows complete learner movement, especially for introductory courses. Movement between

197

course segments should only be allowed when it is instructionally useful (e.g., to review material). Additional details are provided in the discussion below.

Terms, Concepts, Techniques, and Supporting Literature

The user interface is the mechanism, which allows the computer user to interact with the computer program. A Graphical User Interface (GUI) is a type of interface that enables the user to interact with representations of programs, files, and options by means of icons, menus, and dialog boxes on the screen. A computer user directly interacts with a GUI by selecting items on the screen using an input device (e.g., keyboard, mouse, touch screen, etc.). The type of interaction required must be considered when designing the GUI's appearance and functionality. For example, if a pointing device (e.g., mouse) is required, the layout and relative locations of items on the screen should accommodate this functionality so the user can recognize selectable items and easily select them. Selectable items need to be large enough to read and recognize and spaced enough to allow the user to select one without affecting another item on the screen. In computer-based instructional applications, the learner should be able to access segments of the course or information about the course without having to work with special commands.

An easy to use interface is often referred to as "transparent." Transparency "refers to the intuitiveness of the interface to its user" (Tessmer, 1995, p. 132). A transparent interface allows users to interact directly with the system, not via an intermediary. The interface is thus "transparent" so the user can focus on the task at hand rather than on the interface itself. "When an interactive system is well designed, it almost disappears, enabling the users to concentrate on their work or pleasure" (Shneiderman, 1987, p. 9).

Several techniques have been used to design transparent GUIs. One technique is to use perceptual grouping principles, as demonstrated by Gestalt psychologists (e.g., Weiten, 2004, pp. 143-146). Humans tend to perceive items as belonging together if they share characteristics in common (e.g., size, shape, color, theme, or proximity). Nielsen (1993, p. 117) recommends organizing interface items based on these Gestalt principles. Such organization (grouping) of items on the display affects the visual focus of the user and can help to perceptually establish the structure of the interface (Brinck, Gergle, & Wood, 2002, pp. 192-197). Brinck and others

(2002, pp. 194-197) also suggested that one can take advantage of Gestalt grouping principles by reversing them to create perceptual boundaries between the items that should be grouped together and others that belong to a different set. For example, by applying a different background color behind menu options, the menu will stand out from the rest of the content on the page.

All computer programs require a well-designed interface. However, instructional programs need to go beyond just a transparent interface. The design of the interface can actually support learning. For instructional programs, a good interface design reduces the cognitive load of the learner by removing frustrating distractions that may redirect the learner's attention from the instructional content. They can also be designed to help the learner understand the structure of the course and how its various segments support one another.

Various techniques have been used to organize instructional content and represent it on the user interface, such as task-oriented, topic-oriented, or chronologically-oriented. The organization scheme should remain consistent throughout the course (Rosenfeld & Morville, 1998; also see Criteria 5.e, 5.f, and 5.g). It is also important to keep the organization simple, without too much information crammed onto each screen (Brinck, et al., 2002, p. 180).

One way to help ensure that the interface design has good usability and communicates well to the user is to describe the interface in terms of a familiar metaphor or analogy (Eberts, 1994, pp. 143-145; Neilsen, 1993, pp. 126-129). For example, one familiar metaphor is the desktop interface. In this design, the computer desktop is based on artifacts found in a typical office, including: files, folders, and a recycling bin. Another useful metaphor in computer-delivered instruction is the VCR metaphor for controlling videos in the course. In this case, the controls resemble those of a standard VCR (e.g., play, pause, fast forward, rewind, etc.).

When choosing a metaphor or analogy, it is important to choose one that is clear and that will be familiar to most (if not all) users. The intention of the metaphor is to augment the usability of the system by better informing users about how the system works (Nielsen, 1993, pp. 128-129; Eberts, 1994, Chapter 10). "For an interface metaphor to be successful, it must be both usable and informative. It can only be useful if its imagery matches the learner's prior knowledge and experience with the metaphor as well as with the multimedia system's functionality" (Tessmer, 1995, p. 134).

Shneiderman (1998, pp. 204-205) explained that good use of a metaphor helps to prevent the user from over or under-extension of the system's capabilities relative to the user's mental models and expectations of what the system can do. Good metaphors improve the user's ability to learn and remember how to interact with the system, whereas a system with no metaphor (or a poorly designed one) requires the user to retain in memory the meaning of each icon or term used in the system.

Nielsen (1993, pp. 43-48) recommended that interfaces should be designed to support both novice and expert users. He explains that there are three dimensions that explain how users differ: 1) computer experience in general; 2) knowledge of the task domain or topic; and 3) experience using a specific interface. Due to the variability in interface designs, expertise in one interface may or may not be helpful when using a new interface. This is especially true for computer-delivered instruction. Even computer experts may not have any experience in a specific content domain and may require help to understand the structure of the course. This is one reason why every instructional application should include a tutorial and a help function that explain all controls and capabilities (see Criteria 5.b and 5.c below).

Content Maps. A technique that can help make the organization of the content apparent to the learner is to use a content map or a site map (Ross, 1998). This can be in the form of an outline, showing major segments, lessons, or topics and how they relate to one another. This is much like a table of contents in a book. However, as discussed in Criterion 1.a, developers must take care that learners (especially introductory learners) are guided through the course rather than are allowed to browse topics in any order (Jones and Okey, 1995). For learners who are taking refresher training or those that want to review a previously completed course, more freedom to select topics can be provided.

Managing Complex Content. Complex content may sometimes overload the cognitive processing capabilities of the learners. This is especially true when various presentation media and modalities are combined. Ross (1998) suggested several tools that can help learners to manage content:

1. *Glossary*: definitions of technical terms, links to original location in the course to provide context; perhaps a

"pronounce" button to demonstrate correct pronunciation of terms.

2. *Index*: list and brief overview of the major topics; "tracking" function to show what parts of the course have been completed (This is similar to the content or site maps discussed in sections 1.g. and 5.f.)

3. *Bookmarking*: to allow learners to return to the area of the course they last visited

4. *Searching*: to help learners find specific information quickly and efficiently

5. Detailed *resource lists*: categorized by subject area.

6. *Notebook*: An electronic resource with a print and edit feature to allow learners to summarize and paraphrase course material. A float, pop-up window could be used to allow learners to move through course pages, while still having access to the notebook.

7. *On-line help*: In addition to a built-in help function (see section 5.a), on-line help can allow learners to ask detailed questions about course operation or content. This could also include a course facilitator's e-mail address, but care must be taken to provide timely responses to questions.

5.b. Tutorial is Available to Explain Navigation and Operation Features

A tutorial is a "mini" course that provides instruction on how to use the navigation and operation features to optimize the learning experience.

Using the Scale

This scale is used to evaluate how many of the navigation and operation features are covered by a tutorial to help the learner to understand how to use the navigation and operation features. Use the scale as a guide during development and as a diagnostic tool during later ISD stages. The anchor statements and list of ways to design tutorials should be used to help assign a rating on this criterion. Additional information on this criterion can be found in the discussion below.

Terms, Concepts, Techniques, and Supporting Literature

Prior to beginning a course, learners should be provided with a tutorial that explains all of the navigational features. The tutorial should also explain how the learner should set up his or her computer to optimally view text, graphics, videos, and other presentation formats (see Criterion 7.c).

The tutorial should provide "hints" and suggestions for how to use the power of each navigational feature as support for the instruction. The tutorial should also provide guidance on the appropriate setup of the computer (e.g., level of screen resolution).

Some possible ways to design tutorials include:

- Walk-through with text and narration
- Animation of moving cursor with text narration
- Animated "guide" (e.g., avatar)
- Text and graphics

5.c. Help Function is Available to Explain Navigation and Operation Features

A help function is a mechanism that allows a learner to seek information on the use of a specific navigation or operation feature.

Using the Scale

This scale is used to evaluate the course on the presence and usefulness of a help function. Use the scale as a guide during early ISD stages and as a diagnostic tool during later ISD stages. Use the anchor statements and list of ways to access help as guides in assigning a rating on this criterion. Additional information on this criterion is provided in the discussion below.

Terms, Concepts, Techniques, and Supporting Literature

A help feature should always be available if a learner forgets how or when to use a given feature. Replaying short segments from the tutorial might provide this targeted help.

Ross (1998) suggested that an on-line help function can allow learners to ask detailed questions about course operation or content. This could also include a course facilitator's e-mail address. Care must be taken to provide timely responses to e-mail questions lest learners become frustrated and lose interest in the course. An alternative might be a "call-in" help desk. However, a help desk must be maintained and monitored as long as the course is in use.

5.d. Includes all Necessary Navigation and Operation Controls

The learner needs to be able to move through the course as efficiently as possible. Furthermore, when arriving at the desired location, he or she should be able to easily operate any controls needed to interact with the course (e.g., play a video, answer a question, interact with a simulation, etc.).

Using the Scale

This scale is used to rate the course in terms of the number of navigation and operation controls provided in the course, as well as the degree of control provided to the learner. Use the scale as a guide during the development of navigation and operation controls. During later ISD stages, assign a score on the scale and use the score to diagnose and correct problems. The anchor statements and list of navigation and operation controls found below the scale should be used as guides for assigning a score on this criterion. Consult the discussion below for additional information on this criterion.

Terms, Concepts, Techniques, and Supporting Literature

When it is appropriate for the learner to control navigation or the operation of a delivery medium (e.g., video) a mechanism to access these features should be provided. This access can be made available in various ways (e.g., buttons, highlighted text, voice commands, etc.), but whichever method one selects, it should remain consistent throughout the course. Table 13 is a list of possible navigation and operation controls with a short description of their function. In general, most of these controls should be included in any computer-delivered course.

Table 13:
Possible Navigational and Operation Controls
in Computer-Delivered Courses

Control Name	Description of Function
Start/Play	Used to begin the course or a section within the course. Can also be used to begin a video or audio segment or begin an interactive exercise.
Stop	Used to end a section or any activity within a section (e.g., a video).
Pause	Used to suspend (pause) an ongoing segment of the course. This might be narration, a video, or an interactive exercise.
Resume	Used to restart (resume) a paused activity. In some cases this is done by hitting the "start/play" button again.
Go Forward (by screen)	Used to move to the next screen of instruction.
Go Backward (by screen)	Used to move back to the previous screen of instruction.
Go Forward (by lesson)	Used to move forward to the next lesson.
Go Backward (by lesson)	Used to move back to the previous lesson.
Return to Beginning	Used to return to the beginning of the course.
Return to Main Menu	Used to go to the main menu of the course (table of contents or lesson outline).
Bookmark	Used to mark the learner's place in the course so he or she may return to that specific screen.
Print Screen	Used to print the current screen.
Print Selected Text	Used to print a selected segment of the text. Some courses also allow the learner to print the entire text and/or narration script.
Take Notes	Enables the learner to take notes or make comments about the current instruction.
Save Copy	Enables the learner to save and retrieve any notes or activities (e.g., computations) made during the course.
Volume control for audio	Used to adjust the volume for audio presentations.
VCR-type controls (for videos)	Used to control any videos used in the course. Should resemble controls on standard Video Cassette Recorders (VCRs). Should include: play, stop, pause, rewind, fast forward, etc.

As discussed under the topic of content presentation (Chapter 3, Criterion 1.a), learner control is a double-edged sword. Too much control can be detrimental to effective learning (Clark, R., 2003, p. 14; Niemiec, et al., 1996), but some level of control can be beneficial (Doherty, 1998). Providing the ability to control pacing and movement within a lesson (e.g., replaying a section or controlling a video presentation) is a positive design goal. However, in most cases, the structure and order of instructional content should not be left in the hands of the learner. In the context of this criterion, "necessary" controls are those that support the navigation through the course and allow control of content presentation. For example, "necessary" controls for a video presentation are those that allow the learner to access and control the video (e.g., start, stop, rewind, or pause). If there are no video presentations, these controls are not necessary.

5.e. Navigation and Operation Controls are Clearly and Consistently Labeled

Using the Scale

This scale is used to rate the course on how many of the navigation and operation controls are clearly and consistently labeled. The scale should be used as a guide during development and as a diagnostic tool during later ISD stages. Use the anchor statements below the scale to help assign your rating on this criterion. Additional information on this criterion is provided in the discussion below.

Terms, Concepts, Techniques, and Supporting Literature

Consistency is essential to establish commonality and unity across the various content pages of the course (Brinck, et al., 2002, pp. 110-112; Nielsen, 1993, pp. 132-134). Gestalt psychologists have demonstrated that humans perceive items to be grouped together if they are located close to one another and share common features (e.g., colors, shapes, font styles, etc.; Weiten, 2004, pp. 143-146). Following these principles, the grouping of navigation and operation controls can help the learner understand their functions and prepare for taking actions (Adam, Hommel, & Umiltà, 2003; Borchers, Deussen, Klingert, & Knörzer, 1996).

Fitts (1954) demonstrated that the rate of performance in a given task is approximately constant over a range of movement. However, the performance rate falls off outside the optimal range of movement. Thus, grouping controls not only helps the learner understand their function, such grouping can also help in the speed and accuracy of actions (Eberts, 1994; Shneiderman, 1998).

Whichever design is chosen for navigation controls, each should be clearly and consistently labeled. In no case should the appearance or label of a control be different in different course segments. Consistency is regarded as one of the most important usability issues in any computer interface (Molich and Nielsen, 1990). This is true for this criterion in terms of consistency of labeling. It is also true for the next two criteria, consistency of location (Criterion 5.f) and consistency of operation (Criterion 5.g).

Designers should consider using standard browser controls as much as possible. Standard browser controls are those that are used by almost all software that allows users to access the Internet. Most computer users are familiar with how these controls are labeled, so they should be able to more easily adapt to their use in instructional applications. Even these standard controls should be clearly labeled (e.g., easily seen). When additional controls are needed, they should also be clearly labeled and these labels should be consistent.

5.f. Navigation and Operation Controls are Located in a Consistent Place

Just as navigation and operation controls should have a consistent appearance, they should also be located in a consistent place on the computer screen.

Using the Scale

This scale is used to evaluate how consistently navigation and operation controls are located on the computer screens throughout the course. The scale should be used as a guide during development and as a diagnostic tool during later ISD stages. Use the anchor statements below the scale as guides in assigning a rating on this criterion. The discussion below provides additional information on this criterion.

Terms, Concepts, Techniques, and Supporting Literature

It is often useful to cluster navigational controls in a single "control panel," but this panel should always be found in the same place. The specific place is not as important as maintaining a consistent location. Operation controls should also be located in a consistent place. For example, if videos are used in the course, the controls should be located near the video display window (usually under the window).

The Gestalt grouping principles discussed under Criteria 5.a and 5.e.) also support this criterion (Weiten, 2004). The research conducted by Adam and his colleagues (2003) demonstrated the close association between perception and action. Once the learner has learned to deal with common controls in a certain location, a change in this location would require relearning and would likely be a distraction from the learning experience.

5.g. Navigation and Operation Controls Operate Consistently

Using the Scale

This scale is used to evaluate how consistently the controls function in different places in the course. It should be used as a guide during courseware development and as a diagnostic tool during implementation and evaluation. Use the anchor statements below the scale to assist in assigning a rating on this criterion. Additional information is provided in the discussion below.

Terms, Concepts, Techniques, and Supporting Literature

Consistency of function is also very important for navigation and operation controls. The learner should understand exactly what will happen any time he or she activates a navigational control and the resulting action should operate reliably. It is also important that the interface provide a visual or audio cue that the program has registered his or her choice and that the action is taking place or the learner is going someplace (Jones and Okey, 1995, citing Nicol, 1990).

Consistency in the actions of navigation and operation controls is just as important as consistency in the location of controls (Shneiderman, 1998 p. 74). As mentioned in the discussion on location consistency, functional consistency can also be achieved by using standard browser buttons as often as possible.

5.h. Course Show's Learner's Location

As the learner moves through a course, he or she can benefit from any cues that help integrate the many separate items of information that needs to be learned. Knowing his or her current location and how he or she arrived there (see Criterion 5.i below) can be powerful tools to assist the learner in this integration. This criterion and the next evaluate these two capabilities.

Using the Scale

This scale is used to evaluate how easily a learner can determine his or her location in the course. The scale should be used as a guide during development. During implementation and evaluation, it should be used as a diagnostic tool. Use the anchor statements and the list of example techniques found below the scale to help assign a rating on this criterion. Additional information is provided in the discussion below.

Terms, Concepts, Techniques, and Supporting Literature

Utting and Yankelovich (1989) reported that computer users frequently complain about being lost in an interactive program. A learner can waste valuable instructional time trying to determine his or her location in the course. This may even lead to a loss of the motivation to continue the instruction.

As discussed under content presentation (Chapter 3, Criterion 1.a), learners should be provided with a content map (site map) or other aid that helps them understand where they are in a course and how they will proceed. According to Ross (1998), a site map is a detailed hierarchical structure of the course with the following features:

- It allows learners to quickly obtain an overview of the course's structure.

- It should ideally be available from every page.
- It should show where the learner is currently located (e.g., by highlighting the current screen on the map).
- It should help the learner "track" his or her progress by showing completed topics.

5.i. Course Show's How Learner Arrived at Location

As mentioned above, knowing how he or she moved from topic to topic to arrive at a given location can help the learner to understand the interrelationship among various items of information.

Using the Scale

This scale is used to evaluate how easy it is for the learner to understand how he or she arrived at their current location in the course. Use the scale as a guide during courseware development and as a diagnostic tool during implementation and evaluation. Use the anchor statements and list of techniques found below the scale to help assign a rating on this criterion.

Terms, Concepts, Techniques, and Supporting Literature

As important as knowing where they are currently located in the course (Criterion 5.h), learners should also understand the instructional path that led them to their current location. This will help them integrate the new instructional information with their previously developed knowledge structures. This can also help learners get back to previous locations when they wish to review material.

5.j. Course Show's Estimated Time Required for Each Module

Using the Scale

This scale is used to evaluate how often time estimates for completing course modules are provided. During development the scale should serve as a guide. During formative evaluations, the scale should sensitize the development team to create and test time estimates for each courseware module. During implementation and evaluation, the scale should be used to diagnose problems with time estimates that should be corrected. Use the anchor statements and list of example techniques below the scale to assist in assigning a rating on this criterion.

Terms, Concepts, Techniques, and Supporting Literature

One of the strengths of computer-based or web-based instruction is the capability for learners to take the instruction at their job sites or on their own time. They may want to take the instruction during slack times, break times, or lunch. They need to know how long it will take to complete a module in order to schedule their instructional time. In most cases, it is important for learners to complete a module and the associated assessment and feedback before taking a break from the course. Therefore the course designer should provide estimated times for each module to facilitate scheduling. These time estimates should be derived from formative evaluations.

One method to show the learners the estimated time to complete a module is to provide a statement of this estimated time at the beginning of each module. Another method is to use a bar diagram or some other symbolic indicator of how much of the module has been completed.

Chapter 9:
Content Presentation

The user interface is the mechanism for presentation of the instructional content. How the various methods of presentation are used can either support or distract from the instruction. The following criteria are used to help ensure that the presentation supports the instruction.

6.a. There are No Sensory Conflicts

Using a variety of delivery modalities (e.g., video, graphics, audio) can make a course more engaging and more informative. However, if there are conflicts between different modalities, learning effectiveness can suffer. Sensory conflicts occur when different content is presented simultaneously in two or more modalities or when the same content is not properly synchronized across modalities.

Using the Scale

This scale is used to evaluate how often sensory conflicts are encountered when the course delivers the content using multiple modalities (e.g., audio and video). During early ISD stages (early formative evaluations) the scale should be used as a guide so sensory conflicts can be avoided. During later ISD stages, the scale should be used to identify sensory conflicts so these can be eliminated. Use the anchor statements and examples of sensory conflicts found below the scale to assist in assigning a rating on this criterion. Additional information is provided in the discussion below.

Terms, Concepts, Techniques, and Supporting Literature

Some cognitive psychologists (e.g., Baddeley, 1992; Paivio, 1990; Penny, 1989) theorized that humans' working memory includes separate processes for different sensory modalities (e.g., auditory, vision, etc.). According to these theorists, the separate processes have separate amounts of processing resources and can either reinforce or inhibit each other.

Course designers often try to use a variety of presentation media (audio, text, graphics, or video) to present instructional content. This is beneficial only if the media work with one another in a supportive fashion. If they do not, they can become distractions. A learner cannot simultaneously attend to multiple presentations of different information. Nor can the learner determine which medium to attend to or which information is most important. For example, if using audio to supplement textual presentation of content, the two media should present the same information. This does *not* mean word-for-word duplication. However, reinforcing important points in the narration by using textual bullets may improve learning.

Some research indicates that people learn better when narration is supplemented with pictures, videos, illustrations, or animations (Mayer, 2003). Other research has shown that combining audio explanations with visual instructions can have negative consequences due to this concurrent information causing cognitive overload (Kalyuga, 2000). This overload can be avoided if the concurrent instructional messages do not contain extraneous words, pictures, or sounds (Mayer, 2003).

In general, research has shown that conflicting auditory messages should not be provided simultaneously (Cherry, 1953; Gray & Wedderburn, 1960; Moray, 1959; Moray, Bates, & Barnett, 1965; Treisman, 1964). For example, Moreno and Mayer (2000a) examined the impact on performance of adding background sounds and music to a multimedia instructional message. While reviewing instructional material on the formation of lightning, learners in different groups received background music, environmental sounds, both, or neither. After completing the instruction, participants completed a retention task that asked them to explain the lightning process (e.g., "What could you do to decrease the intensity of lightning?"). Participants who experienced background music recalled less verbal material and performed worse on the transfer test than those who experienced no background music. Participants who received both music and sounds performed worse than all the other three groups. The results of a second experiment, teaching the operation of hydraulic braking systems, were similar to the first experiment. The authors conclude that auditory adjuncts can overload the learner's auditory working memory and are detrimental to learning.

It is difficult to attend to a single voice when multiple voices are present. Rudmann, McCarley, and Kramer (2003) examined the impact of presenting a video image of a target speaker to help participants identify words spoken by that speaker. In their study, participants in different groups listened to multiple speakers (a target speaker and 2, 3, or 4 distracting speakers). Their task was to focus on the target speaker and identify target words spoken by the target speaker while trying to ignore the distracting speakers. Participants in each group either received or did not receive a video-displayed image of the target speaker. Results indicated that the performance of the participants declined when the number of distracting speakers increased. Furthermore, the participants' "ability to track target words declined regardless of whether or not a display of the target speaker was provided. However, when the video display was not provided, performance declined at a faster rate" (Rudmann, et al., 2003, p. 332). These results demonstrate that for tasks requiring attention to multiple speakers (e.g., air traffic control), including supporting media (e.g., video images) may help task performance. However, for instructional applications, it is probably better to use only one speaker at a time.

6.b. All Media are Clear and Sharp

No matter which medium is used, learners cannot attend to instructional information if it is presented in a manner that does not allow them to perceive it.

Using the Scale

This scale is used to evaluate how many of the media used in the course are presented in a format that is easily perceived by the learner (e.g., they are clear and sharp). It should be used as a guide during development and as a diagnostic tool during implementation and evaluation. Use the anchor statements and list of examples of clear and sharp media found below the scale to help assign a rating on this criterion. Additional information is provided in the discussion below.

Terms, Concepts, Techniques, and Supporting Literature

If the learner cannot understand the narration, read the text, or see the important portions of a graphic or video, the instructional message will be garbled. Developers should always ensure that the instructional information is actually being conveyed by the chosen medium. They should also ensure that the media do not become distractions (e.g., annoying soundtracks, blinking lights, irrelevant animations; Nash, 2003). Regardless of the specific medium, it is a good general principle to try to avoid the need for the learner to scroll either horizontally or vertically.

The use of different types of media involves different issues. The following discusses some of the presentation issues for different media types.

Text. Text should be designed to enhance readability and comprehension (Bostock, 2004). Only readable (legible) fonts should be used (e.g., those that are large enough to avoid eye strain and are displayed clearly on the computer screen at the recommended level of resolution). The tutorial or setup module (5.b) should include guidance for setting up the proper screen resolution and the setup should be confirmed with an "optimization" test (Chapter 10, Criterion 7.c).

Morkes and Nielsen (1997; 1998) observed that persons reading web pages generally prefer writing that is:

- Concise (e.g., makes its points quickly).
- Easy to scan (e.g., uses inverted pyramid style like news articles "in which the news and conclusions are presented first, followed by details and background information" [p. 13 of 27] and uses headings, bold face, and other cues).
- Objective (rather than promotional).

They found that rewriting web pages combining these three changes resulted in 124% higher measured usability in their first study (1997) and 159% higher usability in their second study (1998).

Although text has been the primary instructional medium for centuries, displaying text on a computer screen can cause problems (e.g., eye strain). During the initial introduction of computers, it was generally found that reading efficiency (e.g., reading speed) was lower from a standard computer display than from paper (e.g., Mutter, Latrémouille, Treurniet, & Beam, 1982). Neilson (1997) reported that most people only read 50% of the text on a screen and at a rate about 25% slower compared to reading the same text on paper. He also maintains that readers tend to scan rather than read all the text on a screen. Therefore, Nielson (1997) and many others (e.g., Thibodeau, 1997; ANSI/ADA, 2002) recommended limiting the amount of text on a screen.

Computer displays, combined with various enhancements (e.g., double spacing, negative contrast, bold face, etc.) have been shown to reduce the performance differences between readers of paper- and computer-displayed text. Mutter and Maurutto (1991) examined the differences between reader performance when using an enhanced computer display and those using paper. They found no differences in reading speed and comprehension between the two groups. They concluded that computer display capabilities and presentation techniques were now mature enough to make computer-displayed text a viable option.

The reader often prefers using larger font sizes on the computer display. For example, Chen, Jackson, Parsons, Sindt, Summerville, Tharp, Ullrich, and Caffarella (1996) found no differences in reading comprehension between groups presented 10, 12, 14, or 16-point fonts. However, most of the participants preferred either the 14 or 16-point fonts (97.78% and 83.78% respectively). Pacheco, Day, Cribelli, Jordan, Murry, and Persichitte (1999) found similar results. They found that readers preferred larger fonts and double spacing in both scrolled and not scrolled displays.

Harpster, Freivalds, Shulman, and Leibowitz (1989) compared the search speeds for persons reading text on a computer or on paper. The participants viewed a large pattern of numbers and were required to locate four specified numbers in this pattern. They found performance differences between the computer and paper conditions when a low-resolution computer display was used, but no differences when the text was shown on a high-resolution display.

Garland and Noyes (2004) found no differences in the test performance of learners who read from paper or a computer screen. These results are difficult to interpret because the font size on the computer display is not provided. They did find differences in the way participants in the two groups retrieved knowledge. Over 7 sessions, the computer group took longer to shift from episodic memory ("remember") to semantic memory ("know") than the paper group. The authors speculate that the computer presentation may interfere with the learning process. However, this conclusion should be considered very tentative due to the lack of detail provided on experimental procedures.

Lee and Boling (1999) summarized screen design guidelines from 77 books and articles. Their guidelines on typography (pp. 10-21) include:

- Be consistent in the use of textual cues and signals to the learner. Consistency in these typographical signals can establish and convey clear visual messages to the learners that they are now reading a certain subject or section of the course content. These cues can include the use of titles and subtitles to improve comprehension by providing structure and to signal the flow of ideas.

- Use both upper and lower case letters (i.e., capitals only for indicating the first letter of a sentence or a proper name) for increased legibility. All upper case characters should only be used occasionally (e.g., for purposes of emphasis).

- Use high contrast between letters and background.

- Left-justify text, but do not right-justify it.

- Limit text to approximately 65 characters per line (cpl), or a maximum of 8-10 words per line. Dyson and Hasselgrove (2001) confirmed this general guideline. They found that reading comprehension was better when line length was 55cpl as compared to 100cpl. Readability can also be improved by presenting text in columns that are no wider than a person's comfortable eye span.

- Use highlighting techniques conservatively and carefully when trying to attract the learner's attention. Blinking, flashing, or the use of reverse video (e.g., white on black) can be used to attract attention. However, overuse of these techniques can interfere with legibility.

- Select a font with a simple, clean style and use only a few different font sizes on any one screen.

Thibodeau (1997) recommended the following techniques when formatting text for display on a computer screen:

- Use white (blank) space to separate blocks of textual information

- Convert sentences containing serial items to lists

- Use upper case only for titles and emphasis

- When using highlighted or bold text, limit this to 10% of total screen text

- Text should never "blink" except temporarily to attract attention

- Use no more than one attention-getting technique per screen

Nielson (1997) added the following recommendations for the use of headings to help the reader:

- Use 2 or even 3 levels of headings
- Use meaningful, not "cute" headings – these should be the same as in the table of contents
- Use highlighting or other methods to emphasize the headings and catch the learner's eye

Here are a few additional suggestions. Moreno and Mayer (2000b) demonstrated that instructional text written in first and second person resulted in better learning than when the text was written in a more impersonal tone. All technical words should be explained and included in an easily accessible glossary (Bostock, 2004). A balance between text and graphics can add to the aesthetic appeal of the course.

Audio. Ross (1998) suggested three ways audio can be used to support instruction. *Audio messages* can be used to emphasize important points or serve as reminders for learners (e.g., "Pay particular attention to sections 1-6."). *Audio lectures* can be used to present short explanations of important concepts. Audio can also be used to *pronounce glossary terms.* This can be very effective when learners are not fluent in English or are not familiar with technical terms. All audio presentations should be easily understood. Also, some research indicates that learning is improved when narrators speak in a conversational style (Mayer, 2003) and with a standard accent rather than a machine voice or foreign accent (Mayer, 2003).

The authors' experience strongly suggests that multiple voices should be used for narration. There are two main reasons for this recommendation:

1. Use of multiple voices provides variety and helps maintain the learner's attention
2. When revising a course, it is not likely that the original speaker will be available to change the narration. Therefore, a new voice will not distract the learner because it is one of many.

In terms of language style, the narrator should speak in "plain English." The use of technical terms should only be used when necessary to support the content, not to sound "important." Jargon should never be used. Furthermore, the narrator should never talk "at the learner," rather he/she should talk "to the learner."

One of the main goals of narration should be to cognitively engage the learner with the content (e.g., make them think about it). Therefore, the narration should include important questions about the content and attempt to draw the learner into a deeper understanding of the material.

Graphics. Bostock (2004) stated that images used in instructional products should always be unambiguous. That is, they should directly support the instructional objectives and be visually sharp enough that the learner can see all the necessary information in the graphic.

Levie and Lentz (1982) discussed four functions of graphics:

- *Attentional:* graphics can attract attention to important content and direct attention within the content.
- *Affective:* graphics can enhance enjoyment and stimulate emotions and attitudes.
- *Cognitive:* graphics can be used to increase comprehension (i.e., providing elaboration for textual explanations), improve retention, improve recollection, and provide information that is not otherwise available.
- *Compensatory:* graphics can assist poor readers by adding pictorial clues to decode text.

Lee and Boling (1999) provided the following guidelines for use of graphical images (p. 21):

- Use simple, clear images. Images with too much detail can be lost when presented at a small scale like a computer screen.
- Only use graphics for instructional, motivational, or attention-focusing effects. Never include gratuitous graphical images.
- Make sure all of the key components of the graphical image are labeled. Use captions or titles for labeling the key elements.
- Avoid sexist, culturally insensitive, or other potentially offensive imagery.
- Obey any existing conventions (e.g., standard symbols in a circuit diagram or top-to-bottom or left-to-right order for a flow chart).

Levie and Lentz (1982) reviewed 46 experimental comparisons of reading with and without pictures. They found that the presence of relevant illustrations significantly helped the learning of text information in 85% of the cases. On the average, groups reading with relevant pictures learned 1/3 more than groups reading text alone.

Anglin, Towers, and Levie (1996) reviewed a large body of literature on the learning effects of static and dynamic illustrations. They concluded that "static visual illustrations can facilitate the acquisition of knowledge when they are presented with text materials" (p. 766). They further concluded that the instructional effectiveness of dynamic illustrations (e.g., animations) is positive when motion is a critical attribute of the concept being presented and motion is used to cue or draw the learner's attention to the material being presented.

Mayer, Bove, Bryman, Mars, and Tapangco (1996) conducted three separate experiments comparing lessons in which detailed text explained the visuals to lessons that only included summary text and visuals. Learners who read the summary text performed better on tests of retention and transfer than those who read the detailed passages. The graphics appeared to positively supplement the summary text.

Color and Unused Space. Use of colors can enhance the impact and readability of text by highlighting important words and definitions (Bostock, 2004). The inclusion of white or unused space can also reduce clutter and enhance readability. Grabbinger (1993) found that multimedia screens that used white space were rated higher by viewers than more crowed screens.

In general, background colors or patterns should not detract from or obscure text and graphics. Hall and Hanna (2004) examined the impact of text-background color on readability and retention of information on web pages. Participants viewed either an educational or commercial web page for ten minutes. Then, they completed a quiz/questionnaire about the content of the web sites. The participants were assigned to one of four font/background color conditions: black/white, white/black, light blue/dark blue, and cyan/black. Results generally showed that the pages with high contrast color combinations (B/W and W/B) lead to greater readability. Ratings of readability were positively related to retention for the educational web site, but not for the commercial web site. Participants indicated that they preferred the blue color schemes on the commercial site. This preference was positively related to their intention to purchase a product. These results highlight the importance of readability for instructional applications. They also demonstrate the differences between commercial and instructional web sites in terms of their intended purpose.

Screens should be free from flickering, moving, or blinking words or graphics except for specific functions to gain attention. When using color to cue the learner, Tognazzini (2003) recommended that clear, secondary cues (e.g., boldface) should also be provided to convey information to learners who may be colorblind.

The following are Lee and Boling's (1999) guidelines for the use of color (pp. 21-22):

- Use color in a conservative way (e.g., limit the number and amount of colors used to a maximum of three to seven colors per screen).

- Keep color coding consistent (e.g., use the same colors for menus, titles, buttons, etc.).

- Use colors selectively to manipulate attention (e.g., a bright color to cue the learner to new information).

- Use cool, dark, low-saturation colors (e.g., olive green, gray, blue, brown, dark purple, black, etc.) for backgrounds. Use hotter, lighter, and more highly saturated colors (e.g., lemon yellow, pink, orange, red, etc.) for foregrounds.

- Avoid the use of complementary colors (e.g., blue/orange, red/green, violet/yellow).

- Use commonly accepted colors for particular actions (e.g., red for stop, green for go). However, remember that such colors may be appropriate only for a specific culture or social system.

- Use higher levels of brightness for distinguishing colors when designing for younger audiences.

Animation and 3-D Graphics. Based on their review of the literature on teaching equipment procedures, Hamel and Ryan-Jones (1997) concluded that "Emerging technologies such as 3-D graphics and animation create new visualizations of equipment and support more natural interaction with the computer" (p. 85). They cautioned, however, that these approaches "should be applied selectively based on the cognitive requirements of procedural tasks" (p. 86).

Hamel and Ryan-Jones (1997) provided several guidelines for using animations and 3-D graphics. Some of these guidelines include:

- Allow learners to have control over views of a 3-D object and additional textual elaboration. Guidance on effective viewing strategies should be provided.
- The learner's attention should be directed to the important parts of the animated instruction.
- When using 3-D objects, provide aids to enhance the interpretation of the object. For example, one might provide additional 2-D views of an image to help the learner interpret the 3-D view.
- When rotating objects, rotate at a slow rate (about equal to the viewer's rate of mental rotation). Sollenberger and Milgram (1993) found support for this guideline. They found that visualizations of a tree structure of blood vessels in the brain was better at slower rotational rates as long as the rate was not so slow as to remove the apparent motion effect.
- Use animations as a visual analogy or cognitive anchor for the instruction of problem solving (see also Mayer & Anderson, 1992).
- Include practice and feedback in animated instruction when feasible. For example, an exercise, based on an animation could use a version of the animation to highlight errors and direct the learner to correct the procedure.

Video. The use of video can provide useful support for many instructional approaches, including:
- "Talking Heads" for lectures or expert testimonials
- "Show and Tell" for demonstrations
- Panel discussions
- Simulations (especially of processes)
- "Walk Throughs" of facilities or events

Thibodeau (1997) provided the following recommendations when using video:
- Ensure the video is relevant to the content (e.g., only if content requires showing movement)
- Avoid sensory (modality) conflicts (see Criterion 6.a)
- Show the consequences of improper performance
- Make sure the area of focus is well lighted

- Make sure there are no distracting movements, such as someone walking by in the background (the learner's eye will be attracted to the movement)
- Use long, medium, and then close-up shots to establish the visual introduction
- Use close-ups to get the learner's attention and indicate that the video is important
- Don't use video for static shots (use photographs)
- Zoom-in is useful to focus learners' attention on a specific object or area while still maintaining their visual bearings
- When introducing something new, be sure to focus on the object or area long enough to "register" with the learner

6.c. Screens are Aesthetically Pleasing

Learners are more likely to attend to and be motivated by instructional presentations that are aesthetically pleasing. Although an individual's aesthetic preferences are, in some part, subjective, there are some general principles that can enhance the aesthetics of media presentations.

Using the Scale

This scale is used to evaluate how many of the screens in the course are aesthetically pleasing. It should be used as a guide during design and development and as a diagnostic tool during implementation and evaluation. Use the anchor statements and examples of aesthetic principles that are found below the scale to help assign a rating on this criterion. Additional information is provided in the discussion below.

Terms, Concepts, Techniques, and Supporting Literature

An aesthetic experience is one, which has "a satisfying emotional quality because it possesses internal integration and fulfillment reached through ordered and organized movement" (Dewey, quoted in Misanchuk, Schwier, & Boling, 2000, p. 2 of 10). Misanchuk and colleagues (2000) observed that aesthetics are not a quality of objects. They are rather found in one's experience when viewing or working with an object. Nevertheless, artists have worked for centuries to develop techniques that increase the aesthetic appeal of their work. Many of these techniques can be used to increase the aesthetic appeal of instructional content and the learners' engagement with the content (Graham, et al., 2000). Likewise, the study of human perception has helped our understanding of how to present instruction that supports rather than conflicts with the ways that learners perceive.

Screen Complexity. Coll and Wingertsman (1990) found that the relationship between screen complexity and user performance and preference follows an inverted U-shaped curve. In their first experiment, participants were assigned to one of three screen density conditions in which they had to complete the same task. Screen density referred to the amount of information presented on a screen and the number of operations available to the user on the screen. Three levels of screen density were used in the study (24%, 37%, and 64%). The highest density screen contained more information and allowed the users to complete more operations from that initial screen. Alternatively, the low-density screens contained less information and required the users to navigate through multiple screens to access the same information provided on the first page of the high-density screen. The time for task completion was fastest and appeal scores were highest in the 37% condition. In either the lowest or highest complexity conditions, they found that performance times were longer and appeal scores were lower.

In their second experiment, they asked participants which screen density they would prefer in a learning application. Sixty percent of the subjects chose the medium-complexity (37%) screen. The authors concluded that medium complexity screen designs should result in both better performance and higher preferences from users.

Screen Design Principles. Skaalid (1999) and Misanchuk, et al. (2000) compiled screen design guidelines for multimedia and web-based instruction. These guidelines are based on:

- "Classic graphic design theory." These include elements of graphic design (e.g., use of lines, shapes, textures, colors, and shapes) and principles of graphic design (e.g., movement, balance, emphasis, and unity).
- Gestalt principles of perception (e.g., figure and ground, similarity, proximity, continuity, closure, area, and symmetry).

- Human-computer interface design principles (e.g., from sources such as Norman, 1988; Nielsen, 1994; and Schneiderman, 1998).

There is not sufficient space in this book to provide details on all of these design topics. It is strongly recommended that Instructional Developers and Managers ensure that their development teams have copies of these guidelines. This will enable the teams to access specific guidance to support the design needs of their instructional products. Below are a few brief samples of guidance from each of the three areas. It should be remembered that the three areas are not separate, but strongly interact with and influence one another.

Classic Graphic Design Theory. One of the most important aspects of aesthetically pleasing instructional design is *simplicity.* Research reported by Reeves and Nass (1996) led them to conclude that "People like simplicity.... Rather than empowering through endless choices, media can empower through ease of use, and that often means freedom from choice.... 'Simple' also means predictable.... When people know what to expect, they can process media with a greater sense of accomplishment and enjoyment" (p. 254). Misanchuk et al. (2000) recommend that the instructional message be presented as simply as possible, without any confounding or superfluous elements that can distract the learner. For example, complex or "busy" backgrounds should be avoided and diagrams or pictures should provide just enough visual information to support the instruction. Too much information can become "noise," distracting the learner from the important portions of the instruction.

Another important aspect of aesthetically pleasing instructional design is the use of color. Misanchuk et al. (2000) provided several reasons to use or not to use color (color, pros and cons, p. 2 of 3). Some of the *reasons to use color* include:

- Color may be necessary to convey important instructional information (e.g., how a diseased organ looks compared to a normal one).
- Color may help learners to organize instructional content and help them process and retrieve information.
- Learners like color.

Some of the *reasons not to use color* include:

- Many instructional materials, especially text on a screen, do not require color.
- Color can be a distraction to the learner.

- Not all learners have a computer that will present the colors correctly (monochrome is the lowest common denominator).
- Some learners may be colorblind or have difficulty distinguishing certain color differences.

Principles of Perception. Two perceptual principles that are well supported by research are *proximity* and *similarity.* "The Principle of Proximity suggests that objects that are close together are interpreted as being related, while objects that are apart are viewed as being unrelated" (Misanchuk, et al., 2000, perceptual principles, p. 2 of 24). Thus, locating related objects close together on a computer screen provides cues to help the learner perceive this relationship. "The Principle of Similarity states that objects that look alike are perceived as belonging together" (p. 6 of 24). Similarity is so powerful that it can sometimes override proximity. These two principles should be used in tandem to help the learner perceive patterns in the instructional content. These patterns help in both learning and retrieval of the content.

Human-Computer Interface Design Principles. Over the years, researchers have learned many things about how people interact with computers. This knowledge has been accumulated into computer interface design principles. One of the most widely used set of principles is the usability heuristics recommended by Molich and Nielsen (1990) and Nielsen (1993). Many of these were listed in the Introduction to Section III. Although these heuristics are focused on any type of computer interface, they can easily be adapted to meet the interface design requirements of computer-delivered instruction. Applications of these heuristics are also discussed under other criteria (especially Criteria 5.e, 5.f, and 5.g).

6.d. Multi-modal Presentation of Content is Used

Computer-delivered instruction can present instructional material that is focused on different senses or combinations of senses (e.g., visual, auditory). Instruction that uses various senses is sometimes referred to as multi-modal.

Using the Scale

This scale is used to evaluate how often different presentation modes are used to reinforce and clarify instructional information. Use the scale as a guide during development to remind developers to include multi-modal presentation of content. During implementation and evaluation, use the scale as a tool to identify instances where multi-modal presentation could enhance the courseware. Use the anchor statements and the list of examples of multi-modal presentation found below the scale to help assign a rating on this criterion. Additional information is provided in the discussion below. Remember, if you give a one (1) rating on this criterion, you <u>must</u> also rate the next criterion (6.e) as a one (1).

Terms, Concepts, Techniques, and Supporting Literature

Some research (e.g., Moreno and Mayer, 1999) shows that learners benefit when instruction is presented using multiple sensory modalities (e.g., vision, sight, hearing). However, as mentioned above (6.a), there are large risks of creating sensory conflict if the information is different across the modalities.

Sharon Oviatt (1999) discussed "myths" about multimodal interaction that she terms "currently fashionable among computationalists" (p. 75). These "myths" are all refuted to some degree by empirical data. She discusses most of the "myths" in the context of operational systems, but nonetheless, some have some relevance for multi-modal presentation of instructional content. For example:

- *Myth: If you build a multi-modal system, users will interact multi-modally.* Even though they like to interact multi-modally, users do not always do so. They often use a mix of uni- and multi-modal commands, depending on the nature of the action. Instructional interface designers should carefully determine the input options they provide for their course. Standard, point and click inputs are probably sufficient.

- *Myth: Multi-modal input involves simultaneous signals.* Users of operational systems often synchronize their multi-modal inputs, but synchrony does not imply simultaneity. Simultaneous presentation of instructional content risks overloading the learner with information. Designers should use different modalities to reinforce important items of information and help tie them together. The specific timing of each modality needs to be determined by the nature of the information to be presented.

- *Myth: Multi-modal integration involves redundancy of content between modes.* "The dominant theme in user's natural organization of input actually is complementarity of content, not redundancy" (Oviatt, 1999, p. 78). Instructional designers should search for a balance between redundancy (repetition to aid deeper learning) and complementarity (helping learners link pieces of instructional information or procedural steps together).

- *Myth: All users' multi-modal commands are integrated in a uniform way.* Individual differences in the way individuals integrate multi-modal interactions require careful choices in modes and mixtures of modes for content presentation.

- *Myth: Different input modes are capable of transmitting comparable content.* "Different modes basically vary in the degree to which they are capable of transmitting similar information with some modes relatively more comparable (speech and writing) and others less so (speech and gaze)."

6.e. Multi-media Presentation of Content is Used

Computer-delivered instruction affords many presentation options. These presentation options include: text, graphics, video, animations, and others. Collectively, these presentation options are often referred to as multi-media.

Using the Scale

This scale is used to evaluate how many different media are used in the course. During early ISD stages it should serve as a guide. During later ISD stages it should be used as a diagnostic tool. The anchor statements and list of example instructional media, found below the scale, should be used to assist in assigning a rating on this criterion. Additional information is presented in the discussion below. Remember, if you rated Criterion 6.d as a one (1), you *must* also rate this criterion as a one (1).

Terms, Concepts, Techniques, and Supporting Literature

Multi-media is "a computer-driven interactive communication system for various types of textual, graphic, video, and auditory information" (Tessmer, 1995, p. 128; see also Gayeski, 1992, p. 9). A multi-media presentation can be instructionally beneficial if it enhances the content and makes it easier to understand and remember. Media should never be included gratuitously because they can become distractions. Furthermore, as noted in Criteria 6.a and 6.d, designers should ensure that media do not present information in conflicting sensory modalities.

Media integration refers to how well different media are combined to produce an effective whole or how they work together to form one cohesive program. Jones and Okey (1995) suggested that media be should be designed so that learners can search for information across different media. They also observed that some types of media may be perceived as more credible than others (e.g., text over video).

A number of researchers have reviewed research on multi-media effects on learning (e.g., Mayer, 2001). Below are some instructional design principles that have resulted from these efforts.

- *Media Choice Principle*: Choose the medium that best communicates the information to be learned (Najjar, 1998). For example:
  - For a small amount of information to be remembered for a short time, audio is better than text.
  - Text is better than sound for longer retention.
  - Pictures are useful for presenting spatial information.
  - Simple illustrations with captions are more effective than text for summarizing information (Mayer, Bove, Bryman, Mars, & Tapangco, 1996).

- *Multimedia Principle*: Learners learn better from words and pictures than from words alone (Mayer, 2003, p. 37; Mayer & Anderson, 1991).

- *Spatial Contiguity Principle*: Learners learn better when corresponding words and pictures are presented near rather than far from each other on the page or screen (Mayer, 2003, p. 49).

- *Temporal Contiguity Principle*: Learners learn better when corresponding words and pictures are presented so they coincide meaningfully (Mayer, 2003, p. 51; Mayer & Anderson, 1992).

- *Irrelevancy Principle*: Learners learn better when extraneous words, pictures, and sounds are excluded rather than included (Mayer, 2003, p. 33; Harp & Mayer, 1998; Moreno & Mayer, 2000a). Gratuitous use of media can detract from learning. As Levie and Dickie (1973) put it, "Realism cues which are not relevant to the learning task may produce divergent responses especially under conditions of high information loads" (p. 875). Unrelated illustrations "may actually decrease learning" (Najjar, 1998, p. 313).

- *Modality Principle*: People learn better from animation and narration than from animation and on-screen text (Mayer, 2003, p. 35). This has been called the "split attention effect" (Mayer & Moreno, 1998; Mousavi, Low, & Sweller, 1995). However, this general principle must be tempered by specific guidance on the type of material to be learned and the conditions in which a given modality is applied. For example, Rieber (1990) found that fourth- and fifth-grade students learned science principles better from animated presentations only if practice was provided. Thus, the specific conditions that improve learning of specific material must be understood before decisions are made to use one modality over another. Another important issue when delivering instructional information using multiple modalities is the timing of delivery. Kalyuga (2000) found that combining a diagram, text, and narration can result in cognitive overload and reductions in learning if the text and narration are presented simultaneously. When it is "necessary" for narration to be redundant with text, Kalyuga recommended that written materials be delayed and presented after the auditory narration has been fully articulated. Another technique to avoid this problem is to present text as "bullets" rather than full text.

- *Redundancy Principle*: "Learning is facilitated by increasing the redundancy of relevant cues and reducing the number of cues that are irrelevant to the learning task" (Levie and Dickie, 1973, p. 875; Mayer, 2003, p. 45). Media should elaborate the instructional information (Najjar, 1998, p. 313; Kalyuga, Chandler, & Sweller, 1999; Clark, R. C., & Mayer, 2003; Moreno & Mayer, 2002), but should not include features that are interesting but not relevant (Harp & Mayer, 1997; Mayer, Heiser, & Lonn, 2001). Fox (2004) found support for this principle. Using signal detection methods, she found that subjects were better able to discriminate information from video news stories with redundant visuals than from news stories with dissonant visuals.

• *Interaction Principle*: A cognitively engaging, interactive user interface "appears to have a significant positive effect on learning from multimedia" (Najjar, 1998, p. 314).

• *Prior Knowledge Principle*: Media design effects are stronger for learners with low-knowledge of subject area and lower aptitudes (Mayer, & Gallini, 1990). High knowledge and high aptitude learners seem to benefit from almost any media design. (Mayer, 2003, p. 43).

• *Voice Principle*: People learn better from narration when the voice is human (rather than a machine voice) and speaks with a standard accent (Mayer, 2003, p. 53).

• *Personalization Principle*: Learning is facilitated in multimedia lessons when the words are in conversational style rather than formal style (Mayer, 2003, p. 39).

• *Pretraining Principle*: People learn better from multimedia when they already know something about the topic (e.g., names and functions of components) (Mayer, 2003, p. 41; Mayer, Mathias, & Wetzell, 2002).

• *Signaling Principle*: Multimedia explanations using narrated animations should include highlights of the key steps, section headings that correspond to the key steps, and/or other techniques to signal the importance of the information (Mayer, 2003, p. 47).

• *Pacing Control Principle*: The cognitive load imposed on the learner can be reduced and deeper learning can be achieved by allowing the learner to control the rate of presentation (Mayer & Chandler, 2001).

• *Appropriate Instructional Cues Principle*: The instructional medium or mix of media should be chosen on the basis of the media attributes that will facilitate the learning of specific tasks. Levie and Dickie (1973) summarized the need for additional research on which specific media attributes should be used for instruction on specific tasks. "No single level of independent variable is consistently superior" (p. 877). They recommend that instructional researchers should direct their efforts toward "discovering the conditions under which different levels of attributes are differentially effective. What media attributes will facilitate learning for what kinds of tasks?" (p. 877).

6.f. Media are Easy to Use

If instructional media are not easy to use, it may lead to frustration, distraction, and loss of learner motivation.

Using the Scale

This scale is used to evaluate how often the media in the course are easy to use. During development the scale can be used to sensitize developers to the importance of making the media easy to use. During later ISD stages, the scale should be used to identify instances where the media are difficult to use so these can be corrected. The anchor statements and list of examples of easy-to-use media, found below the scale, should be consulted to help assign a rating on this criterion. Additional information is provided in the discussion below.

Terms, Concepts, Techniques, and Supporting Literature

Learners should not have to struggle to operate an instructional delivery medium. Controls should be easily located, clearly labeled, and easy to operate. Media will be easy to use if designers follow the requirements of Criteria 5.d, 5.e, 5.f, and 5.g (Chapter 8). One example of a difficult-to-use medium would be if the control for a video presentation were hidden by another window.

6.g. External Hyperlinks are Kept to a Minimum

The author has met some people who believe that one of the strengths of web-delivered instruction is the ability for learners to link to other web sites for additional information. Including hyperlinks to other web sites can increase the learner's frustration if these links do not function properly or if the sites have been modified since the course was developed. It is the position of this criterion that external hyperlinks should be few or not used at all.

Using the Scale

This scale is used to evaluate how many external hyperlinks are used in the course. During development the scale should be used as a guide to help minimize hyperlinks. During implementation and evaluation, it should be used to identify instances of unnecessary hyperlinks so these can be reduced or eliminated. It is assumed that fewer external hyperlinks is always to be preferred. The anchor statements below the scale should be used to help assign a rating on this criterion. Additional information is provided in the discussion below.

Terms, Concepts, Techniques, and Supporting Literature

Informational sites are usually designed to sell a product or provide information chosen by the user. On the other hand, instructional sites are designed to provide structured instructional information and to assess whether the learner has mastered this information. Acknowledging these differences, there is still much to be learned from commercial web sites.

Many links used on web sites fail to make clear their destinations. Borges, Morales, and Rodriguez (1998) investigated users' ability to predict the destinations of 50 links randomly selected from 10 commercial web sites. They found that "in approximately one fourth of the cases, the link names suggested a wrong idea about the content of a page" (p. 145, cited in Farkas & Farkas, 2000, p. 5 of 21). "Even in well-designed Web sites, users will periodically follow a link to an unwanted node or will sit and ponder whether to follow a link. But designers should work hard to minimize these frustrating occurrences" (Farkas & Farkas, 2000, p. 5 of 21).

"Entropy is the enemy of the Web, which tends toward disorder. Your sites—and the outside Web sites you link to—get dated, changed, or reorganized. Inevitably, links break. In their initial enthusiasm, many new Web authors add dozens of external links to their sites. Unfortunately, each of those links soon becomes a maintenance issue" (Lynch & Horton, 1997, p. 117). Links to websites that do not support LOs could reflect poorly on your instruction. Furthermore, if the links are not properly maintained, they could provide incorrect or irrelevant information. In any case, external links introduce possible problems because they are outside of your control.

Chapter 10:
Installation and Registration

The following criteria refer to any special actions that the learner needs to complete to begin a course and receive credit for successful completion. In all cases, care should be taken to make these actions as easy as possible.

7.a. Course Does not Require Installation or Learners Can Install the Course without Assistance

Using the Scale

This scale is used to evaluate how difficult it is to install a course on the learner's computer. During development the scale should be used as a guide and during implementation and evaluation, it should be used as a diagnostic tool. Use the anchor statements below the scale to help assign a rating on this criterion. Additional information is provided in the discussion below.

Terms, Concepts, Techniques, and Supporting Literature

Some computer-delivered courses must be downloaded from an external source (e.g., the internet) and installed on the learner's computer. Others are delivered to the learner on an electronic medium (e.g., CD ROM) and then have to be installed on his or her computer. Other courses do not require installation.

When installation is required, as it often is to ensure the learner obtains credit for the course, it should be easily accomplished. Easy installation will minimize distractions for the learner and also avoid demotivating the learner by putting him or her through excessive, frustrating actions. The installation process should be fully explained and be completed in a short time. It is important to get the learner to the instructional content as quickly as possible.

A related issue is that the learner may start a course from one location (e.g., work) and wish to continue or complete it at another location (e.g., home). If this is the case, he or she should be able to restart the course from different computers without losing his or her place in the course or having to retake completed lessons.

7.b Minimal "Plug-ins" are Required

Using the Scale

This scale is used to evaluate how many plug-ins (extra software programs) are required to run the course. Use the scale as a guide during early ISD stages and as a diagnostic tool during later ISD stages. Use the anchor statements found below the scale to assist in making your rating on this criterion. Additional information is provided in the discussion below.

Terms, Concepts, Techniques, and Supporting Literature

"Plug-ins" are software programs that are needed to perform functions within the course. An example is a program to play video clips. In general, the course should be self-contained. All of the necessary plug-ins should be included with the course or the learner should be provided with easy instructions to download the plug-in. These instructions should be easy from the perspective of the learner, not the computer programmer. The learner should not be required to install a large number of plug-ins, nor should he or she be required to locate the plug-ins prior to installation.

Many plug-ins are included in standard browser software. It is strongly recommended that developers only use standard plug-ins. There should be a compelling reason to use a unique plug-in. For example, if a 3-D view is needed to demonstrate a procedure and only a special-purpose plug-in will work, then it must be used. However, in no case should a special-purpose plug-in be used because it is easier for the developer or because the developer is more familiar with it. The decision to use a plug-in should be based on what will be easier for the learner and what will support the learning objectives of the course.

7.c. "Optimization" Test is Available

Using the Scale

This scale is used to evaluate how well the optimization test provides a tryout of all features and provides directions to set up the computer to display the course in the most effective manner. The scale should be used as a guide when designing and developing the "optimization" test. It should be used to diagnose problems with the "optimization" test during later ISD stages. Use the anchor statements below the scale to assist in assigning a rating on this criterion. Additional information is provided in the discussion below.

Terms, Concepts, Techniques, and Supporting Literature

Many computers differ in small ways that can change the appearance or other functionality of the course. The course instructions or tutorial should include a "test" to help the learner determine if his or her computer is properly set up for the course (also see Chapter 8, Criterion 5.b).

One method to help learners determine if their computer is configured to support the course is to include several test functions. This could be a series of pictures, videos, audio tests, and others. The learner should be prompted as to how the computer should be functioning (e.g., "can you read this text?" or "can you see the red dot?"). If the learner's computer is not functioning properly, he or she should be provided with detailed instructions to properly configure the computer.

7.d. Technical Support is Available

Most learners are not computer experts. When encountering a problem with the course, it is important that they have access to technical support. This technical support needs to get them back to the instructional experience as soon as possible.

Using the Scale

This scale is used to evaluate how much technical support is available and how effective it is for the learner. Use the scale as a guide during early ISD stages and as a diagnostic tool during later ISD stages. Use the statements below the scale and the list of characteristics of effective technical support to help assign a rating on this criterion. Additional information is provided in the discussion below.

Terms, Concepts, Techniques, and Supporting Literature

Technical support needs to be "learner-centric." This means that the needs of the learner are paramount and the most important function of the technical support staff is to get the learner into the course as quickly and painlessly as possible.

7.e. Registration is Simple and Straightforward (Or Not Required)

Using the Scale

This scale is used to evaluate how easy it is to register for the course, if registration is required. Use the scale as a guide during development and as a diagnostic tool during later ISD stages. Use the anchor statements below the scale to help assign a rating on this criterion. Additional information is provided in the discussion below. Note: If *no* registration is required for the course, assign a score of five (5) on this criterion.

Terms, Concepts, Techniques, and Supporting Literature

Learners are usually required to register for a course. This is often to ensure that they have completed any prerequisites and also to ensure that they receive credit for completing the course. In many cases, organizations use learning management systems to register and track learners. In other cases, the course may include software that records and transmits registration information. Either way, registration should be as easy as possible for the learner. He or she should be able to quickly accomplish the task and move on to the course itself. Upon completion, he or she should be able to easily receive credit for the course.

SECTION IV:
Adaptations and Uses of the Method

This final section provides information to help tailor the Method to be more relevant to the needs of each user. One way to increase its relevance is to adapt it to address a user's specific instructional approach. The use of instructional games is one of the fastest growing instructional approaches. Therefore, Chapter 11 presents several adaptations of the Method so it can be used to evaluate Instructional Games.

Another way to make the Method more relevant to user needs is to provide guidance for applying it appropriately. The Method can be used for both formative and summative evaluations depending on which stage of instructional systems development (ISD) is the current focus of user energy. Chapter 12 provides discussions on how to use the Method at each ISD stage and includes brief discussions of how the Method can be improved.

CHAPTER 11:
Adaptations of the Method for Instructional Games

There is growing interest in business, healthcare, education, and the military services in using games and game-based technologies as instructional tools. However, there are too many individuals who assume that all games are effective instructional tools and should be the preferred delivery method for all instructional applications. In support of this assumption, there is some empirical evidence that games can be effective instructional tools if they are appropriately designed and used. However, there is also evidence that games, if used inappropriately, can consume large amounts of resources (e.g., time, money) with little or no instructional gain (see Hays, 2005; 2006 for a review of both sides of this research). This chapter discusses the important issues that must be considered when choosing to use an instructional game. It also provides some adaptations of the Method so it can be used to evaluate the design and use of instructional games.

Developing, Selecting, and Using Instructional Games

The purpose of this chapter is to present and discuss some adaptations of the Method so instructional developers and instructional program managers can develop, select, and use games to help meet their instructional goals. Following the procedures in this chapter will help one understand and make decisions on the basis of:

1. The factors that influence when and why to choose an instructional game.
2. Ways to determine if the selected game is an effective instructional tool.
3. Why a game may be the preferred instructional tool when compared to other approaches.

Possible Instructional Benefits of Games

For many years, claims have been made about the instructional benefits of games. These claims include:

1. Games can increase the motivation and interest of learners.
2. Games can improve learning.
3. Games can improve the learner's attitudes about the subject matter

Greenblat (1981) summarized the empirical data that supported these claims and Hays (2005; 2006) updated this summary with more recent empirical data. The first claim (games can improve motivation) has strongest empirical support. In most cases, learners enjoy games and are willing to invest their time and energy in game play. However, there is only weak empirical support for the second claim (games can improve learning). Although data show that some games result in learning, there are also data that show less positive results. Some games have been shown to be detrimental to learning while others provided no more benefits than other forms of instruction. The third claim (games can improve learners' attitudes about the subject matter) also has mixed support. The empirical evidence has shown that games can increase both positive and negative attitudes toward the subject matter. As with any instructional tool, the characteristics of the game and how it is used are the prime determinants of learner's attitudes about the game and its instructional effectiveness (e.g., Briedemeier, Bernstein, & Oxman, 1982; Leutner, 1993; Mayer, Mautone, & Prothero, 2002; Hays, 2006).

When Will a Game Provide Effective Instruction?

Positive support for the instructional value of games (the second and third claims) has been found when:

1. The game is used in a well-designed program of instruction.
2. The purpose of the game is explained to the learners in terms of how it supports their learning objectives.
3. Learners are given performance feedback after playing the game. This feedback must provide the learners information about the quality of their performance and how the game activities supported their learning objectives.

It can be concluded from the empirical data on the instructional effectiveness of games that games are not always the preferred approach. However, games can be effective if they are designed to support instructional objectives and are appropriately incorporated into a program of instruction.

The Importance of Understanding the Definitions of Terms

Greenblat (1981), Rieber (1996), Thomas, Cahill, & Satilli (1997) and Hays (2005; 2006) pointed out that there is confusion on the use of various terms in the literature on games. The terms model, simulation, game, and simulation-game are often used interchangeably. Confusion about these terms may lead to incorrect decisions about what instructional approach or combination of approaches to select. Below are definitions of these important terms.

Models and Simulations. A *model* can be defined as "a physical, mathematical, or otherwise logical representation of a system, entity, phenomenon, or process" (Department of Defense, 1997, p. 138). Models represent selected aspects of the real world for specific purposes. They do not represent all aspects of any real-world phenomena. If a model represented all these aspects, it would not be a model—it would be the real thing. Models are the foundation for dynamic simulations by providing the rules and the data that allow a simulation to function in a specific way to meet a specific purpose.

A *simulation* is "a method for implementing a model over time" (Department of Defense, 1997, p. 160). Chapter 5 (Instructional Activities) included discussions of simulations as instructional tools.

Game. After reviewing many definitions, Hays (2005; 2006) provided the following definition of a game.

> *A game is an artificially constructed, competitive activity with a specific goal, a set of rules and constraints that is located in a specific context.*

There are four important parts of this definition.

1. A game is "*artificially constructed.*" A game is not real. Rather, it is a representation of reality. Therefore it is a simulation, based on a model of reality. Although *all games are simulations, not all simulations are games.* It is vital that the user of an instructional game understands the model upon which it is based. Are the instructional objectives realistically supported by the characteristics of the model underlying the game?

Here are three simple examples. First, if a weapon is used in the game, its performance should replicate the real world in terms of number of rounds, ballistic effects, and effects on the target. Second, if simulated persons are part of the game, they should move realistically (e.g., they should not be able to run at 40mph). Finally, if communications are part of the game, they should be realistic (e.g., one should have to use a communications device to communicate with distant players). There are many other issues that must be decided based on the specific requirements of the instructional task(s).

2. A game is a "*competitive activity.*" Only when a simulation includes competition can it be called a game. Competition can be against other players, against oneself, or against criteria set by the game.

3. A game has a "*specific goal*" established by its "rules and constraints." Both trainers and learners must understand these rules and constraints. Furthermore, they must understand how similar the game's rules are to the real-world constraints of the task.

4. A game is "*located in a specific context.*" This means that each game must be designed, procured, and/or modified to meet one's specific instructional goals. As discussed below, a simulation can be turned into a game if it is used competitively with a set of rules and constraints.

An *instructional game* is specifically designed or modified to meet instructional objectives. It meets these objectives by including rules, constraints, and activities that closely replicate the constraints of the real-world task that must be learned. An instructional game must be incorporated into a program of instruction in a manner that ensures that learners understand the instructional objectives of the game, and receive detailed feedback about their performance in the game and how their performance supported the instructional objectives. In most cases, an instructional game should be considered an instructional aid rather than as a method of stand-alone instruction. There are some instances where an instructional game must be used in a stand-alone mode (e.g., distance or distributed learning). In these cases, the game must be designed to include all of the instructional capabilities that are otherwise provided by an instructor.

Types of Games. There are many types of games that can be used for instructional purposes. There have been many different ways of classifying games (see Hays, 2005 or 2006 for a summary of some of these). It is important that you appreciate the differences among game types in order to choose the gaming approach that most closely meets your instructional goals. Below is a brief overview of some definitions of different types of games. It should be remembered that a given game could be (and often is) a combination of several different game types.

Simulation-based Games. A simulation is not a game; although all games are simulations. Furthermore, some games can be based on existing simulations (e.g., PC flight simulations). Often, the goal of these simulation-based games is to challenge the player to master the simulation (e.g., learn to take off, land, or use the simulated instruments). However, the simulation is not a game unless it includes game-like activities (e. g., specific rules, competition, challenge, feedback, etc.) If the rules and algorithms that govern the simulation are realistic (i.e., match the constraints and requirements of the task in the real word) it may provide effective instruction. This will only be the case if the simulation-based game is incorporated into an instructional program (see subsequent section). Furthermore, care must be takes to ensure that any differences between the real-world constraints and the characteristics of the simulation do not result in negative transfer to the real task.

Hybrid Games. Most games are combinations of various elements from different game types. For example, a tactics game may incorporate simulations of various types of weapon systems or communication equipment. These simulations may be used in realistic scenarios, based on case studies of real events.

Individual or Group Games. Some games are designed to be played by a single individual (competing against the game or against a skill standard) others are designed to be played by groups of people (playing against each other or against a standard). Even if you need to provide instruction on a group task, it may require individual instruction before each learner is ready to interact with a group.

Games of Skill or Games of Chance. Some games are based on skill (e.g., board games, card games, mathematical games, word games, etc.) others are based on chance (e.g., dice games, casino games, bingo, etc.). There is not a clear distinction between these types because chance games may also require certain skills (e.g., knowing

247

when to fold in poker or blackjack). Certain skill games may also incorporate randomly generated events as part of their event scenarios (e.g., how often an opponent's weapons hit and/or destroy the learner's assets).

Computer-based or Live Games. When thinking of games, many people first think of computer-based video games. Although they are very popular, there are many games that involve live individuals (e.g., sports, war game exercises). When a live game has been converted to a video game (like video basketball or football), it is important to determine if it retains the rules and conditions that apply in the real world.

Off-the-shelf or Tailored Games. Many games are available off the shelf. These are often called Commercial Off-The-Shelf (COTS) games. If one chooses to use these COTS games, one must determine if the include the appropriate task characteristics, constraints, and their level of realism. In most cases, they will include some realistic events, but they also may include modified conditions from those that constrain the task in the real world. If game conditions are unrealistic, they may result in persons learning the wrong things or learning to do things the wrong way. Some games may be procured from a commercial source, but designed for a specific Government need. These games are often called Government Off-The-Shelf (GOTS) games. These GOTS games are targeted more narrowly than COTS games, but still must be assessed to determine if they include the appropriate task characteristics and constraints. Finally, a game may be designed for a very specific instructional need. These may be called specific purpose games. When designing and procuring specific purpose games, care must also be taken to include the appropriate task characteristics and constraints and minimize unrealistic task characteristics and constraints.

Uses of Instructional Games. Another way of classifying games is by the type of task to be trained. Like the classifications above, the following are not mutually exclusive.

Skills and Procedures Games. These types of games are intended to help individuals learn specific skills (e.g., how to read a volt meter, how to distinguish between a friend and a foe, how to organize information to support a decision) and procedures (e.g., how to fix or operate a piece of equipment, how to drive a vehicle, how to react to an ambush).

Action Games. Require the learner to react to specific situations and engage in real-time actions (e.g., first-person shooter games, multi-player urban warfare games, [need more here]).

Role-playing Games. The learner participates in a scenario that requires him or her to learn and practice specific activities that are required for a certain task (e.g., team leader, supervisor,

Strategy Games. The learner participates in scenarios that require him or her to learn and practice information analysis, information synthesis, planning, and other strategy skills.

A Systematic Approach to Instructional Game Design and Use

Atkinson (1977) advocated that the design and development of instructional games should follow the same basic systems approach that is required for the development of any instructional aid or activity. This approach is summarized in Figure 6. The first section of the approach includes steps that are exactly the same, no matter what the outcome (e.g., choosing a game or another instructional activity). The first two steps are to identify the instructional problem and the instructional objectives. A problem statement is a general statement of the overall instructional problem (e.g., improve learners overall understanding of and competence in a topic area). Next, specific instructional objectives must be determined. These objectives should be stated in terms of observable learner behaviors, under specific conditions that help the learners reach an acceptable level of performance. These foundational requirements are next used to help determine the possible alternative instructional strategies and/or approaches that can be selected. The choice of a specific instructional strategy is then determined on the basis of the constraints of each instructional situation (e.g., numbers of learners, available facilities, budget, etc.). Only when a gaming approach has been selected from the alternative instructional strategies does one move to the next section: the design or modification of a specific game.

SECTION 1: Understanding the Instructional Environment

Step 1: Develop Problem Statement

Step 2: Develop Instructional Objectives

Identify Constraints

Identify Alternative Strategies

Step 3: Select Game Strategy

SECTION 2: Developing the Game

Step 4: Develop Game Model

Identify Students' Resources

Step 5: Develop Students' Role in Game

Identify Students' Objectives

Step 6: Develop Rules, Events, & Winning Criteria

SECTION 3: Implementing & Evaluating the Game

Step 7: Develop Supporting Game Resources (e.g., player's manuals, teacher's manuals)

Step 8: Evaluate Game Compared to Alternate Instruction

Step 9: Modify Game Based on Results of Evaluation

Figure 6:
A Systematic Approach to Instructional Game Design and Use

The second section of Figure 6 shows the basic steps in developing an instructional game. The fourth step is to develop the game model. As discussed above, any model is a simplified representation of only certain elements of reality. The specific elements chosen for the game model should be selected on the basis of how they will support the instructional objectives already identified. Step 5 is the identification of how the learners will participate in the game. Several questions, like the following, must be answered to support game design. Will each learner play the same role or different roles? Will they play as individuals or as a team? Will learner actions affect the outcome of the game or do they just observe? These and other questions will lead to the development of specific rules and events in the game. Finally, the criteria for winning the game must be developed. Winning the game should involve improved learner performance on the instructional objectives. Sometimes an existing game can be modified for a new instructional situation. Even if an existing game is chosen, it must be modified to meet the specific requirements of the each new instructional situation.

The third section of Figure 6 shows the three main steps involved in the implementation and evaluation of an instructional game. In addition to the game, supporting materials, like learners' instructions and trainers' manuals must be developed. As indicated by the data from studies such as Leutner (1993) and Mayer, Mautone, & Prothero (2002), instructional support that explains the purpose of the game and how to play it can enhance the instructional value of the game. In step 8, the instructional game is evaluated. Ideally this evaluation should compare the effectiveness of the game (as measured by learner performance) to the effectiveness of alternate instructional approaches. If a comparison of the game to an alternative instructional approach is not possible, learner performance should still be evaluated to determine if their performance has improved on task-relevant knowledge and skills. The final step in this process uses the results of the evaluation to modify the game to improve its instructional effectiveness.

A Procedural Checklist for Developing, Selecting, and Using Instructional Games

Although Figure 6 shows a systematic procedure for designing and using an instructional game, additional guidance is needed to help with the individual steps of this procedure. Table 14 is a checklist that can be used to track this procedure. The remainder of the chapter is a series of discussions of the activities identified in the checklist. These activities should be carefully completed by anyone attempting to use game-based technologies to achieve specific learning objectives. The next section provides discussions of these issues to help ensure that if a game is selected, it will be an effective instructional tool.

Discussions of Activities on the Checklist

The following discussions provide information about each activity that must be performed on the checklist (Table 14).

Before You Select a Game: The Planning Stage (1)

The first section of the checklist (Table 12) consists of activities that must be completed before deciding to use a game or a game-based approach. The following discussions explain these important activities.

Document Instructional Objective(s) (1.1)

The first activity is to understand and document the nature and requirements of each task to be trained. This is accomplished by documenting the instructional objective(s) of your program of instruction (POI). Chapter 4 included in-depth discussions about why it is important for learners to understand the purpose of a course and how the activities within the course support its instructional objectives. It is just as important that learners understand the purpose of playing an instructional game. The game should clearly support the instructional objectives of the program of instruction and these objectives should be made clear to the learners.

Table 14:
Checklist for Selecting and Using Instructional Games

Activity	Completed?
1. Planning Stage (do not check off until all sub-activities have been completed)	
1.1 Document Instructional Objective(s)	
1.1.1 Review existing documentation of instructional objectives (in terms of activities, conditions, and standards for each instructional objective).	
1.1.2 If existing documentation is incomplete, develop new instructional objectives (that include complete descriptions of activities, conditions, and standards for each objective).	
1.2 Review Current Instruction	
1.2.1 Document Deficiencies in Current Instruction	
2. Selecting a Game (do not check off until all sub-activities have been completed)	
2.1 Review Game Events (in terms of their relationship to instructional objectives [1.1] and deficiencies in current instruction [1.2])	
2.2 Review Requirements of Game (what the learner must do)	
2.3 Determine Whether to Use an Existing Game or Develop a New Game	
2.4 Develop Introductory Materials for the Game	
3. Using a Game (do not check off until all sub-activities have been completed)	
3.1 Insert the Game into Your Program of Instruction	
3.2 Deliver an Introduction for the Game	
3.2.1 Explain How to Play the Game	
3.2.2 Explain How Game Events Support Instructional Objectives	
3.3 Measure Performance	
3.4 Deliver Performance Feedback	
4. Evaluating the Game's Effectiveness (do not check off until all sub-activities have been completed)	
4.1 Determine if Learners Performance Has Improved	
4.2 Determine if the Instructional Program is More Efficient	

Characteristics of a Good Instructional Objective. A good instructional objective (Hays, Stout, & Ryan-Jones, 2005; Depart of Defense, 2001; Dick & Cary, 1996; Clark, 1995) must include three main parts:

1. A description of an *observable action* in terms of performance or behavior.
2. At lease one *measurable criterion (standard)* that states the level of acceptable performance in terms of quantity, quality, time, or other measures.
3. The actual *condition(s)* under which the task will be conducted.

Chapter 4 (Criterion 1.c) included detailed information on the parts of an instructional (learning) objective. It also included a discussion on how different instructional objectives relate to one another. If your POI includes instruction for multiple tasks, you must document complete instructional objectives for each task and determine how they support each other.

Review Existing Documentation of Instructional Objectives (1.1.1). If the instructional objectives been documented in existing documents (e.g., task analyses, handbooks, Task Lists, etc.), you should review these documents to ensure that they contain complete descriptions of each instructional objective in terms of actions, conditions, and standards. The *actions* are what the person must do when using the knowledge and skills you intend to impart to them. The *conditions* are the environmental and other constraints (e.g., time) under which the task must be accomplished in the real world. The *standards* are used to determine if the learners have successfully accomplished the task. The instructional objective should also indicate whether an individual or a group conducts the task and whether this is introductory, refresher, or enhancement instruction. Introductory instruction is the initial presentation of the knowledge and skills to the learners. Refresher instruction helps reinforce the required knowledge and skills. Enhancement instruction helps an individual practice to improve his or her knowledge and skills by using them in realistic exercises.

Develop New Instructional Objectives (1.1.2). If the task is not fully described in existing documentation or if the task has changed, you must develop new instructional objectives. These objectives must include descriptions of actions, conditions, and standards. If this is a new task, you may need to review the instruction for similar tasks.

Review Current Instruction (1.2)

Before you decide to use an instructional game, you must understand how instruction is currently conducted. This begins by reviewing current instructional materials and collecting inputs from current instructors.

Review Current Instructional Materials and Approaches (1.2.1). Unless the instruction is for a totally new task, some form of instruction probably exists. You need to understand this current instruction if you are to improve it by adding gaming technologies. The current instructional materials (e.g., books, slides, animations, simulations, etc.) should be reviewed to determine their effectiveness. It will be useful to interview current instructors and have them indicate the strengths and weaknesses of the current instruction.

Document the Deficiencies in the Current Instruction (1.2.2). If you are considering using a game for instruction, there must be some deficiency or deficiencies in the current instruction or there may be no current instruction for some task or tasks. These deficiencies can be determined by reviewing the information collected in activity 1.2.1 above. By understanding the current instructional deficiencies you will be able to forecast how a game may help to correct them. For example:

- A game could introduce new terms in a more realistic context

- A game could allow the learners to practice new skills more efficiently than current instruction.

- A game could allow the learners to integrate knowledge and skills in realistic scenarios.

- A game could provide more efficient (i.e., faster) instruction.

If a game cannot help correct current instructional deficiencies, you should not consider using a game.

Selecting a Game (2)

There are several sub-activities that must be completed before you select any game. The most important activity is to determine the events that the learner will experience in the game and determine how closely they match your instructional objectives. Understanding the events in the game will help you determine if an existing game can be used or whether you need to modify the existing game or develop a new game.

Review Game Events (2.1)

Any game consists of a series of events that are governed by rules and constraints (see the definition of a game above). It is important that the specific game you select meets as many of the instructional objectives of the task as possible. The more overlap between your instructional objectives and game activities the greater the probability of effective instruction (Hays, 2005; 2006). This is illustrated in Figure 7. In order to determine this overlap, you must understand the relationship between the instructional objectives and the events that occur in the game. As discussed above (1.2.2), you should also understand how the game events reduce or eliminate the deficiencies in the current instruction.

Review the Requirements of the Game (2.2)

Before a learner can play a game, he or she must be able to function in the game world. This may require them to learn various skills that are game-specific. Almost as important as the incorporation of realistic task requirements in the game is the elimination of as many unrealistic game requirements as possible. If learners are required to spend too much intellectual energy on learning and performing game activities that are not task related, they will not be able to focus on the task-relevant game activities. Game requirements that do not support instructional objectives need to be recognized and explained to the learners during their performance review session (After Action Review). This is discussed in greater detail below.

Determine Whether to Use an Existing Game or Develop a New Game (2.3)

If there is enough overlap between game events and instructional objectives you may be able to use an existing game. Before deciding to use an existing game, you must carefully review the existing game to confirm the realism of the game's rules and constraints and determine if they support your instructional objectives. If they do not, you may need to develop a new game that includes more realistic game events.

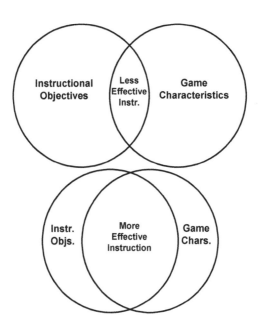

Figure 7:
Instructional Effectiveness as Degree of Overlap
among Instructional Objectives and Game Characteristics

Develop Introductory Materials for the Game (2.4)

Once you have selected an instructional game, you need to develop the materials that you will use to introduce learners to the game. The characteristics and requirements of the game will determine the requirements of these introductory materials. The introductory materials should help the learners focus on the events of the game that support the instructional objectives. They should provide cues and aids to help the learners complete game-specific activities with the least amount of attention so they can get on with the instructional purposes of the game.

Using a Game (3)

How a game is used is as important as the characteristics of the game itself (Hays 2005; 2006). You need to plan how to use the game as a tool in your program of instruction. In very few cases can one effectively use a game as a stand-alone instructional tool. If a game must be used in a stand-alone mode (e.g., delivered over the internet), it must be designed to include the same types of instructional support that would be provided by a live instructor. These include performance assessment and feedback. In any case, the instructional program must provide the learner with the necessary prerequisite knowledge and skills that will make the game instructionally meaningful.

Insert the Game into Your Program of Instruction (3.1)

You need to have a clear plan for how the game will be used in your program of instruction. For example, you need to decide at which point the game will be used and how many game sessions will be required. You might want to conduct a series of game sessions with feedback and discussions between sessions. You may want to use the game for both instruction and assessment. These decisions must be made prior to using the game so the learners can obtain the most instructional benefits from their gaming experiences.

Deliver an Introduction for the Game (3.2)

Allowing learners to engage in game activities (events) is the purpose of an instructional game. It is important that learners focus on the game events rather than wasting time and energy on learning how to play the game or on activities that do not support their instructional objectives. Your introduction should be based on the plans and materials developed in activity 2.4.

Explain How to Play the Game (3.2.1). The introduction to the game should supply the learners with all of the information and assistance necessary for them to begin playing the game rather then wasting time on trying to figure out and learn game-specific skills. Their focus should be on their experiences during important game events.

Explain How Game Events Support Instructional Objectives (3.2.2). In order to effectively use a game as an instructional tool, the learners must understand why they are playing the game and how their activities support their instructional objectives. This should also be explained both during the introduction to the game and during performance feedback (see below).

Measure Performance (3.3)

The only way to determine if someone has learned new knowledge or skills is to measure their performance (Hays, 2006). After playing the game, learners should be able to perform better using the knowledge and skills learned in the game. You should measure their performance using either existing performance measures (e.g., tests or evaluation activities) or newly developed performance measures (e.g., evaluation game sessions). If their performance has not improved, the learners probably need additional instruction or game sessions or you may need to change how you use the game.

Deliver Performance Feedback (3.4)

After engaging in game activities, learners need to receive detailed feedback that explains how well they performed in the game and how the events and activities in the game supported their learning objectives. Without such feedback, a learner may believe her or she performed adequately and learned what was required. Data have shown that people tend to hold overly favorable views of their performance (e.g., Kruger & Dunning, 1996; Maki, 1998). Feedback that highlights the learners' performance in the game and shows how it relates to the learning objectives of the game will help the learners more accurately evaluate their performance so they can improve their knowledge and skills.

Evaluating the Game's Effectiveness (4)

Just as you must evaluate the performance of your learners who play the game (activity 3.3), you must also evaluate the effectiveness of the game itself. The effectiveness of the game should be determined in two ways: improved performance and improved efficiency.

Determine if Learners' Performance Has Improved (4.1)

If an instructional game is effective, the average performance of learners should show improvement. Records of performance obtained during the use of the game (activity 3.3) should be accumulated and the average performance improvements should be documented. If the average performance of your learners has decreased, you should discontinue the use of the game and use an alternate instructional approach. Even if the average performance of learners is the same as with other instructional approaches, you may still wish to use the game is to improve the efficiency of your POI.

Determine if the Instructional Program is More Efficient (4.2)

If the average performance of your learners has improved or remained the same, an instructional game may still be the preferred instructional method because it has improved the efficiency of your POI. You can determine if this is the case by comparing your POI using the game with your POI using an alternate or previous instructional approach. Some of the measures of efficiency you might use include:

- Time to complete the POI
- Number of learners who can complete the POI in a given time period
- Learner reactions to the POI

Another way to help ensure that a systematic procedure is followed when selecting and using instructional games to adapt some of the scales presented in Chapter 2 to evaluate instructional games. These scales and discussions are shown below.

Instructional Game Evaluation Scales

Hays, Stout, and Ryan-Jones (2005) developed a tool to evaluate the instructional quality of computer-delivered instruction. It consists of a series of rating scales that target the criteria that have been shown to lead to effective instruction. Several of the scales from this tool have been adapted to be used to evaluate the instructional quality of a game. The scales are shown below followed by a brief discussion of each scale.

The scales can be used during each stage of game development and during its incorporation into an instructional program. During the early conceptual development phases, the scales serve as guides to help focus on important issues that will increase the probability that the game will be instructional effective. At later development stages the scales should be used to focus on specific game characteristics that can be improved prior to final delivery. After the game has been developed, the scales should be used to help incorporate the game into an instructional program and to help evaluate its effectiveness. The scales are divided into three sections: (1) instructional issues (2) technical issues, and (3) playability issues.

The Scales

Instructional Issues

The first group of scales (1-6) directly addresses the instructional design and use of games.

1. Instructional Objectives (Goals) are Clearly Stated

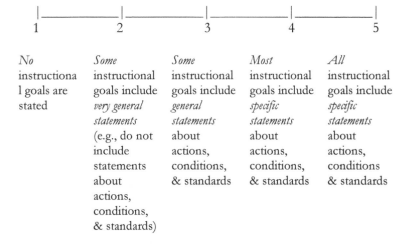

1	2	3	4	5
No instructional goals are stated	*Some* instructional goals include *very general statements* (e.g., do not include statements about actions, conditions, & standards)	*Some* instructional goals include *general statements* about actions, conditions, & standards	*Most* instructional goals include *specific statements* about actions, conditions, & standards	*All* instructional goals include *specific statements* about actions, conditions & standards

Discussion. The first rating scale helps determine if the instructional objectives of the game are understood and communicated to the learners. At the early development stage, the scale should be used to ensure that game developers fully understand and document the instructional goals of the game. Once a game has been developed and is being inserted into a program of instruction, the instructional goals will guide how the game will be used. At this stage, the scale can be used to determine how well these instructional goals are communicated to the learner prior to any interaction with the game.

2. Includes Instructions on How to Play the Game

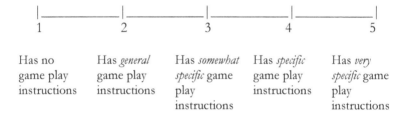

1	2	3	4	5
Has no game play instructions	Has *general* game play instructions	Has *somewhat specific* game play instructions	Has *specific* game play instructions	Has *very specific* game play instructions

Discussion. It should always be remembered that the purpose of the game is to provide task-relevant instruction, not to be played only for enjoyment. Although some game enthusiasts enjoy learning to play the game, this is not an efficient use of instructional time. Data have demonstrated that games are more instructionally effective if they include guidance about how to play the game (Hays, 2006). Such guidance allows the learners to focus their energy on game activities rather that learning how to play the game.

3. Game Activities Support Instructional Goals (Objectives)

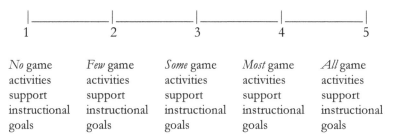

1	2	3	4	5
No game activities support instructional goals	*Few* game activities support instructional goals	*Some* game activities support instructional goals	*Most* game activities support instructional goals	*All* game activities support instructional goals

Discussion. A game can include many different activities. The instructional effectiveness of a game will be enhanced to the extent that game activities overlap with the instructional goals of the game (see Hays, 2006 for a more extensive discussion of this issue).

4. Game Activities are Realistic (conforms to real-world conditions)

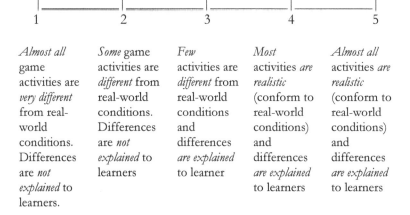

1	2	3	4	5
Almost all game activities are *very different* from real-world conditions. Differences are *not* *explained* to learners.	*Some* game activities are *different* from real-world conditions. Differences are *not* *explained* to learners	*Few* activities are *different* from real-world conditions and differences *are explained* to learner	*Most* activities *are* *realistic* (conform to real-world conditions) and differences *are explained* to learners	*Almost all* activities *are* *realistic* (conform to real-world conditions) and differences *are explained* to learners

Discussion. The goal of instruction is to help learners improve the knowledge and skills that will allow them to successfully perform the

263

task in the real world. Like any instructional tool (e.g., simulations, case studies), a game should provide realistic activities that conform to real-world conditions. If game activities are not realistic, game experiences may result in negative transfer to the work environment. In this case, learners may need to relearn or unlearn these activities when they perform the task.

5. Game Includes Assessments of Learner Actions

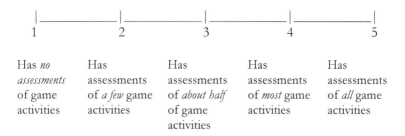

1	2	3	4	5
Has *no* assessments of game activities	Has assessments of *a few* game activities	Has assessments of *about half* of game activities	Has assessments of *most* game activities	Has assessments of *all* game activities

Discussion. A game will be more effective if it includes assessments and summaries of learner actions. During the debrief session, these assessments should be used by the instructor to explain how the learner's performance met or failed to meet instructional goals. Learners can benefit from mistakes made during the game if they can be made to understand the implications of the mistakes and are given the opportunity to correct them (see the next scale).

6. Game Provides Feedback on Learner Actions

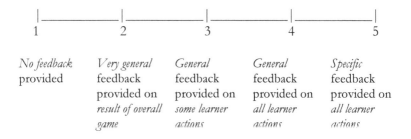

1	2	3	4	5
No feedback provided	*Very general* feedback provided on *result of overall game*	*General* feedback provided on *some learner actions*	*General* feedback provided on *all learner actions*	*Specific* feedback provided on *all learner actions*

Discussion. Related to the above scale, the results of the assessments of his or her performance need to be communicated to the learner. Ideally, the instructor will communicate this feedback during the game debrief. Some feedback can also be provided during the game to allow the learner to learn from mistakes and correct his or her actions. If a game is used without an instructor, the quality of the feedback needs to be even higher.

Technical Issues

This group of scales (7-11) addresses how the game is presented to the learner in terms of its technical quality.

7. Game Graphics are Clear and Sharp

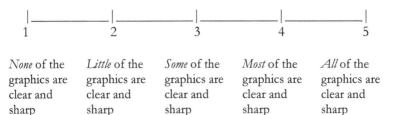

1	2	3	4	5
None of the graphics are clear and sharp	*Little* of the graphics are clear and sharp	*Some* of the graphics are clear and sharp	*Most* of the graphics are clear and sharp	*All* of the graphics are clear and sharp

Discussion The graphics used in computer games can range from very simple line drawings, through cartoon-like representations, to photo realistic representations. Depending on the instructional goals of the game, the graphics should be clearly presented. For example, if the instructional goal is to help someone learn to read and interpret a display on a piece of equipment, the graphics need to clearly depict the display. On the other hand, if the instructional goal is to teach someone to locate the display, the clarity of the graphics will not have to be as high. In all cases, supporting graphics and text should be clear and sharp.

8. Game Audio is Clear and Sharp

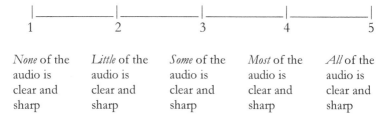

1	2	3	4	5
None of the audio is clear and sharp	*Little* of the audio is clear and sharp	*Some* of the audio is clear and sharp	*Most* of the audio is clear and sharp	*All* of the audio is clear and sharp

Discussion. Some tasks require the learner to hear and understand certain sounds (e.g., equipment sounds or communications). In these cases, the audio should provide the necessary clarity to support task performance. Audio can also be used to direct game play or provide feedback during game play. This type of audio should always be clear and sharp.

9. Game Video is Clear and Sharp

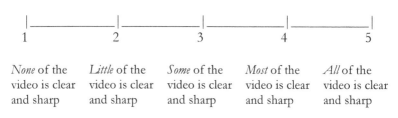

1	2	3	4	5
None of the video is clear and sharp	*Little* of the video is clear and sharp	*Some* of the video is clear and sharp	*Most* of the video is clear and sharp	*All* of the video is clear and sharp

Discussion. Games may incorporate video clips showing real task activities or guidance from task experts. In all cases these videos should be clear and sharp so learners can see all of the necessary details that support instructional goals.

10. There are No Sensory Conflicts in the Game

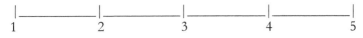

1	2	3	4	5
Different information is *always* presented simultaneou sly in two or more modalities	Different information is *often* presented simultaneous ly in two or more modalities	Different information is *sometimes* presented simultaneo usly in two or more modalities	Different information is *seldom* presented simultaneous ly in two or more modalities	Different information is *never* presented simultaneo usly in two or more modalities

Discussion. Learners use all of their senses during game play. Learning can be improved if information is transmitted in multiple sensory modes (e.g., visual and auditory). This is only true if the information transmitted in the different sensory modes is mutually supportive. On the other hand, if different or conflicting information is presented in the different sensory modes it will likely result in sensory conflict and reduce the instructional effectiveness of the game.

11. Game Installation is Easy or not Required

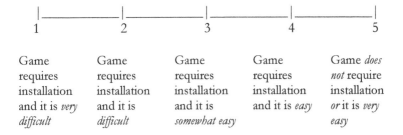

1	2	3	4	5
Game requires installation and it is *very difficult*	Game requires installation and it is *difficult*	Game requires installation and it is *somewhat easy*	Game requires installation and it is *easy*	Game *does not* require installation *or* it is *very easy*

Discussion. Sometimes games must be installed on the learner's computer. Installation of the game should be avoided whenever possible. If this is necessary, the installation should be easy.

267

Playability Issues

The last two scales address issues that affect the playability of the game (i.e., how much learners enjoy playing the game).

12. Game Screens are Aesthetically Pleasing

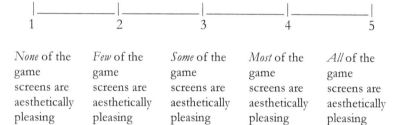

1	2	3	4	5
None of the game screens are aesthetically pleasing	*Few* of the game screens are aesthetically pleasing	*Some* of the game screens are aesthetically pleasing	*Most* of the game screens are aesthetically pleasing	*All* of the game screens are aesthetically pleasing

Discussion. Game will likely be more enjoyable if the screen displays are designed using accepted artistic principles. These include using compatible colors and aesthetic shapes (see Chapter 9 for a discussion of the aesthetics of screen design).

13. Game Activities are Fun & Engaging (Attract & Maintain Learner Attention)

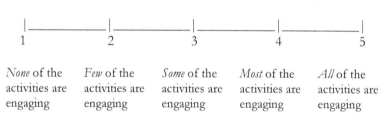

1	2	3	4	5
None of the activities are engaging	*Few* of the activities are engaging	*Some* of the activities are engaging	*Most* of the activities are engaging	*All* of the activities are engaging

Discussion. Learners must attend to (engage with) instructional information if learning is to occur. One of the possible benefits of an instructional game is that it will be fun to play, thus engaging the learner with the activities that support instructional objectives. Csikszentmihalyi (1990) studied the factors that make an activity enjoyable. He found that people enjoy many different activities, including: sports, other games, dance, art, thinking, and many others. He labeled the feeling of peak enjoyment "flow" and documented the components that combine to produce this experience. The process of flow is shown in Figure 8. The two main variables of the flow experience are challenges and skills. These are shown on the axes of the figure. One may experience flow when the task offers little challenge and one's skills are not well developed (A1). As one develops higher skill levels, the task will become boring because it no longer provides a challenge (A2). On the other hand, one may experience anxiety if the task is too difficult (A3). If, however, one gradually develops higher skill levels as the task becomes more difficult (A4), it is possible to maintain the flow experience. The challenge of an instructional game is to keep the learner in the flow channel by increasing the challenge of the game as the learner's skills improve.

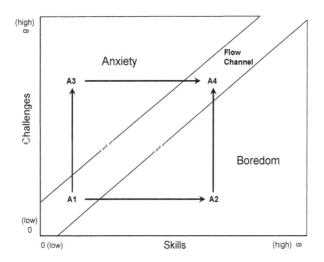

Figure 8:
The Process of "Flow"

CHAPTER 12:
Details on How to use the Method and Recommended Improvements

The instructions accompanying each evaluation scale and the discussions about each scale included brief statements about how the scales should be used for formative and summative evaluations. This chapter includes more in-depth discussions about the roles of different individuals who use the Method and how they should view the scales during each stage of the instructional systems development (ISD) process. These discussions begin with an overview of ISD and some of the people who engage in major parts of the ISD process.

Instructional Systems Development

Instructional Systems development (ISD) is a controlled process for designing instructional systems and evaluating their effectiveness. An instructional system can be defined as follows:

> *An instructional system is the planned interaction of people, materials, and techniques, which has the goal of improved performance as measured by established criteria.*

These criteria are usually established by educational standards and on-the-job requirements (Hays & Singer, 1989; Hays, 1992; Hays, 2006). Table 15 lists the major elements of an instructional system under the three categories mentioned in the above definition.

The *interactions*, which take place in ISD occur during each stage of the development and delivery cycle. ISD is a process that consists of a series of iterative steps, stages, or phases. Various authors have summarized the ISD process using different numbers of stages (e.g., Branson, Rayner, Cox, Furman, King, & Hannum, 1975 discuss five stages). Figure 9 shows a four-stage depiction of the ISD cycle and some correspondences between its four stages and the steps of the scientific method.

Table 15:
The Major Elements of an Instructional System

People	Materials	Techniques
• Learners (students) • Instructors (teachers) • Course/content Developers • Program Developers • Computer programmers • Administrators • Budget Analysts • Logistics Managers • Subject Matter Experts • Instructional consultants • Instructional Aids, Equipment, & Simulator Developers • On-the-job Supervisors • Instructional System Researchers	• Instructional content • Instructional Aids, Equipment, & Simulators • Instructional Requirements Documents • Evaluation Instruments • Instructional Development Tools (e.g. authoring systems)	• Instructional Design Approaches • Instructional Strategies and Techniques • Development Methods • Instructional Aids, Equipment, & Simulation Design Methods • Needs Analysis Techniques • Effectiveness Evaluation Methods • Performance measurement tools • Instructional quality evaluation methods • Return on Investment Analysis Methods

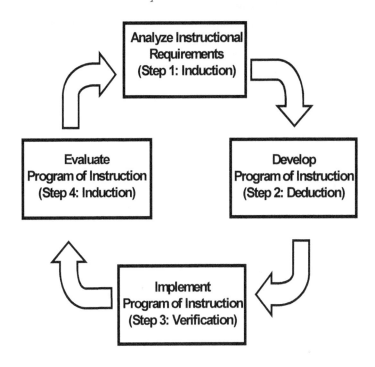

Figure 9:
Stages of Instructional Systems Development
and the Steps of the Scientific Method

The ISD cycle normally begins with an analysis of instructional needs. This corresponds to the first step of the scientific method, induction, or observations of objects and events in the real world. Next, a program of instruction is developed. This stage is often separated into design and development (this separation results in the acronym ADDIE as opposed to ADIE). In the four-stage cycle depicted in Figure 9, development corresponds to the second step of the scientific method, deduction, or developing ideas about how the program of instruction is expected to work. The implementation of the program of instruction corresponds to the third step of the scientific method, verification. Here the program is tried out in an instructional context to verify whether the program can be implemented (e.g., are the facilities sufficient, does all the software work, will policy allow implementation). Finally, when implemented, the program of instruction is evaluated. This corresponds to the fourth step of the scientific method, induction based on controlled observations. This takes us back to the beginning of the instructional system development cycle where we can apply what we have learned to improve the instructional program or future programs.

This conceptualization is for illustrative purposes only. One should not regard these correspondences as exact. However, the guiding principles behind the scientific method are the same as those behind the ISD process. Both are cyclic and never ending. Both rely upon logical reasoning, controlled observations, and iterative improvements.

As discussed in earlier chapters the Method provides a literature-based, quantitative method to evaluate the instructional quality of computer-delivered instruction. The anchored evaluation scales are intended to cover all of the critical areas that can affect the quality of instruction. However, the scales should be used differently depending on who is conducting the evaluation, the purpose of the evaluation, and during which ISD stage the evaluation is conducted.

Using the Method

Each of the types of people listed in Table 15 can benefit from considering and using the Method (i.e., the evaluation scales). The following discussion focuses on three important types of people: program managers, instructional developers, and instructors. Each of these types people plays different roles at different stages of ISD and should use the scales differently. Sometimes an instructional development effort requires a single individual in these roles and sometimes teams of individuals engage in the effort. Sometimes the roles are combined in a single individual or a single team. To simplify the following discussions, these three roles will be discussed as if they are single individuals. Table 16 summarizes some of the ways program managers, instructional developers, and instructors should use the Method during each stage of ISD.

Table 16:
Uses of the Method During Each ISD Stage

ISD Stage	Role	How to Use the Method
Analysis	**Program Manager**	Use the scales as <u>guides</u> to: • Ensure that complete task requirements information is collected • Ensure that complete task information is documented in terms of actions, conditions, and standards • Include use of the Method as a proposal requirement • Evaluate proposals and select development team • Select development teams with alternate approaches (when feasible) • Ensure that requirements information is converted into complete instructional objectives
	Instructional Developer	Use the scales as <u>guides</u> to: • Focus on important requirements information • Develop proposals that address all of the important instructional issues and demonstrate plans to apply the "best" instructional approaches • Translate instructional requirements into instructional objectives
	Instructor	Use the scales as <u>guides</u> to: • Select and provide information on current instructional approaches and deficiencies

Table 16:
(Continued)

ISD Stage	Role	How to Use the Method
Development	Program Manager	Use the scales as <u>guides</u> to: Evaluate progress of development team (e.g., review instructional approaches, review storyboards)
	Instructional Developer	Use the scales as <u>guides</u> to: • Select instructional strategies • Select instructional activities • Select sensory modalities and combinations • Develop assessment strategies • Develop feedback strategies • Design user interface • Conduct formative evaluations of all the above
	Instructor	Use the scales as <u>guides</u> to: • Select information to give to program manager and development team
Implementation	Program Manager	Examine the results of <u>detailed formative evaluations</u> to ensure deficiencies are identified and corrected
	Instructional Developer	Use the scales to: • Identify formative evaluation areas • Conduct detailed formative evaluations
	Instructor	Use the scales to: • Focus on important implementation issues • Insert courseware into larger POI

Table 16:
(Continued)

ISD Stage	Role	How to Use the Method
Evaluation	Program Manager	• Ensure that the scales are used to conduct <u>detailed summative evaluations</u> • Provide report(s) to sponsors and higher level management
	Instructional Developer	Use scales to: • Conduct detailed summative evaluations • Report results to program manager
	Instructor	Use the scales to: • Explain the results of the summative evaluations to the program manager

The Analysis Stage

During the analysis stage, the requirements of the instructional system (i.e., the courseware) are identified and documented so they can guide the efforts at subsequent ISD stages. Each of the three persons discussed above contribute differently to the success of the requirements analysis and documentation.

The Program Manager. Program managers typically control the budget and schedule for an instructional development effort. Ultimately, it is the program manager is responsible for the success of the effort. He or she is responsible for assigning roles to other individuals engaged in the effort and monitoring their performance. The first and perhaps most important task of a program manager is to ensure that the instructional requirements are complete and in a form that will support subsequent ISD tasks. The Method can help the program manager understand the importance of instructional requirements and how these requirements should be converted into instructional objectives.

Instructional requirements information is normally collected from instructors and other subject matter experts. The Method should be used as a guide to help the program manager ensure that these individuals supply all of the necessary information on the instructional task and the current instructional approach or approaches. It can also help the program manager to ensure that the experts focus on the most important aspects of the instructional requirements. For example, the information should address why current instruction is deficient and how a new approach or product is expected to correct these deficiencies.

In almost all instances, program managers do not actually develop instructional courseware. However it is usually the program manager's job to select the individuals who will develop the courseware. Once the program manager is sure that all requirements are understood and documented, he or she can use the Method to help select a development team. The Method could be identified in the RFP (request for proposals) as one of the ways the proposals will be evaluated. During proposal evaluations, the program manager and his or her proposal evaluation team could then use the criteria identified in the Method to choose among competing instructional developers. This choice should be based on which developer best explains his or her plans to address the most important issues that will affect the quality of their courseware (or other instructional product). Once an instructional developer is selected, the program manager should use the Method to track their progress during the remainder of the analysis stage and the subsequent ISD stages.

The Instructional Developer. The first task of the instructional developer is to be awarded the job of building the courseware. This involves an analysis of both the instructional requirements and the contractual process. The instructional developer must submit a proposal to demonstrate his or her ability to successfully meet the objectives of the project. The Method can help the developer focus on the most important requirements information and also demonstrate how they will use the information to create the highest quality courseware. The criteria used in the Method and the discussions of the scales to identify the most effective instructional practices based on the theoretical and empirical literature. Including discussions of the criteria identified in the Method will demonstrate the developer's commitment to the activities that will result in higher quality instruction.

After he or she has been awarded a contract, the instructional developer must translate the instructional requirements into instructional objectives. As discussed in Chapter 4, a complete instructional objective must include three important pieces of information: 1) a description of an observable action in terms of performance or behavior; 2) at least one measurable criterion (standard) that states the level of acceptable performance in terms of quantity, quality, time, or other measures; and 3) the actual condition(s) under which the task will be performed. The Method can be used as a guide in developing the instructional objectives and also as a way to demonstrate to the program manager that efficient development methods are being used.

The Instructor. During the analysis stage, the instructor is primarily a source of information on task requirements and current instructional approaches. The Method can guide instructors to select and report the information that will be most beneficial to the program manager and the instructional developer.

The Development Stage

During the development stage, the actual instructional product (i.e., courseware) is designed and developed. It is very important that formative evaluations be conducted during development to identify and correct problems at the earliest possible time. Later in the ISD process it will probably be much more expensive and time consuming to correct the problems. If problems are not identified or corrected during development, they will compromise the instructional effectiveness of the courseware when it is implemented.

The Program Manager. During development, the program manager must track the progress of the instructional development team. The program manager should use the Method (the scales) during product and process reviews as a "roadmap" to guide his or her monitoring efforts. The evaluation criteria should be to set the agenda and establish the discussion points for review meetings. The Method can also be used as guides to assign resources for project activities and to help evaluate interim products. For example, during storyboard reviews, the program manager should expect the plans for the courseware to detail how the courseware will communicate the purpose of the course to the learners.

The Instructional Developer. The instructional developer (development team) is the main player during this ISD stage. He or she should use the Method to organize the development efforts to focus on the activities that will have the greatest impact on the quality of the courseware. Some of these activities include:

- Selection of the instructional strategies that will be incorporated into the courseware.

- Selection and design of the instructional activities that will engage the learner with the material to be learned.

- Selection and design of ways to deliver the instructional information using different sensory modalities.

- Selection and development of strategies to assess learner performance to determine if the desired learning has occurred.

- Selection and development of feedback strategies to reward or remediate learner performance.

- The design and development of the user interface for the courseware.

These activities should be formatively evaluated beginning with concept formulation all the way through design and development. The Method should be used as a guide to conduct these formative evaluations.

The Instructor. The instructor's level of involvement will depend on the goals of the specific courseware development project. As a minimum, the instructor should serve as a consultant to the instructional development team. The experiences of an instructor who has actually taught the subject matter can be extremely beneficial during courseware development. Instructor involvement is important regardless of whether the courseware will be used as an aid for an instructor or as a stand-alone product without the presence of an instructor. In the former case, the instructor can use the Method to select the information the development team needs about the classroom environment and how the courseware can be integrated into other classroom activities. Sometimes courseware is designed for use without an instructor (e.g., we-delivered instruction). In this case, the instructor can help the development team include all instructor functions in the courseware. These functions include monitoring interactive activities, assessing performance, and providing feedback.

The Implementation Stage

During the implementation stage, the courseware is installed and tested in the actual environment where it will be used. It is during this stage that various activities must be completed so that the instructional process can be conducted. Many of the formative evaluations that are conducted during this stage focus on these support activities. Other formative evaluations focus on the way learners interact with the courseware and whether their performance improves as a result of these interactions.

The Program Manager. One of the tasks of the program manager during implementation is to ensure that the courseware is delivered on time and that the implementation and formative evaluation team focus on the correct activities and have the resources to accomplish their tasks. The Method should be used as a guide when reviewing implementation plans.

The Instructional Developer. During this stage, the courseware developed by the instructional development team is installed in a real-word instructional environment. Formative evaluations should be guided by the Method to focus on important installation and delivery issues. For example, there are many information technology (IT) barriers that must be successfully overcome before learners can access computer-delivered courseware. Computers must be both available to the learners and they must be capable of running the courseware. This is true whether the courseware is run on a single computer or is accessed over a local network or the Internet. The user interface evaluation criteria under installation and registration (Section 7) directly address some of these IT issues.

The Instructor. During implementation, the instructor can help the program manager and instructional developer to focus on important implementation issues. For example, the courseware will probably need to be inserted into a larger program of instruction. The instructor can advise how this insertion can be accomplished most efficiently and effectively.

The Evaluation Stage

It is during this stage that summative evaluations are conducted. Summative evaluations focus on the outcome of an instructional program. Kirkpatrick (1996) identified four levels of outcome evaluations. A level-1 evaluation (reaction) is typically conducted at the end of a course. It evaluates how the learners felt about the course. It does not measure whether learning occurred. A level-2 evaluation (learning) is also conducted at the end of the course. It measures the immediate learning of principles, facts, and techniques. A level-3 evaluation (behavior) focuses on the behavior of learners after they return to the job (or move on to a subsequent course).

Finally, a level-4 evaluation assesses how the instructional program affected the larger organization in terms of lower costs, higher quality products, increased production, reduced absenteeism, etc. This type of evaluation is sometimes called a cost-effectiveness or return-on-investment evaluation.

The Method should be used "formally" during this stage. The scores obtained on the literature-based evaluation criteria can serve a diagnostic function. The Method can highlight the specific strengths and weaknesses that resulted specific levels of performance. These strengths can be built upon in subsequent editions of the courseware. The weaknesses can be corrected before the courseware is more widely implemented. Scores should be assigned on each of the evaluation scales. It is recommended that at least three evaluators take the course and assign scores. They should then meet and discuss their ratings until they reach consensus scores on every criterion.

The Program Manager. The program manager should use the Method to ensure that detailed "formal" evaluations are conducted. He or she should then report the results of the evaluation to sponsors and higher-level managers. If the scores indicate that the courseware is of high quality, the program manager can used the report to publicize the courseware and follow similar developmental processes for other instructional products. If the courseware is not of high quality, the program manager has the opportunity to revise the product before it is implemented in additional locations.

The Instructional Developer. During this stage, the instructional developer has already completed most of his or her work. However, it is still possible that deficiencies will be identified that need to be corrected. In addition, the lessons learned during development can be highlighted using the Method as an organizational tool.

The developer may or may not serve as a member of the evaluation team. Nevertheless, he or she can consult with the evaluators to explain why certain approaches were taken when developing the courseware. The Method can be a useful tool to help organize these explanations.

The Instructor. An instructor might be assigned as one of the members of the evaluation team. It is not recommended that the entire team be instructors. This is because instructors probably know the subject matter too well to view the course the same way a learner would. Nevertheless, an instructor can bring a unique point of view to the evaluation and should at minimum be a consultant during the evaluation.

Recommended Improvements of the Method

The Method has been under development for several years. This development started by surveying various approaches to instructional quality and identifying the evaluation criteria which capture the most relevant aspects of computer-based courseware that contribute to its instructional quality (Hays, et al., 2003). The second phase of development focused on developing the anchored rating scales for the criteria and documenting the theoretical and empirical literature that supports the criteria (Hays, et al., 2005). This book includes enhanced discussion sections and has begun to explore some adaptations of the Method so it can be used to evaluate the quality of instructional games (see Chapter 11). There are several additional developments that would make the Method more valid and reliable and that would allow individuals to use it to evaluate and improve a wider variety of instructional products and approaches. It is recommended that the Method be improved through at least the following efforts.

Expand the User Interface Discussion Sections

Readers should have noticed that the discussion sections for the instructional evaluation criteria contain much more detail than the discussions for the user interface evaluation criteria. The main reason for this disparity is that there is a much larger literature base that supports the instructional features criteria. Most user interface research has focused on usability issues (e.g., Norman, 1988; Molich & Nielsen, 1990; Nielsen, 1993; and Schneiderman, 1998). Empirical data on other aspects of user-interface and screen appearance (e.g., aesthetics) needs to be collected and interpreted to use for design guidance. Furthermore, gaps in the empirical support for both the user interface and instructional features criteria should be identified to provide a "road map" for future instructional research.

Conduct Formal Reliability and Validity Tests of the Criteria

The content validity and construct validity of the evaluation scales have been informally evaluated during the development of the

Method. Informal reliability assessments of the scales were also conducted during development and during group discussions among evaluators who tried the Method. Unfortunately, the Method has, as yet, not undergone any formal reliability and validity testing. It is recommended that the criteria be used to evaluate a variety of instructional programs and products and that formal reliability and validity tests be conducted. Quantitative reliability and validity data will increase evaluators' confidence in the Method.

Conduct Additional Formative Evaluations of the Method

The Method should be tried out by diverse groups of evaluators to determine the most effective ways to conduct evaluations. Currently a group evaluation, using a consensus approach is the recommended approach. However, additional formative research may not support this recommendation in all cases. Also, formative evaluations can provide insights on how to apply the Method during different phases of instructional product development. Finally, the formative evaluations can support the development of special and specific guidance that may be needed for different "types" of evaluators (e.g., instructional developers versus instructional program managers).

Develop Weightings for the Criteria

Not all evaluation criteria are created equal. Some may be more important for certain types of content or for certain instructional approaches. Additional reviews of empirical research and discussions with instructional development experts can contribute to the development of a weighting scheme for the criteria. This weighting scheme can be used to "tailor" the evaluation criteria to the specific needs of a given instructional program. The criterion weightings will then need to be empirically tested and modified as appropriate.

Develop or Adapt the Criteria for Classroom and Other Types of Instruction

The Method currently is designed to focus on computer-delivered instruction without an instructor present. Computer-delivered instruction can also be used as an adjunct to classroom instruction (e.g., as a way to administer task-relevant exercises). An instructor could also serve as an on-site facilitator to help learners engage more effectively with the computer-delivered instruction. The Method needs to be adapted to effectively evaluate these variations in computer-delivered instruction.

Chapter 11 presented some adaptations of the Method to evaluate instructional games. Additional adaptations of the Method should be developed so it can be used to evaluate various types of instruction and instructional approaches.

Examine Computerized Scoring and Reporting

Chapter 2 contained a brief discussion of ways to interpret and present the results of an instructional quality evaluation. In this discussion, it was recommended that results be presented graphically to make them easier to interpret. If the Method included computerized scoring and reporting, it might allow evaluators to concentrate on understanding the criteria and assigning scores rather than focusing on adding scores and deciding how to report them. Such a computerized scoring system would keep track of the scores on all criteria, sum the scores, interpret the scores, and generate the evaluation summary. If weightings are developed for the criteria, this system could also assign these weightings based on a few questions about the specific nature of the course (e.g., knowledge or skill based; introductory or refresher, etc.).

Final Comments

The instructional quality evaluation method presented in this book is the result of many years and many people's efforts. However, it is still in its infancy. In addition to the recommended developments summarized above, the Method needs the contributions of both researchers and practitioners. The design of any tool can be improved through the knowledge gained during its use. I urge people to use this Method—not only because it will help them improve the quality of their computer-delivered courseware, but also because their experiences can help to improve the Method. I believe that there are four main groups who need to interact to produce high quality courseware: instructional developers, instructors, procurement officials, and researchers. I challenge these groups to use the Method and to interact with each other about it. Everyone wants higher quality instruction, whether delivered by computer courseware or other means. Working together, we can make it happen.

References

AAHE. (2004). *9 principles of good practice for assessing student learning.* American Association for Higher Education. Retrieved on February 9, 2003 from http://www.aahe.org/assessment/principl.htm.

AAR Toolkit (Ver. 1.2) [DVD]. (2003). Washington, DC: U.S. Army FA-57 Proponent Office, Office of the Deputy Chief of Staff, G-3/5/7, Battle command, Simulation and Experimentation Directorate.

Adam, J. J., Hommel, B, & Umiltà, C. (2003). Preparing for perception and action (I): The role of grouping in the response-cuing paradigm. *Cognitive Psychology, 46,* 302-358.

Alessi, S. M., & Trollip, S. R. (1991). *Computer based instruction: Methods and development.* Englewood Cliffs, NJ: Prentice Hall.

American Psychological Association (2001). *Publication manual of the American Psychological Association* (5th ed.). Washington, DC: Author. (ISBN 1-55798-790-4)

Anderson, J. R., & Bower, G. H. (1972). Recognition and retrieval processes in free recall. *Psychological Review, 79*(2), 97-123.

Anderson, J. R., & Bower, G. H. (1973). *Human associative memory.* Washington, DC: Winston & Sons.

Anderson, J. R., & Bower, G. H. (1974). A prepositional theory of recognition memory. *Memory and Cognition, 2*(3), 406-412.

Anderson, R. C., Kulhavy, R. W., & Andre, T. (1972). Conditions under which feedback facilitates learning from programmed lessons. *Journal of Educational Psychology, 63,* 186-188.

Anette, J. (1969). *Feedback and human behavior.* Baltimore, MD: Penguin Books.

Anglin, G. J., Towers, R. L., & Levie, W. H. (1996). Visual message design and learning: The role of static and dynamic illustrations. In D. H. Jonassen (Ed.), *Handbook of research for educational communication and technology: A project of the Association for Educational Communications and Technology,* (pp. 755-794). New York: Macmillan LIBRARY Reference USA, Simon & Schuster Macmillan and London: Prentice Hall International.

ANSI/ADA. (2002). *Guidelines for the design of educational software* (American National Standard/American Dental Association Specification No. 1001).

Atkinson, R. K. (2002). Optimizing learning from examples using animated pedagogical agents. *Journal of Educational Psychology, 94*(2), 416-427.

Ausubel, D. P. (1960). The use of advance organizers in the learning and retention of meaningful verbal material. *Journal of Educational Psychology, 51*, 267-272.

Ausubel, D. P. (1963). *The psychology of meaningful verbal learning: An introduction to school learning.* New York: Grune and Straton.

Ausubel, D. P. (1968). *Educational psychology: A cognitive view.* New York: Holt, Rinehart, & Winston, Inc.

Ausubel, D. P., & Youssef, M. (1963). The role of discriminability in meaningful parallel learning. *Journal of Educational Psychology, 54*(6), 331-336.

Baddeley, A. (1992). Working memory. *Science,* New Series, *255*(5044), 556-559.

Bangert-Drowns, R. L., & Kozma, R. B. (1989). Assessing the design of instructional software. *Journal of Research on Computing in Education, 21*(3), 241-262.

Bardwell, R. (1981). Feedback: How does it function? *The Journal of Experimental Education, 50*, 4-9.

Baron, R., Byrne, D., & Kantowitz, B. (1978). *Psychology: Understanding behavior.* Philadelphia: W. B. Saunders Company.

Baum, D. R., Riedel, S., Hays, R. T., & Mirabella, A. (1982). *Training effectiveness as a function of training device fidelity* (ARI Technical Report 593). Alexandria, VA: U.S. Army Research Institute.

Baylor, A. L., & Ryu, J. (2003). The effects of image and animation in enhancing pedagogical agent persona. *Journal of Educational computing Research, 28*(4), 373-394.

Bell, J. (2005). *Evaluating psychological information: Sharpening your critical thinking skills* (4th ed.). Boston: Pearson Education, Inc.

Bilodeau, E. A., Bilodeau, I. McD., & Schumsky, D. A. (1959). Some effects of introducing and withdrawing knowledge of results early and late in practice. *Journal of Experimental Psychology, 58*(2), 142-144.

Boettcher, J. V. (2003). Designing for learning: The pursuit of well-structured content. *Syllabus: Technology for Higher Education.* Retrieved on July 30, 2004 from http://www.syllabus.com/print.asp?ID=7092.

Bonk, C. J. (1999). *Part II: Online learning: Opportunities for assessment and evaluation.* Retrieved on June 20, 2005 from

http://www.trainingshare.com/download/vincennes/op_as
ses_eval.ppt.

Borchers, J., Deussen, O., Klingert, A., & Knörzer, C. (1996). Layout
rules for graphical web documents. *Computers and Graphics,
20*, 415-426.

Borges, J. A., Morales, I., & Rodriguez, N. J. (1998). Page design
guidelines developed through usability testing. In C.
Forsythe, E. Grose, & J. Ratner (Eds.), *Human factors and web
development* (pp. 137-152). Mahwah, NJ: Lawrence Erlbaum
Associates.

Bostock, S. (2004). *Learning technology: Draft evaluation criteria for content-
based web sites.* Retrieved on April 29, 2005 from
http://www.keele.ac.uk/depts/cs/Stephen_Bostock/docs/
webevaluation.htm.

Botha, J. (2000). *Conceptions of quality and web-based learning in higher
education.* Retrieved on April 1, 2004 from
http://www.upe.ac.za/citte2000/docs/jbotha.doc.

Botha, J. (2004). *Software evaluation: The process of evaluating software and
its effect on learning.* Retrieved from
http://hagar.up.ac.za/catts/learner/eel/Conc/conceot.htm
on January 30, 2004.

Bower, G. H., Clark, M. C., Lesgold, A. M., & Winzenz, D. (1969).
Hierarchical retrieval schemes in recall of categorized word
lists. *Journal of Verbal Learning and Verbal Behavior, 8*, 323-343.

Bransford, J. D., Sherwood, R., Vye, N., & Rieser, J (1986). Teaching
thinking and problem solving: Research foundations.
American Psychologist, 41(10), 1078-1089.

Bransford, J. D., Franks, J. J., Vye, N. J., & Sherwood, R. D. (1989).
New approaches to instruction: because wisdom can't be
told. In S. Vosniadou & A. Ortony (Eds.), *Similarity and
analogical reasoning.* New York: Cambridge University Press.

Branson, R. K., Rayner, G. T., Cox, J. L., Furman, J. P., King, F. J., &
Hannum, W. H. (1975). *Interservice procedures for instructional
systems development* (5 vols.), (TRADOC Pam 350-30 and
NAVEDTR 106A). Ft. Monroe, VA: U.S. Army Training
and Doctrine Command.

Bredemeier, M. E., Bernstein, G., & Oxman, W. (1982). BA FA BA
FA and dogmatism/ethnocentrism: A study of attitude

change through simulation-gaming. *Simulation & Gaming,* *13*(4), 413-436.

Brinck, T., Gergkem D., & Wood, S. D. (2002). *Usability for the web: Designing web sites that work.* San Francisco, CA: Morgan Kauffman Publishers.

Broadbent, B., & Cotter, C. (2002). *Evaluating e-learning* (Appears in the *2003 Pfeiffer Annual: Training*). Retrieved on April 29, 2005 from http://www.e-learninghub.com/articles/evaluating_e-learning.html.

Broadbent, D. E. (1958). *Perception and communication.* Oxford: Pergamon Press.

Broadbent, D. E. (1963). Flow of information within the organism. *Journal of Verbal Learning and Verbal Behavior, 2*, 34-39.

Brookfield, S. (1995). Adult learning: An overview (web version). *International Encyclopedia of Education.* Oxford: Pergamon Press. Retrieved on May 26, 2004 from http://www.digitalschool.net/edu/adult_learn_Brookfield.html.

Brown, R., & McNeill, D. (1966). The "tip-of-the-tongue" phenomenon. *Journal of Verbal Learning and Verbal Behavior, 5*, 325-337.

Brunner, J. S. (1960). *The process of education.* New York: Vintage Books.

Carrier, M., & Pashler, H. (1992). The influence of retrieval on retention. *Memory and Cognition, 20*(6), 633-642.

Catrambone, R. (1998). The subgoal learning model: Creating better examples so that students can solve novel problems. *Journal of Experimental Psychology: General, 127*(4), 355-376.

Cavalier, J. C., & Klein, J. D. (1998). Effects of cooperative versus individual learning and orienting activities during computer-based instruction. *Educational Technology Research and Development, 46*(1), 5-17.

Chen, M., Jackson, W. A., Parsons, C., Sindt, K. M., Summerville, J. B., Tharp, D. D., Ullrich, R. R., & Caffarella, E. P. (1996). The effects of font size in a hypertext computer based instruction environment. In *Proceedings of Selected Research and Development: Presentations at the 1996 National Convention of the association for Educational Communications and Technology* (18th, Indianapolis, IN). Educational Resources Information Center (ERIC) Document Reproduction Service No.: ED 397 784; IR 017 972.

References

Cherry, E. C. (1953). Some experiments on the recognition of speech, with one and with two ears. *Journal of the Acoustical Society of America, 25*(5), 975-979.

Chesebro, J. L., & McCroskey, J. C. (1998). The relationship of teacher clarity and teacher immediacy with students' experiences of state receiver apprehension. *Communication Quarterly, 46*, 446-456.

Chi, M. T. H. (1996). Constructing self-explanations and scaffolded explanations in tutoring. *Applied Cognitive Psychology, 10*, S33-S49.

Chi, M. T. H., Feltovich, P. J., & Glaser, R. (1981). Categorization and representation of physics problems by experts and novices. *Cognitive Science, 5*, 121-152.

Chi, M. T. H., Siler, S. A., Jeong, H., Yamauchi, T., & Housmann, R. G. (2001). Learning from human tutoring. *Cognitive Science, 25*, 471-533.

Clark, D. (1995a). *Big Dog's ISD Page.* Retrieved on June 23, 2003 from http://www.nwlink.com/~donclark/hrd/sat.html.

Clark, D. (1995b). Instructional system design – design phase. In *Big Dog's ISD Page.* Retrieved from http://www.nwlink.com/~donclark/hrd/sat.html on June 23, 2003.

Clark, D. (1995c). Developing instruction or instructional design. In *Big Dog's ISD Page.* Retrieved on June 18, 2004 from http://www.nwlink.com~donclark/hrd/learning/development.htm.

Clark, R. (2003). What works in distance learning: Instructional strategies. In H. F. O'Neil, *What works in distance learning* (report to the Office of Naval Research) (pp. 13-31). Los Angeles: University of Southern California, Rossier School of Education.

Clark, R. C. (2001). Online strategies to improve workplace performance. *Performance Improvement, 40*(8), 24-30.

Clark, R. C. (2003). *Building expertise: Cognitive methods for training and performance improvement* (2nd ed.). Washington, DC: International Society for Performance Improvement. ISBN 1-890289-13-2

Clark, R. C., & Mayer, R. E. (2003). *E-learning and the science of instruction: Proven guidelines for consumers and designers of multimedia learning.* San Francisco, CA: John Wiley & Sons, published by Pfeiffer.

Clark, R. E. (1994). Media will never influence learning. *Educational Technology Research and Development, 42*(2), 21-29.

Coll, R., & Wingertsman, J. C. III. (1990). The effect of screen complexity on user preference and performance. *International Journal of Human-Computer Interaction, 2*(3), 255-265.

Coursestar. (2003). *Procedures for evaluating computer courseware.* Retrieved from http://www.coursestar.org/ku/aust/t1729/m2_Integration/Lessons/L3_Software_Evaluation/t102c3_02008.html on March 11, 2003.

Craik, F. I. M, & Lockhart, R. S. (1972). Levels of processing: A framework for memory research. *Journal of Verbal Learning and Verbal Behavior, 11*, 671-684.

Csikszentmihalyi, M. (1990) *Flow: The psychology of optimal experience.* New York: Harper & Row, Publishers.

Dembo, M. H., & Junge, L. G. (2003). What works in distance learning: Learning strategies. In H. F. O'Neil, *What works in distance learning* (report to the Office of Naval Research) (pp. 55-79). Los Angeles: University of Southern California, Rossier School of Education.

Dempster, F. N. (1996). Distributing and managing the conditions of encoding and practice. In E. L. Bjork & R. A. Bjork (Eds.), *Memory* (pp. 317-344). San Diego, CA: Academic Press.

Department of Defense. (1997, Dec.). *DoD Modeling and Simulation (M&S) Glossary* (DoD 5000.59-M). Alexandria, VA: Defense Modeling and Simulation Office.

Department of Defense. (2001). *Handbook: Instructional Systems Development/Systems Approach to Training and Education* (part 2 of 5 parts) (MIL-HDBK-29612-2A).

deWinstanley, P. A., & Bjork, R. A. (2002). Successful lecturing: Presenting information in ways that engage effective processing. In D. F. Halpern and M. D. Hakel (Eds.), *Applying the science of learning to university teaching and beyond, New directions for teaching and learning, 89* (pp. 19-31). San Francisco, CA: Jossey-Bass.

Dick, W., & Carey, L. (1996). *The systematic design of instruction*, (4th Ed.). New York: Harper-Collins.

References

Dickinson, J. (1978). Retention of intentional and incidental motor learning. *Research Quarterly, 49*(4), 437-441.

Doherty, P. B. (1998). Learner control in asynchronous learning environments. *ALN Magazine, 2*(2). Retrieved on March 8, 2005 from http://www.sloan-c.org/publications/magazine/v2n2/doherty.asp.

Driscoll, M. P. (2002). Psychological foundations of instruction design. In R. A. Reiser, & J. V. Dempsey (Eds.), *Trends and issues in instructional design and technology* (pp. 57-69). Upper Saddle River, NJ: Merrill Prentice Hall.

Druckman, D., & Bjork, R. A. (Eds.). (1994). *Learning, remembering, believing: Enhancing human performance.* Washington, DC: National Academy Press.

Duncan, C. P. (1951). The effect of unequal amounts of practice on motor learning before and after rest. *Journal of Experimental Psychology, 42*, 257-264.

Dyson, M. C., & Haselgrove, M. (2001). The influence of reading speed and line length on the effectiveness of reading from screen. *International Journal of Human-Computer Studies, 54*, 585-612.

Eagly, A. H., Wood, W., & Chaiken, S. (1978). Causal inferences about communicators and their effect on opinion change. *Journal of Personality and Social Psychology, 36*(4), 424-435.

Eberts, R. E. (1994). *User interface design.* Englewood Cliffs, NJ: Prentice Hall.

Elwell, J. L., & Grindley, G. C. (1938). Effects of knowledge of results on learning and performance: I. A co-ordinated movement of both hands. *British Journal of Psychology, 1*, 39-54.

Farkas, D. K., & Farkas, J. B. (2000). Guidelines for designing web navigation. *Technical Communication, 47*(3), 341-358.

Fitts, P. M. (1954). The information capacity of the human motor system in controlling the amplitude of movement. *Journal of Experimental Psychology, 47*, 381-391. Reprinted. (1992). *Journal of Experimental Psychology: General, 121*(3), 262-269.

Flaxman, R. E., & Stark, E. A. (1987). Training simulators. In G. Salvendy (ed.), *Handbook of human factors* (pp. 1039-1058). John Wiley & Sons, Inc.

Fleishman, E. A. (1972). On the relationship between abilities, learning, and human performance. *American Psychologist, 27*, 1017-1032.

Fox, J. R. (2004). A signal detection analysis of audio/video redundancy effects in television news video. *Communication Research, 31*(5), 524-536.

Fry, E. (1963). *Teaching machines and programmed instruction.* New York: McGraw-Hill.

Gagné, E. D., Yekovich, C. W., & Yekovich, F. R. (1993). *The cognitive psychology of school learning* (2nd ed.). HarperCollins College Publishers. ISBN 0-673-46416-4

Gagné, R. M. (1968). Learning hierarchies. *Educational Psychologist, 6*(1), 1-6.

Gagné, R. M. (1973). The domains of learning. *Interchange, 3*, 1-8.

Gagné, R. M. (1985). *The conditions of learning and theory of instruction* (4th ed.). New York: Holt, Rinehart & Winston.

Gagné, R. M., & Briggs, L. J. (1979). *Principles of instructional design* (2nd ed.). New York: Holt, Rinehart and Winston.

Gagné, R. M., & Rohwer, W. D., Jr. (1969). Instructional psychology. *Annual review of Psychology, 20*, 381-418.

Garner, R., Gillingham, M. G., & White, C. S. (1989). Effects of "seductive details" on macroprocessing and microprocessing in adults and children. *Cognition and Instruction, 6*(1), 41-57.

Garland, K. J., & Noyes, J. M. (2004). CRT monitors: Do they interfere with learning? *Behaviour & Information Technology, 23*(1), 43-52.

Gayeski, D. M. (1992). Making sense of multimedia: Introduction to special issue. *Educational Technology, 32*(5), 9-14.

Glaser, R, & Bassok, M. (1989). Learning theory and the study of instruction. *Annual Review of Psychology, 40*, 631-666.

Grabbinger, R. S. (1993). Computer screen designs: Viewer judgments. *Educational Technology Research and Development, 41*(2), 35-73.

Graham, C., Cagiltay, K., Craner, J., Byung-Ro, L, & Duffy, T. M. (2000). *Teaching in a web based distance learning environment: An evaluation summary based on four courses* (CRLT Technical Report No. 13-00). Bloomington, IN: Center for Research on Learning and Technology, Indiana University. Retrieved from http://crlt.indiana.edu/publications/crlt00-13.pdf on March 12, 2004.

References

Gray, J. A., & Wedderburn, A. A. I. (1960). Grouping strategies with simultaneous stimuli. *Quarterly Journal of Experimental Psychology, 12,* 180-184.

Greenblat, C. S. (1981). Teaching with simulation games: a review of claims and evidence. In C. S. Greenblat & R. D. Duke (Eds.), *Principles and practices of gaming-simulation* (pp. 139-153). Beverly Hills, CA: Sage Publications.

Hagman, J. D., & Rose, A. M. (1983). Retention of military tasks: A review. *Human Factors, 25*(2), 199-213.

Hairston, M., & Ruszkiewicz, J. J. (1996). The Scott, Foresman handbook for writers (4th ed.). New York: HarperCollins College Publishers. (ISBN 0-673-99728-6)

Hall, R. H., & Hanna, P. (2004). The impact of web page text-background colour combinations on readability, retention, aesthetics and behavioural intention. *Behaviour & Information Technology, 23*(3), 183-195.

Halpern, D. F., & Hakel, M. D. (2003). Applying the science of learning to the university and beyond: Teaching for long-term retention and transfer, *Change,* July/August, 36-41.

Hamel, C. J., & Ryan-Jones, D. L. (1997). Using three-dimensional interactive graphics to teach equipment procedures. *Educational Technology Research and Development, 45*(4), 77-87.

Hamel, C. J., Ryan-Jones, D. L., & Hays, R. T. (2000). Guidelines for evaluation of internet-based instruction. *Proceedings of the Interservice/Industry Training, Simulation, and Education Conference* (pp. 537-543). Orlando, FL: National Training Systems Association.

Hannafin, R. D., & Sullivan, H. D. (1995). Learner control in full and lean CAI programs. *Educational Technology Research and Development, 43*(1), 19-30.

Hansen, F. C. B., Resnick, H., & Galea, J. (2002). Better listening: Paraphrasing and perception checking—A study of the effectiveness of a multimedia skills training program. Co-published simultaneously in *Journal of Technology in Human Services, 20*(3/4), 317-331 and H. Resnick & P. S. Anderson (Eds.), *Human services technology: Innovations in practice and education* (pp. 317-331). Haworth Press, Inc.

Harp, S. F., & Mayer, R. E. (1997). The role of interest in learning from scientific text and illustrations: On the distinction between emotional interest and cognitive interest. *Journal of Educational Psychology, 89*(1), 92-102.

Harp, S. F., & Mayer, R. E. (1998). How seductive details do their damage: A theory of cognitive interest in science learning. *Journal of Educational Psychology, 90*(3), 414-434.

Harpster, J. L., Freivalds, A., Shulman, G. L., & Leibowitz, H. W. (1989). Visual performance on CRT screens and hard-copy displays. *Human Factors, 31*(3), 247-257.

Haskell, R. E. (2001). *Transfer of learning: Cognition, instruction, and reasoning.* New York: Academic Press.

Hays, R. T. (1992). Systems concepts for training systems development. *IEEE Transactions on Systems, Man, and Cybernetics, 22*(2), 258-266.

Hays, R. T. (2001). *Theoretical foundation for Advanced Distributed Learning Research* (TR 2001-006). Orlando, FL: Naval Air Warfare Center Training Systems Division. (Defense Technical Information Center No. ADA 390 504)

Hays, R. T. (2005, Nov.). *The effectiveness of instructional games: A literature review and discussion* (Technical Report 2005-004). Orlando, FL: Naval Air Warfare Center Training Systems Division. (Defense Technical Information Center No. ADA 441 935)

Hays, R. T. (2006). *The science of learning: A systems theory perspective.* Boca Raton, FL: BrownWalker Press. (ISBN 1-59942-415-0)

Hays, R. T., Jacobs, J. W., Prince, C., & Salas, E. (1992). Flight simulator training effectiveness: A meta-analysis. *Military Psychology, 4*(2), 63-74.

Hays, R. T., Ryan-Jones, D. L., & Stout, R. (2003). Raising the Bar for instructional quality. *Proceedings of the Interservice/Industry Training, Simulation, and Education Conference* (pp. 1295-1304). Orlando, FL: National Training Systems Association.

Hays, R. T., Ryan-Jones, D. L., & Stout, R. (2005). *Quality evaluation tool for computer- and web-delivered instruction* (Technical Report 2005-002). Orlando, FL: Naval Air Warfare Center Training Systems Division. (Defense Technical Information Center No. ADA 4435 294)

Hays, R. T., & Singer, M. J. (1989). *Simulation fidelity in training system design: Bridging the gap between reality and training.* New York: Springer-Verlag.

References

Henke, H. (2001). *Evaluating web-based instructional design.* Retrieved on December 17, 2003 from http://www.chartula.com/ evalwbi.pdf.

Hiemstra, R., & Sisco, B. (1990). Moving from pedagogy to andragogy. Adapted and updated from *Individualizing instruction.* San Francisco: Jossey-Bass. Retrieved from http://www-distance.syr.edu/andraggy.html on April 26, 2004.

Hogan, K., & Pressley, M. (1997). *Scaffolding student learning: Instructional approaches and issues.* Cambridge, MA: Brookline Books, Inc. ISBN 1-57129-036-2

Holding, D. H. (1965). *Principles of training.* Oxford: Pergamon Press.

Holding, D. H. (1987). Concepts of training. In G. Salvendy (Ed.), *Handbook of human factors,* (pp. 939-962). New York: John Wiley & Sons.

Howard, R. W. (2000). Generalization and transfer: An interrelation of paradigms and a taxonomy of knowledge extension processes. *Review of General Psychology, 4*(3), 211-237.

Iidaka, T., Anderson, N. D., Kapur, S., Cabeza, R., & Craik, F. I. M. (2000). The effect of divided attention on encoding and retrieval in episodic memory revealed by Positron Emissions Tomography. *Journal of Cognitive Neuroscience, 12*(2), 267-280.

Iseke-Barnes, J. M. (1996). Issues of educational uses of the Internet: Power and criticism in communications and searching. *Journal of Educational Computing Research, 15*(1), 1-23.

Johnson Laird, P. N., Legrenzi, P., & Girotto, V. (2004). How we detect logical inconsistencies. *Current Directions in Psychological Science, 13*(2), 41-45.

Jones, M. G., & Okey, J. R. (1995). *Interface design for computer-based learning environments [online].* Retrieved on December 18, 2003 from http://ddi.cs.uni-potsdam.de/HyFISCH/ Multimedia /Learning/InterfaceDesignJones.htm.

Jones, M. K. (1989). *Human-computer interaction: a design guide.* Englewood Cliffs, NJ: Educational Technology Publications.

Kalyuga, S. (2000). When using sound with a text or picture is not beneficial for learning. Australian Journal of Educational Technology, 16(2), 161-172. Retrieved from http://www.ascilite.org.au/ajet/ajet16/kalyuga.html on March 12, 2003

Kalyuga, S., Chandler, P., & Sweller, J. (1999). Managing split-attention and redundancy in multimedia instruction. *Applied Cognitive Psychology, 13*, 351-371.

Kalyuga, S., Chandler, P., Tuovinen, J., & Sweller, J. (2001). When problem solving is superior to studying worked examples. *Journal of educational Psychology, 93*(3), 579-588.

Kanfer, R., & Mccombs, B. L. (2000). Motivation: Apply current theory to critical issues in training. In S. Tobias & J. D. Fletcher (Eds.), *Training and retraining: a handbook for business, industry, government and the military* (pp. 85-108). New York: Macmillan Reference USA.

Keller, J. M. (1983). Motivational design of instruction. In C. M. Reigeluth (Ed.), *Instructional design theories and models: An overview of their current status* (pp. 383-434). Hillsdale, NJ: Lawrence Erlbaum.

Keller, J. M. (1987). Development and use of the ARCS model of motivational design. *Journal of Instructional Development, 10*(3), 2-10.

Kinkade, R. & Wheaton, G. (1972). Training device design. In H. Vancoff and R. Kinkade (Eds.), *Human engineering guide to equipment design* (pp. 667-699). Washington, DC: American Institutes for Research.

Klatsky, R. L. (1975). *Human memory: Structures and processes.* San Francisco, CA: W. H. freeman and Company.

Kluger, A., & DiNisi, A. (1998). Feedback interventions: Toward the understanding of a double-edged sword. *Current Directions in Psychological Science, 7*(3), 67-72.

Knowles, M. S. (1989). *The making of an adult educator.* San Francisco: Jossey-Bass.

Kruger, J., & Dunning, D. (1999). Unskilled and unaware of it: How difficulties in recognizing one's own incompetence lead to inflated self-assessments. *Journal of Personality and Social Psychology, 77*(6), 1121-1134. Electronic version retrieved on April 20, 2004 from http://www.apa.org/journals /psp/psp7761121.html.

Lane, D. M., & Tang, Z. (2000). Effectiveness of simulation training on transfer of statistical concepts. Journal of Educational Computing Research, 22(4), 383-396.

Lee, S. H., & Boling, E. (1999). Screen design guidelines for motivation in interactive multimedia instruction: A survey and framework for designers. *Educational Technology*, May-June, 19-26.

Leutner, D. (1993). Guided discovery learning with computer-based simulation games: Effects of adaptive and non-adaptive instructional support. *Learning and Instruction, 3*, 113-132.

Levie, W. H., & Dickie, K. E. (1973). The analysis and application of media. In R. M. W. Travers (Ed.), *Second handbook of research on teaching* (pp. 858-882). Chicago: Rand McNally.

Levie, W. H., & Lentz, R. (1982). Effects of text illustrations: A review of research. *Educational Communication and Technology Journal, 30*(4), 195-232.

Lewin, K. (1935). *A dynamic theory of personality*. New York: McGraw-Hill.

Locke, E. A. (2000). Motivation, cognition, and action: An analysis of studies of task goals and knowledge. *Applied Psychology: An International Review, 49*(3), 408-429.

Locke, E. A., & Bryan, J. F. (1966). Cognitive aspects of psychomotor performance: The effects of performance goals o level of performance. *Journal of Applied Psychology, 50*(4), 286-291.

Lorch, R. F., Jr., & Lorch, E. P. (1996). Effects of organizational signals on free recall of expository text. *Journal of Educational Psychology, 88*(1), 38-48.

Lynch, P. J., & Horton, S. (1997). Imprudent linking weaves a tangled web. *Computer, 30*, 115-117.

Magill, R. A. (1980). *Motor learning: Concepts and Application*. Dubuque, IA: Wm. C. Brown Company Publishers.

Maki, R. H. (1998). Test predictions over text materials. In D. J. Hacker, J. Dunlosky, & A. C. Graesser (Eds.), *Metacognition in educational theory and practice* (pp. 117-144). Mahwah, NJ: Erlbaum.

Malcolm, S. E. (2000). Stating the obvious: Most training is boring, ineffective, of both. Retrieved from http://www.performance-vision.com/articles/art-boring.htm on December 23, 2003.

Martens, R. L., Gulikers, J., & Bastiaens, T. (2004). The impact of intrinsic motivation on e-learning in authentic computer tasks. *Journal of Computer Assisted Learning, 20*, 368-376.

Mautone, P. D., & Mayer, R. E. (2001). Signaling as a cognitive guide in multimedia learning. *Journal of Educational Psychology, 93*(2), 377-389.

Mayer, R. E. (2001). *Multi-media learning.* Cambridge, UK: Cambridge University Press.

Mayer, R. E. (2002). *The promise of educational psychology: Volume II: Teaching for meaningful learning.* Upper Saddle River, NJ: Pearson Education, Inc.

Mayer, R. E. (2003). What works in distance learning: Multimedia. In H. F. O'Neil (Ed.), *What works in distance learning* (Office of Naval Research Award Number N00014-02-1-0179) (pp. 32-54). Los Angeles: University of Southern California, Rossier School of Education.

Mayer, R. E. (2004). Teaching of subject matter. *Annual Review of Psychology, 55*, 715-744.

Mayer, R. E., & Anderson, R. B. (1991). Animations need narrations: An experimental test of a dual-coding hypothesis. *Journal of Educational Psychology, 83*(4), 484-490.

Mayer, R. E., & Anderson, R. B. (1992). The instructive animation: Helping students build connections between words and pictures in multimedia learning. *Journal of Educational Psychology, 84*(4), 444-452.

Mayer, R. E., Bove, W., Bryman, A., Mars, R., & Tapangco, L. (1996). When less is more: Meaningful learning from visual and verbal summaries of science textbook lessons. *Journal of Educational Psychology, 88*(1), 64-73.

Mayer, R. E., & Chandler, P. (2001). When learning is just a click away: Does simple user interaction foster deeper understanding of multimedia messages? *Journal of Educational psychology, 93*(2), 390-397.

Mayer, R. E., Dow, G. T., & Mayer, S. (2003). Multimedia learning in an interactive self-explaining environment: What works in the design of agent-based microworlds? *Journal of Educational Psychology, 95*(4), 806-812.

Mayer, R. E., & Gallini, J. K. (1990). When is an illustration worth ten thousand words. *Journal of Educational Psychology, 82*(4), 715-726.

Mayer, R. E., Heiser, J., & Lonn, S. (2001). Cognitive constraints on multimedia learning: When presenting more material results in less understanding. *Journal of Educational Psychology, 93*(1), 187-198.

Mayer, R. E., Mathias, A., & Wetzell, K. (2002). Fostering understanding of multimedia messages through pre-training: Evidence for a two-stage theory of mental model construction. *Journal of Experimental Psychology: Applied, 8*(3), 147-154.

Mayer, R. E., Mautone, P., & Prothero, W. (2002). Pictorial aids for learning by doing in a multimedia geology simulation game. *Journal of Educational Psychology, 94*(1), 171-185.

Mayer, R. E., & Moreno, R. (1998). A split-attention effect in multimedia learning: Evidence for dual processing systems in working memory. *Journal of Educational Psychology, 90*(2), 312-320.

McKenzie, J. (1999). Scaffolding for Success. *From Now On: The Educational Technology Journal, 9*(4). Retrieved from http://fno.org/dec99/scaffold.html on March 9, 2004.

McLoughlin, C., & Luca, J. (2001). Quality in online delivery: What does it mean for assessment in e-learning environments? *Proceedings of ASCILITE 2001* (pp. 417-426). Retrieved on March 16, 2003 from http://www.ericit.org/fulltext/IR021479.pdf

Merriam, S. B. (2001). Andragogy and self-directed learning: Pillars of adult learning theory. *New Directions for Adult and Continuing Education, 89*, 3-13.

Merrill, M. D. (1983). Component display theory. In C. M. Reigeluth (Ed.), *Instructional design theories and models: An overview of their current status* (pp. 279-333). Hillsdale, NJ: Erlbaum.

Merrill, M. D. (1997). Instructional strategies that teach. *CBT Solutions*, Nov./Dec., 1-11. Retrieved on June 16, 2004 from http://www.id2.usu.edu/Papers/Consistency.PDF.

Merrill, M. D. (2000). Knowledge objects and mental-models. In D. A. Wiley (Ed.), *The instructional use of learning objects: Online version*. Retrieved on 2/19/2004 from http://reusability.org/read/chapters/merrill.doc.

Merrill, M. D. (2002). Instructional strategies and learning styles: Which takes precedence? In R. A. Reiser & J. V. Dempsey (Eds.), *Trends and issues in instructional technology* (pp. 99-106). Upper Saddle River, NJ: Prentice Hall.

Merrill, M. D., & Tennyson, R. D. (1977). *Teaching concepts: An instructional design guide*. Englewood Cliffs, NJ: Educational Technology Publications.

Milheim, W. D. (1995). Learner interaction in a computer-based instructional lesson. Journal of Educational Computing research, 13(2), 163-172.

Miller, G. A., Heise, G. A., & Lichten, W. (1951). The intelligibility of speech as a function of the context of the test materials. *Journal of Experimental Psychology, 41*, 329-335.

Miller, J. G. (1978). *Living systems.* New York: McGraw-Hill Book Company.

Miller, N., Maruyama, G., Beaber, R. J., & Valone, K. (1976). Speed of speech and persuasion. *Journal of Personality and Social Psychology, 34*(4), 615-624.

Misanchuk, E. R., Schwier, R. A., & Boling, E. (2000). *Visual design for instructional multimedia* (CD-ROM). Saskatoon, SK, Canada: University of Saskatchewan.

Molich, R., & Nielsen, J. (1990). Improving a human-computer dialogue. *Communications of the ACM, 33*(3), 338-348.

Moray, N. (1959). Attention in dichotic listening: Affective cues and the influence of instructions. *Quarterly Journal of Experimental Psychology, 11*, 56-60.

Moray, N. (1981). Feedback and the control of skilled behavior, in D. H. Holding (Ed.), *Human Skills.* New York: John Wiley & Sons.

Moray, N., Bates, A., & Barnett, T. (1965). Experiments on the four-eared man. *Journal of the Acoustical Society of America, 38*, 196-201.

Moreno, R., & Mayer, R. E. (1999). Cognitive principles of multimedia learning: The role of modality and contiguity. *Journal of educational Psychology, 91*(2), 358-368.

Moreno, R., & Mayer, R. E. (2000a). A coherence effect in multimedia learning: The case for minimizing irrelevant sounds in the design of multimedia instructional messages. *Journal of Educational Psychology, 92*(1), 117-125.

Moreno, R., & Mayer, R. E. (2000b). Engaging students in active learning: The case for personalized multimedia messages. *Journal of Educational Psychology, 92*(4), 724-733.

Moreno, R., & Mayer, R. E. (2004). Personalized messages that promote science learning in virtual environments. *Journal of Educational Psychology, 96*(1), 165-173.

Morkes, J., & Nielsen, J. (1997). *Concise, scannable, and objective: How to write for the web.* Retrieved from

References

http://www.useit.com/papers/webwriting/writing.html on March 21, 2005.

Morkes, J., & Nielsen, J. (1998). *Applying writing guidelines to web pages.* Retrieved on April 5, 2004 from http://useit.com/papers/webwriting/rewriting.html.

Morris, R., & Thomas, J. (1976). Simulation in training – Part 1. *Industrial Training International, 11*(3), 66-69.

Mousavi, S. Y., Low, R., & Sweller, J. (1995). Reducing cognitive load by mixing auditory and visual presentation modes. *Journal of Educational Psychology, 87*(2), 319-334.

Muter, P., Latrémouille, S. A., Treurniet, W. C., & Beam, P. (1982). Extended reading of continuous text on television screens. *Human Factors, 24*, 501-508.

Mutter, P., & Maurutto, P. (1991). Reading and skimming from computer screens and books: The paperless office revisited? *Behaviour and Information Technology, 10*(4), 257-266.

Najjar, L. J. (1988). Principles of multimedia user interface design. *Human Factors, 40*(2), 311-323.

Nash, S. S. (2003). *Online course quality benchmarks.* Retrieved on March 13, 2004 from http://intercom.virginia.edu/surveysuite/surveys/course_B enchmarks/index2.html.

National Education Association (2000). *A survey of traditional and distance learning higher education members.* Washington, DC: Author.

Naveh-Benjamin, M. Craik, F. I. M., Gravrilescu, D., & Anderson, N. D. (2000). Asymmetry between encoding and retrieval processes: Evidence from divided attention and a calibration analysis. *Memory and Cognition, 21*, 367-374.

Newby, T. J., Ertmer, P. A., & Stepich, D. A. (1995). Instructional analogies and the learning of concepts. *Educational Technology Research and Development, 43*(1), 5-18.

Nielsen, J. (1993). *Usability engineering.* Boston: Academic Press.

Nielsen, J. (1994). Heuristic evaluation. In J. Nielsen & R. L. Mack (Eds.), *Usability inspection methods* (pp. 25-62). New York: John Wiley & Sons.

Nielsen, J. (1997). Be succinct! (Writing for the web). *Alertbox.* Retrieved on June 16, 2004 from http://www.useit.com/alertbox/9703b.html.

Niemiec, R. P., Sikorski, C., & Walberg, H. J. (1996). Learner-control effects: A review of reviews and a meta-analysis. *Journal of Educational Computing research, 15*(2), 157-174.

Nitsch, K. E. (1977). *Structuring decontextualized forms of knowledge.* Unpublished doctoral dissertation, Vanderbilt University, Nashville.

Norman, D. A. (1973). Memory, knowledge, and answering of questions. In R. L. Solso (Ed.), *Contemporary issues in cognitive psychology: The Loyola Symposium* (pp. 135-165). Washington, DC: Winston & Sons.

Norman, D. A. (1976). *Memory and attention: An introduction to human information processing* (2nd ed.). New York: John Wiley and Sons, Inc.

Norman, D. A. (1988). *The design of everyday things.* New York: Currency and Doubleday.

Oviatt, S. (1999). Ten myths of multimodal interactions. *Communications of the ACM, 42*(11), 74-81.

Paas, F. G. W. C. (1992). Training strategies for attaining transfer of problem-solving skill in statistics: A Cognitive load approach. *Journal of Educational Psychology, 84*(4), 429-434.

Pacheco, J., Day, B. T., Cribelli, S., Jordan, J., Murry, B., & Persichitte, K. A. (1999). Web-based menus: Font size and line spacing preferences. In *Proceedings of selected research and Development: Papers Presented at the National Convention of the Association for Educational Communications and Technology (AECT)* (21st, Houston, TX). Educational Resources Information Center (ERIC) Document No.: ED 436 136; IR 019 761.

Paivio, A. (1990). *Mental representations: A dual-coding approach.* New York: Oxford University Press.

Penney, C. G. (1989). Modality effects and the structure of short term verbal memory. *Memory and Cognition, 17*(4), 398-422.

Perry, T. L. (2003). *Evaluating multimedia.* Retrieved from http://www.coastal.com/WhatsNew/online_multimedia.html on March 11, 2003.

Reeves, B., & Nass, C. (1996). *The media equation: How people treat computers, television, and new media like real people and places.* New York: Cambridge University Press.

Reeves, T. C. (1994). Systematic evaluation procedures for interactive multimedia for education and training. In S. Reisman (Ed.),

References

Multimedia computing: Preparing for the 21ˢᵗ century. Harrisburg, PA: Idea Group.

Reigeluth, C. M., & Stein, F. S. (1983). The elaboration theory of instruction. In C. M. Reigeluth (Ed.), *Instructional design theories and models: An overview of their current status*. Hillsdale, NJ: Lawrence Erlbaum.

Reiser, R. A., & Kegelmann, H. W. (1994). Evaluating instructional software: Review and critique of current methods, *Educational Technology Research and Development, 42*(3), 63-69.

Rieber, L. P. (1990). Using computer animated graphics in science instruction with children. *Journal of Educational Psychology, 82*(1), 135-140.

Rieber, L. P. (1996). Seriously considering play: Designing interactive learning environments based on the blending of microworlds, simulations, and games. *Educational Technology Research and Development, 44*(2), 43-58.

Roblyer, M. D., & Ekhaml, L. (2000). How interactive are YOUR distance courses? A rubric for assessing interaction in distance learning. *DLA 2000 Proceedings*. Callaway, GA, June 7-9 2000. Retrieved on February 9, 2004 from http://www.westga.edu/~distance/roblyer32.html

Roblyer, M. D., & Wiencke, W. R. (2003). Design and use of a rubric to assess and encourage interactive qualities in distance courses. *The American Journal of Distance Education, 17*(2), 77-98.

Rosch, E. (1978). Principles of categorization. In E. Margolis and S. Laurence (Eds.), *Concepts: Core readings* (pp. 189-206). Cambridge, MA: MIT Press. Reprinted as Chapter 10 in D. J. Levitin (Ed.) (2002). *Foundations of cognitive psychology: Core readings* (pp. 251-270). Cambridge, MA: Massachusetts Institute of Technology.

Rosenfeld, L., & Morville, K. L. (1998). *Information architecture for the World Wide Web*. Sebastopol, CA: O'Reilly.

Ross, J. L. (1998). On-line but off course: A wish list for distance educators. *International Electronic Journal for Leadership in Learning, 2*(3). Retrieved on March 11, 2004 from http://www.acs.ucalgary.ca/~iejll/volume2/Ross2_3.html

Rothkopf, E. Z., & Billington, M. J. (1979). Goal-guided learning from text: Inferring a descriptive processing model from inspection times and eye movements. *Journal of Educational Psychology, 71*(3), 310-327.

Rotter, J. B. (1972). An introduction to social learning theory. In J. B. Rotter, J. E. Chance, & E. J. Phares (Eds.), *Applications of a social learning theory of personality*. New York: Holt, Rinehart & Winston.

Royer, J. M. (1979). Theories of the transfer of learning. *Educational Psychologist, 14*, 53-69.

Rudmann, D. S., McCarley, J. S., & Kramer, A. F. (2003). Bimodal displays improve speech comprehension in environments with multiple speakers. *Human Factors, 45*(2), 329-336.

Schendel, J. D., & Hagman, J. D. (1982). On sustaining procedural skills over a prolonged retention interval. *Journal of Applied psychology, 67*(5), 605-610.

Schmidt, R. A., & Wulf, G. (1997). Continuous concurrent feedback degrades skill learning: Implications for training and simulation. *Human Factors, 39*(4), 509-525.

Schneider, W. (1985). Training high-performance skills: Fallacies and guidelines. *Human Factors, 27*(3), 285-300.

Scouller, K. (1998). The influence of assessment method on students' learning approaches: Multiple choice question examination versus assignment essay. *Higher Education, 35*, 453-472.

Shneiderman, B. (1987). *Designing the user interface: Strategies for effective human-computer interaction*. Reading, MA: Addison-Wesley Publishing.

Shneiderman, B. (1998). *Designing the user interface: Strategies for effective human-computer interaction* (3rd ed.). Reading, MA: Addison-Wesley Publishing.

Sims, R., Dobbs, G., & Hand, T. (2001). Proactive evaluation: New perspectives for ensuring quality in online learning applications. *ASCILITE 2001: Meeting at the crossroads: Proceedings of the 18th annual conference of the Australasian Society for Computers in Learning in Tertiary Education (ASCILITE)*, 509-517, Melbourn, Victoria, Australia: University of Melbourn.

Skaalid, B. (1999). *Web design for instruction: Research-based guidelines* [on line]. College of Education, University of Saskatchewan. Retrieved on March 9, 2004 from http://www.usask.ca/education/coursework/skaalid/.

Skinner, B. F. (1968). *The technology of teaching*. New York: Meredith Corporation.

References

Slamecka, N. J., & Graf, P. (1978). The generation effect: Delineation of a phenomenon. *Journal of Experimental Psychology: Human Learning and Memory, 4,* 592-604.

Sly, L. (1999). Practice tests as formative assessment improve student performance on computer-managed learning assessments. *Assessment and Evaluation in Higher Education, 24*(3), 339-343.

Sollenberger, R. L., & Milgram, P. (1993). Effects of stereoscopic and rotational displays in a three-dimensional path-tracing task. *Human Factors, 35*(3), 483-499.

Steers, R. M, & Porter, L. W. (1975). *Motivation and work behavior.* New York: McGraw-Hill.

Stepich, D. A., & Newby, T. J. (1988). Analogizing as an instructional strategy. *Performance and Instruction, 27*(9), 21-23.

Stout, R. J., & Sims, E. (2005). Using virtual humans to enhance the e-learning experience. *Proceedings of the Training, Education, & simulation International Conference, Maastricht, The Netherlands.* Kent, UK: Highbury Business.

Stuart, S. A. J., Brown, M. I., & Draper, S. W. (2004). Using an electronic voting system in logic lectures: one practitioner's application. *Journal of Computer Assisted Learning, 20,* 95-102.

Swaak, J., & de Jong, T. (2001). Discovery simulations and the assessment of intuitive knowledge. *Journal of Computer Assisted Learning, 17,* 284-294.

Taylor, H. A., Renshaw, C. E., & Jensen, M. D. (1997). Effects of computer-based role playing on decision making skills. Journal of Educational Computing Research, 17(2), 147-164.

Tessmer, M. N. (1995). Formative multimedia evaluation. *Training Research Journal, 1,* 127-149.

Texas Education Agency. (2003). *Quality of service guidelines for online courses (evaluation matrix).* Houston, TX: Region IV Education Service Center. Retrieved on April 21, 2003 from http://www.iqstandards.info.

Thibodeau, P. (1997). Design standards for visual elements and interactivity for courseware. *T.H.E. Journal Online: Technological Horizons in Education.* Retrieved on May 5, 2004 from http://www.thejournal.com/magazine/vault/articleprintversion.cfm?aid=1536.

Thompson, L. F., & Lynch, B. J. (2003). Web-based instruction: Who is inclined to resist it and why? *Journal of Educational Computing Research, 29*(3), 375-385.

Thomas, R., Cahill, J., & Santilli, L. (1997). Using an interactive computer game to increase skill and self-efficacy regarding safer sex. *Health Education and Behavior, 24*(1), 71-86.

Tognazzini, B. (2003). First principles of interaction design. Nielson Norman Group. Retrieved on March 12, 2004 from http://www.asktog.com/basics/firstPrincipels.html.

Travers, R. M. W. (1972*). Essentials of learning* (3rd ed.). New York: MacMillan.

Treisman, A. M. (1964). Verbal cues, language and meaning in selective attention. *American Journal of Psychology, 77*, 206-219.

Trollinger, V. L. (2003). *ADDIE for music educators: Creating effective multimedia programs for teaching.* Retrieved on March 10, 2003 from http://music.utsa.edu/tdml/conf-VIII-Trollinger.html.

Tuovinen, J. E., & Sweller, J. (1999). A comparison of cognitive load associated with discovery learning and worked examples. *Journal of Educational Psychology, 91*(2), 334-341.

Tweddle, S., Avis, P., Wright, J., & Waller, T. (1998). Towards criteria for evaluating web sites, *British Journal of Educational Technology, 29*(3), 267-270.

Utting, K., & Yankelovich, N. (1989). Context and orientation in hypermedia networks. *ACM Transactions on Information Systems, 7*(1), 58-84.

Valverde, H. H. (1973). A review of flight simulator transfer of training studies, *Human Factors, 15*(6), 510-523.

Van Der Stuyf, R. R. (2002). Scaffolding as a teaching strategy. *Scaffolding Website.* Retrieved from http://condor.admin.ccny.cuny.edu/~group4/ on March 8, 2004.

Van Merrienboer, J. J. G., Clark, R. E., & de Croock, M. B. M. (2002). Blueprints for complex learning: The 4C/ID-model. *Educational Technology Research and Development, 50*(2), 39-64.

Waag, W. L. (1981). *Training effectiveness of visual and motion simulation* (AFHRL-TR-79-72). Brooks Air Force Base, TX: Air Force Human Resources Laboratory.

Webster's New Collegiate Dictionary. (1977). Springfield, MA: G. & C. Merriam Co.

References

Weinberg, D. R., Guy, D. E., & Tupper, R. W. (1964). Variation of postfeedback interval in simple motor learning. *Journal of Experimental Psychology, 67*(1), 98-99.

Weiten, W. (2004). *Psychology Themes and variations* (6th ed.). Belmont, CA: Wadsworth/Thomson Learning.

Wickens, C. E., & Hollands, J. G. (2000). *Engineering psychology and human performance* (3rd ed.). Upper Saddle River, NJ: Prentice Hall.

Wilkinson, R. T. (1963). Interaction of noise with knowledge of results and sleep deprivation. *Journal of Experimental Psychology, 66*, 332-337.

Zarefsky, D. (2001). *Argumentation: The study of effective reasoning* (course guidebook). Chantilly, VA: The Teaching Company.

Zhu, X., & Simon, H. A. (1987). Learning mathematics from examples and by doing. *Cognition and Instruction, 4*(3), 137-166.